RESTORING THE DIASPORA

SOCIETY
OF BIBLICAL
LITERATURE

DISSERTATION SERIES
David L. Petersen, Old Testament Editor
Pheme Perkins, New Testament Editor

Number 144

RESTORING THE DIASPORA
Discursive Structure and Purpose in the Epistle of James

by
Timothy B. Cargal

Timothy B. Cargal

RESTORING THE DIASPORA
Discursive Structure and Purpose
in the Epistle of James

Scholars Press
Atlanta, Georgia

RESTORING THE DIASPORA
Discursive Structure and Purpose in the Epistle of James

Timothy B. Cargal

Ph.D., 1992
Vanderbilt University

Advisor:
Daniel Patte

Library of Congress Cataloging in Publication Data
Cargal, Timothy Boyd.
   Restoring the diaspora: discursive structure and purpose in the
Epistle of James/ Timothy Boyd Cargal.
      p. cm. — (Dissertation series/ Society of Biblical Literature; no. 144)
   Originally presented as the author's thesis (Ph. D.)— Vanderbilt
University, 1992.
   Includes bibliographical references.
   ISBN 1–55540–861–3. — ISBN 1–55540–862–1
   1. Bible. N.T. James—Criticism, interpretation, etc. 2. Bible
N.T. James—Language, style. 3. Semiotics. 4. Discourse analysis.
I. Title.   II. Series: Dissertation series (Society of Biblical
Literature); no. 144.
BS2785.2.C37   1993
227'.9106—dc20   93–10144
                                                       CIP

Printed in the United States of America
on acid-free paper

ACKNOWLEDGEMENTS

When I arrived at Vanderbilt University in the autumn of 1986 to begin my post-graduate studies, Professor Daniel Patte's commentary on the Gospel of Matthew was in the final stages of production. During a seminar that semester, he discussed the implications of a thymic semiotic system for understanding the differences between Matthew and Paul. I posed the question to him after class one day as to whether such differences might contribute to the tensions often noted between James and Paul, since the similarities between James and Matthew are widely acknowledged. Little did I know that in raising such a simple question I was leading myself into a five year study of the Epistle of James that would provide only a part of the preliminary work needed to answer it.

During those years I have benefitted from the instruction of the biblical studies faculty at Vanderbilt far beyond what is evidenced within these pages. Professor Patte has encouraged and supported my various research projects during my tenure at Vanderbilt, and his efforts in aiding my entrance into the "guild" have gone beyond what any student may reasonably expect. Professors Fernando F. Segovia, Mary Ann Tolbert, and Walter Harrelson have each taught me much about the varieties of and interrelationships among the methodologies which increasingly define the contours and structures of the discipline.

I also wish to acknowledge and offer my sincere thanks to the Graduate School of Vanderbilt University for its financial support in the forms of tuition scholarships and travel awards to present my research at professional meetings. These awards made it possible for me to discuss my ideas about the Epistle of James with leading scholars in the field at an early stage in my research. Without this financial support, it would not have been possible for me to pursue post-graduate studies.

Finally, I wish to thank my family for their support, and especially my wife Sherri for her years of patience and sacrifice through my seminary and post-graduate education. I dedicate this dissertation to the memory of my uncle, Don Kennedy, without whose generous financial support of my undergraduate studies I could never have begun the years as a student which are finally drawing to a close. Perhaps had more of the Christians around him proclaimed James's message of God's goodness through their actions on behalf of others he would have had less reservations about the faith of his youth as his life progressed. Certainly by his actions toward his family and those around him, he demonstrated that he himself had heard that message.

CONTENTS

Chapter 4
"WORKS" OF THE "WORD":

Chapter 5
"HUMBLING ONESELF" IN THE LIGHT OF "JUDGMENT":

Chapter 6
"BRINGING BACK" ONE'S "NEIGHBOR":

ABBREVIATIONS

AB	Anchor Bible
ANRW	Hildegard Temporini and Wolfgang Haase, eds., *Aufstieg und Niedergang der römischen Welt*
ATR	*Anglican Theological Review*
BAGD	Walter Bauer, William F. Arndt, F. Wilbur Gingrich, and Frederick W. Danker, *A Greek-English Lexicon of the New Testament and Other Early Christian Literature*
BDF	F. Blass, A. Debrunner, and Robert Funk, *A Greek Grammar of the New Testament and Other Early Christian Literature*
Bib	*Biblica*
BT	*The Bible Translator*
BTB	*Biblical Theology Bulletin*
BZ	*Biblische Zeitschrift*
BZNW	Beihefte zur *Zeitschrift für die neutestamentliche Wissenschaft und die Kunde der älteren Kirche*
CBQ	*Catholic Biblical Quarterly*
CNT	Commentaire du Nouveau Testament
ConNT	Coniectanea neotestamentica
ET	English translation
ETS	Erfurter theologische Studien
EvQ	*Evangelical Quarterly*
ExpTim	*Expository Times*
FB	Forschung zur Bibel

FRLANT	Forschungen zur Religion und Literature des Alten und Neuen Testaments
GBS	Guides to Biblical Scholarship
Hermeneia	Hermeneia—A Critical and Historical Commentary on the Bible
HNTC	Harper's New Testament Commentaries
HTKNT	Herders theologischer Kommentar zum Neuen Testament
HTR	*Harvard Theological Review*
IB	George A. Buttrick, ed., *The Interpreter's Bible*
ICC	International Critical Commentary
Int	*Interpretation: A Journal of Bible and Theology*
JBL	*Journal of Biblical Literature*
JNES	*Journal of Near Eastern Studies*
JR	*Journal of Religion*
JRT	*The Journal of Religious Thought*
JSNTSup	Journal for the Study of the New Testament Supplement Series
JSOT	*Journal for the Study of the Old Testament*
JSS	*Journal of Semitic Studies*
JTS	*Journal of Theological Studies*
LB	*Linguistica Biblica*
LCL	Loeb Classical Library
LSJ	Henry G. Liddell, Robert Scott, and Henry S. Jones, *A Greek-English Lexicon*
LXX	Septuagint
MM	J. H. Moulton and G. Milligan, *The Vocabulary of the Greek New Testament*
NA-26	E. Nestle and K. Aland, *et al.*, eds., *Novum Testamentum Graece*, 26th ed.
NCB	New Century Bible
NF	Neue Folge ("new series")
NICNT	New International Commentary on the New Testament
NIGTC	New International Greek Testament Commentary
NovT	*Novum Testamentum*
NovTSup	Supplements to Novum Testamentum
NRSV	New Revised Standard Version
NT	New Testament
NTS	*New Testament Studies*
OT	Old Testament
PTMS	Pittsburgh Theological Monograph Series

RHPR	*Revue d'histoire et de philosophie religieuses*
ResQ	*Restoration Quarterly*
RevScRel	*Revue des sciences religieuses*
SB	Sources biblique
SBLASP	Society of Biblical Literature Annual Seminar Papers
SBLBMI	Society of Biblical Literature, The Bible and Its Modern Interpreters
SBLSBS	Society of Biblical Literature Sources for Biblical Studies
SBLSS	Society of Biblical Literature, Semeia Studies
SBS	Stuttgarter Bibelstudien
SE	*Studia Evangelica*
SemiotBib	*Sémiotique et Bible*
ST	*Studia theologica*
StBTh	*Studia Biblica et Theologica*
TCGNT	Bruce M. Metzger, ed., *A Textual Commentary on the Greek New Testament*
TDNT	Gerhard Kittel and Gerhard Friedrich, eds., *Theological Dictionary of the New Testament*
TLZ	*Theologische Literaturzeitung*
TMs	Typed Manuscript
TZ	*Theologische Zeitschrift*
UBSGNT	Kurt Aland, *et al.*, eds., United Bible Societies' *The Greek New Testament*, 3rd ed., corrected
WBC	Word Biblical Commentary
WTJ	*Westminster Theological Journal*
WUNT	Wissenschaftliche Untersuchungen zum Neuen Testament
ZKT	*Zeitschrift für katholische Theologie*
ZNW	*Zeitschrift für die neutestamentliche Wissenschaft und die Kunde der älteren Kirche*

"ON READING JAMES"

It has long been a commonplace in modern critical study of the Epistle of James that the book lacked any discernable coherence. One of Marxsen's first statements about the Epistle[1] in his New Testament introduction is that "[w]e are struck immediately by the fact that there seems to be no particular pattern, at least as far as the contents are concerned."[2] Likewise, Perrin commented that the Epistle

> has no discernible structure. It simply moves from theme to theme as the mind of the homilist takes him, on the principle of association of ideas or sometimes merely catchwords. ... The insights we used in our structural analysis of other texts in the New Testament simply do not apply to the homily of James.[3]

---

[1]This study will employ the conventions of using "the Epistle" to refer to "the Epistle of James," and maintaining "James" as the author's self-appellation. The designation "the Epistle" has not been chosen to 'beg' the question of the work's literary genre, but rather as an English shorthand for the traditional title of the book: ΙΑΚΩΒΟΥ ΕΠΙΣΤΟΛΗ. The issues surrounding whether the book belongs to the epistolary genre and the significance of the author's self-appellation "James" will be taken up in the concluding chapter of this study under the heading of "An Overarching Figure: The 'Epistle' of James."

[2]Willi Marxsen, *Introduction to the New Testament: An Approach to its Problems* (Philadelphia: Fortress Press, 1968), 226.

[3]Norman Perrin, *The New Testament, An Introduction: Proclamation and Paraenesis, Myth and History* (New York: Harcourt, Brace and Jovanovich, 1974), 256.

1

Similar comments can be found in virtually any introductory treatment of the Epistle.[4]   Related to this view that the Epistle is merely a conglomeration of loosely strung together paraenetic sayings has been the argument by many scholars that "[t]here is no theme or controlling purpose in this little book."[5]

Yet if we do not somehow manage to move beyond these initial reactions to reading the text of the Epistle, it becomes very difficult—if not impossible—to find meaning within it. The reasons for this have been well stated by James Reese:

> In the actual exercise of language in communicating, context is determi-
> nant for the meaning of the words. In composing a text, a significant
> dimension of this context is the structuring of literary units. How are they
> developed and interrelated? Why do they occur in this order? To what
> literary genre do they belong?[6]

Consequently, various scholars have tried to identify an organizational structure among the sayings within the Epistle, usually on formal grounds (the demands of oral presentation, the epistolary forms of Hellenistic public and private letters, etc.). If the goal of the analysis, however, is to discern an organizational structure that will contribute to an understanding of James's purposes in writing, different criteria than these purely formal characteristics may be necessary.

But we are getting ahead of ourselves. To start at the beginning, we must gain some idea of why we as readers "are struck immediately by the fact that there seems to be no particular pattern, at least as far as the contents are concerned."[7] What is different about this text that pre-vents us from applying "[t]he insights we used in our structural analysis of other texts in the New Testament ... to the homily of James"?[8]

---

[4]Cf. also the comments of Werner Georg Kümmel, *Introduction to the New Testament* (rev. English ed.; Nashville: Abingdon Press, 1975), 404; and Eduard Lohse, *The Formation of the New Testament* (Nashville: Abingdon Press, 1981), 203-204. Elsewhere, Lohse referred to the Epistle as "eine Art Handbüchlein christlicher Ethik" ("Glaube und Werke—Zur Theologie des Jakobusbriefes," in *Die Einheit des Neuen Testaments* [Göttingen: Vandenhoeck und Ruprecht, 1973], 301).

[5]Howard Clark Kee and Franklin W. Young, *Understanding the New Testament* (Englewood Cliffs, New Jersey: Prentice-Hall, Inc., 1957), 319.

[6]James M. Reese, O.S.F.S., "The Exegete as Sage: Hearing the Message of James," *BTB* 12 (1982): 82.

[7]Marxsen, *Introduction*, 226.

[8]Perrin, *Introduction*, 256.

The Problem of Relating Structure and
Purpose in the Epistle of James

The problem most twentieth century readers of the Epistle of James encounter in trying to comprehend the structure of the work arises from the fact that it utilizes some literary conventions which are not frequently found in the writings we customarily read. The convention usually cited first by those writing about the Epistle is its tendency to connect sayings by a "catchword" link, where "one saying is attached to another simply because a word or cognate of the same stem appears in both sayings."[9] Numerous examples of this device can be provided from just the first chapter: χαίρειν/χαράν (vv 1 and 2), λειπόμενοι/λείπεται (vv 4 and 5), πειρασμόν/πειραζόμενος (vv 12 and 13), and θρησκεία/θρησκεία (vv 26 and 27).

The disorientation which arises from the shifts in topic which usually accompany these sayings associated by catchword is only intensified when the cognates which form the link themselves reflect different domains of meaning. For example, whereas the noun πειρασμός in 1:12 seems to refer to a general kind of "trial" or perhaps persecution, the forms of the verb πειράζω in 1:13-14 would most naturally seem to mean "temptation." Occasionally the sayings linked by a catchword even seem to be somewhat contradictory. The saying of 1:2-4 that states that the experience of "trials" initiates a process that makes a person "complete and entire, *lacking* in nothing" is connected to a saying in 1:5 that asserts that "if anyone *lacks* wisdom" it must be received as a gift from God.

This grouping of sayings by formal characteristics, such as catchwords, has another effect which is disorienting for modern readers: sayings with similar content and discussions of a single topic become scattered throughout the book. Both Jas 1:21 and 3:13-18 deal with meekness. Jas 1:26 and 3:3-13 exhort the reader to carefulness in speech. Patient endurance of trials and suffering are encouraged in 1:2-4, 1:12, and 5:7-11. And denunciations of the wealthy can be found in 1:9-11, 2:1-7 and 5:1-6.[10]

Despite the disorientation, we have the sense as readers that all discourses, including paraenetic discourses such as the Epistle of James, exist because an author or speaker desired to communicate something to

---

[9]Martin Dibelius, *James* (rev. Heinrich Greeven; Hermeneia; Philadelphia: Fortress Press, 1975), 6.

[10]See Lohse, *Formation*, 205.

someone, and they are always organized and presented in a fashion that she or he envisions will be meaningful to the anticipated audience. We are haunted by the gnawing suspicion that, as Barton stated it,

> all one has to do is discover or devise conventions of reading which will enable it to have meaning. However odd or disjointed a text may appear, it can be *naturalized*—that is, perceived as belonging to some genre with statable conventions—and so made sense of.[11]

We are convinced by our experiences as readers of a wide variety of texts that the problems of relating the structure and purpose of the Epistle are not insurmountable.

And so our experience of reading the Epistle of James prompts us to ask two fundamental questions. First, how could someone have written such an apparently disorganized and disjointed text? How does one account for the (lack of) structure and organization perceived in the Epistle? And secondly, why would someone have written such a text? What could he or she have hoped to accomplish by writing it in this way? What are the "purposes" or "goals" of this text?

These questions, however, can only be answered from a broader, presuppositional context or paradigm. The choice of such a paradigm must be made very carefully, since it will determine the limits for the kind of answers that can be found to these fundamental questions regarding the structure and purpose of the Epistle. Basically two such paradigms are currently available to us at the close of the twentieth century: an historical paradigm and a linguistic or communication paradigm. We need to consider briefly the basic characteristics of these paradigms.[12]

---

[11]John Barton, *Reading the Old Testament: Method in Biblical Study* (Philadelphia: Westminster Press, 1984), 127. Barton later expands on this idea: "To read any work holistically, as having a unified, coherent 'message', we have to naturalize it, to assign it to a genre, to set conventions within which we are going to understand it" (132).

[12]A more extensive treatment of the characteristic features of these two paradigms can be found in Daniel Patte, *What is Structural Exegesis?* (GBS, NT series; Philadelphia: Fortress Press, 1976), 1-20 and idem, *The Religious Dimensions of Biblical Texts: Greimas's Structural Semiotics and Biblical Exegesis* (SBLSS; Atlanta: Scholars Press, 1990), 3-10 et passim. Basic to his argument in *What is Structural Exegesis?* is the view that our Euro-American society is currently undergoing a "paradigm shift" (see Thomas S. Kuhn, *The Structure of Scientific Revolutions* [2nd ed.; Chicago: University of Chicago Press, 1970]) from the historical paradigm to the linguistic one.

Two Paradigms for Addressing the Problem
of the Epistle's Structure and Purpose

In order to make more explicit the implicit tendencies of exegetical approaches based on these two different paradigms of meaning, it will be helpful to have some kind of lens to refract the light which they each shed on a text, much as a prism makes explicit the various wavelengths of light which implicitly characterize the "white" light which passes through it. Just such a lens is provided for us by the somewhat ambiguous title of this introduction, "On Reading James."

'On Reading James' Historically

The ambiguity in the title of this introduction which refracts the light being shed upon such an extremely brief text is the question of the referent of "James." Does "James" refer to the book "the Epistle of James," or does it refer to its author? Now we quickly resolve this ambiguity as readers by noting the word "reading" within the immediate context, thereby concluding that it must be referring to the Epistle. But the natural tendency of exegetes operating from within an historical paradigm is to begin by assuming that the referent of "James" is the author unless the context makes this assignment of the referent difficult or impossible.

But the significance of this tendency goes beyond a mere predilection to resolve a particular ambiguity in a certain way. In a real sense, historical exegetes ultimately want to read "James" the author even more than they want to read "James" the book. They want to know who James was, what historical circumstances led him to write, what were the sources of his theology and his thought more generally, how did he relate himself to other Christian theologians of the first century. It is not by coincidence that these are the issues addressed in the introductions of historical commentaries on the Epistle. The presupposition at work in this paradigm is that unless at least preliminary answers can be found to these questions about "James" the author, one cannot begin to read "James" the book.

'On Reading James' Linguistically

Conversely, the initial tendency of an exegete operating from within a communication or linguistic paradigm is to first assign the referent of "James" as the Epistle, and not the author. This tendency arises from an interest in "James" the book as an example of the communication process. The concern is with how "James" the book participates in the process of communicating meanings, not with how those particular meanings or ideas might have been generated in the first place by either "James" the author or the community in which he lived. Indeed, studies which operate within this communication paradigm will generally not speak of the 'flesh and blood' author at all. They will rather focus their attention on the persona created within the text itself by that 'flesh and blood' author as part of the communication process—a persona often referred to as the "implied author."

Comparing Historical and
Linguistic Readings

We can gain a sense of the implications of these different paradigms by comparing the approaches to the text of the Epistle taken by methodologies drawn from the two models. Since one of the trends in historico-critical research on the Epistle of James is redaction criticism, let us take it as our example of historical methods. For our example of a methodology grounded in a communication paradigm, let us consider structural exegesis.

The concerns and methods of redaction criticism have been well summarized by Dan Via:

> Redaction criticism is concerned with the interaction between an inherited tradition and a later interpretive point of view. Its goals are to understand why the items from the tradition were modified and connected as they were, to identify the theological motifs that were at work in composing a finished [text], and to elucidate the theological point of view which is expressed in and through the composition.[13]

Thus, redaction criticism begins with the traditions that lie behind the text and seeks to explicate how the authors/redactors develop their theology out of this tradition. That is to say, it begins outside the text (with the extra-textual phenomena of tradition, socio-historical setting, etc.) and moves from there into the text itself. This is clearly evidenced by considering, for example, Peter Davids's research on the relationship

---

[13]Dan O. Via, forward to *What is Redaction Criticism?*, by Norman Perrin (GBS, NT series; Philadelphia: Fortress Press, 1969), vi-vii. It was Via's immediately following comment that redaction criticism could be applied to New Testament books other than the Gospels that prompted Davids, the first self-conscious redaction critic of the Epistle of James, to use this method in his study of the Epistle (see Peter H. Davids, *The Epistle of James* [NIGTC; Grand Rapids, Michigan: William B. Eerdmans Publishing Company, 1982], xi).

between the Epistle of James and the "Jesus Tradition,"[14] and Ralph Martin's repeated references to the redactor of the Epistle applying the traditions stemming from James the Just to the situations facing the Syrian church.[15]

The approach of structural semiotics, however, is precisely the opposite. Rather than using the traditions as a foil for isolating the author's theology, a structural exegesis begins by isolating the author's beliefs so that they may be employed as a foil for understanding why particular traditions were chosen to express those beliefs.[16] How this task is accomplished will be examined, in brief, in chapter two. But notice that the chief concern is with how an author *communicates* certain beliefs to the readers, not with how the author or the recipient community came to hold such beliefs in the first place. Thus, the text is read as it were from the inside out; the exegete begins with the system of the author's convictions as expressed within the text and other communication processes at work within the text and moves out to the relationship with extra-textual traditions, social conditions, etc.

---

[14]See Peter H. Davids, "James and Jesus," in *The Jesus Tradition Outside the Gospels*, ed. David Wenham (Sheffield: JSOT Press, 1984), 63-84. Davids has elsewhere dealt with James's use of other traditional materials; see idem, "Themes in the Epistle of James that are Judaistic in Character," (Ph.D. dissertation, University of Manchester, 1974), and idem, "Tradition and Citation in the Epistle of James," in *Scripture, Tradition, and Interpretation*, E. F. Harrison Festschrift, ed. W. W. Gasque and W. S. LaSor (Grand Rapids: William B. Eerdmans Publishing Company, 1978), 113-126. Cf. also Rudolf Hoppe, *Der theologische Hintergrund des Jakobusbriefes*, FB 28 (Würzburg: Echter Verlag, 1977), "Jakobusbrief und Jesusüberlieferung," 119-148; and Patrick J. Hartin, *James and the Q Sayings of Jesus*, JSNTSup 47 (Sheffield: JSOT Press, 1991).

[15]See Ralph Martin, *The Epistle of James* (WBC 48; Dallas: Word Books, 1988), lxix-lxxvii et passim.

[16]It was confusion on precisely this point that led to Stanton's misunderstanding of Patte's references to the "readers' old knowledge" in the latter's commentary on Matthew. For Stanton, the "old knowledge" of the readers simply equated with the traditions from Mark and Q used by the author/redactor of Matthew. See Graham Stanton, review of *The Gospel According to Matthew*, by Daniel Patte, in *Int* 43 (1989): 185. But for Patte, the "old knowledge" of the readers was composed of the beliefs and ideas that the author presupposed the imaginary audience of the Gospel to hold, i.e. the "system of convictions" of the enunciatee as opposed to the "convictions" of the enunciator. See Daniel Patte, *The Gospel According to Matthew: A Structural Commentary on Matthew's Faith* (Philadelphia: Fortress Press, 1987), 12-13, for comments relative to the use of source material and historical setting in a structural exegesis.

Summary: Choosing a Paradigm
for Our Study

Before choosing one of these paradigms for addressing our questions regarding the relationship between the organizational structure and purposes of the Epistle of James, we should consciously remind ourselves that while these two paradigms may be competing for primacy within our culture, they are not mutually exclusive. Both a communication paradigm and an historical paradigm provide legitimate readings of the text of the Epistle. Nevertheless, they do have different strengths and weaknesses, and indeed certain "blindspots." Thus, we need to assess these respective strengths and weaknesses, compare them to our own interests for studying the Epistle (specifically the problem of relating its structure and purpose), and then choose the paradigm we expect to be most beneficial for fulfilling those interests. Chapter one will review exegetical approaches grounded in the historical paradigm, and chapter two will examine methodologies arising from a communication paradigm and propose a reading strategy for this study.

READING JAMES FROM THE OUTSIDE IN: HISTORICAL CRITICISM

I have likened historical criticism to reading a text "from the outside in" because of its tendencies to focus on the historical circumstances which influenced the author and to emphasize such extra-textual phenomena as the traditional sources behind the text, its socio-historical setting, and so on. Yet it may seem that questions regarding how a text is structured and organized, if not also questions about its purpose, can only be answered on the basis of the text itself and not with regard to things external to it. The present chapter will examine how the Epistle has in fact been read "from the outside in" by historical critics seeking to analyze its structure and purpose. Moreover, we shall see how another extra-textual concern, namely ethical theories, have influenced how historical critics assess the value of different proposals regarding the structure and purpose of the Epistle of James.

Sketching the History of the Historical Criticism of the Epistle of James

It is quite arguably the case that in the past century of historico-critical exegesis the discussion of no other book of the New Testament has been more controlled by the work of a single commentator than has the Epistle of James. Martin Dibelius's commentary first appeared in 1921 as the seventh edition of the "Meyers Kommentar" on the Epistle and has dominated the scholarly discussion of the book since that time. The fact that the then more than fifty year old study was translated for inclusion in the highly regarded English "Hermeneia" commentary series is ample testimony to its preeminence in the field.

Dibelius applied the "form critical" method[1] to the Epistle and concluded that it consisted of a series of paraenetic sayings of more or less extended nature that had been gathered together without any overall pattern of organization. Indeed, he considered the "stringing together" of sayings one of the characteristic features of paraenetic literature.[2] He maintained that a related characteristic of paraenesis was that it collected traditions from a wide range of sources and periods with the consequence that its admonitions do not fit any single audience or particular historical circumstance or situation. These conclusions were basically consistent with the findings of the other major commentaries of the early twentieth century (namely those by Joseph Mayor and James Ropes[3]), and came to form a majority opinion among commentators into the 1970's (cf. Sophie Laws and E. M. Sidebottom,[4] and to a lesser degree Jean Cantinat, Franz Mußner, and Bo Reicke[5]).

Some scholars, however, attempted to isolate some type of organizational pattern within the contents of the Epistle. Arnold Meyer[6] (followed with slight modification by Gerhard Hartmann and B. S. Easton[7]) argued that the Epistle was based on a Jewish onomasticon

---

[1]Dibelius was one of the leading figures in the development of form criticism. See Martin Dibelius, *From Tradition to Gospel* (New York: Charles Scribner's Sons, 1935).

[2]Dibelius, *James*, 6.

[3]Joseph B. Mayor, *The Epistle of St. James. The Greek Text with Introduction and Commentary* (3rd ed.; London: MacMillan and Co., 1910) and James Hardy Ropes, *A Critical and Exegetical Commentary on the Epistle of St. James* (ICC; New York: Charles Scribner's Sons, 1916).

[4]Sophie Laws, *A Commentary on the Epistle of James* (HNTC; San Francisco: Harper and Row, 1980); and E. M. Sidebottom, *James, Jude, 2 Peter* (NCB; Grand Rapids, Michigan: William B. Eerdmans Publishing Company, 1967).

[5]Jean Cantinat, *Les Epîtres de Saint Jacques et de Saint Jude* (SB; Paris: Libraire Lecoffre, 1973); Franz Mußner, *Der Jakobusbrief* (HTKNT, XIII/1; Freiburg und Basel: Herder, 1964); and Bo Reicke, *The Epistles of James, Peter and Jude* (AB 37; Garden City, New York: Doubleday, 1964). Each of these scholars felt it may be possible to isolate a setting for the letter, though Cantinat and Mußner would place it in the mid-first century in Jerusalem, whereas Reicke would place it in the late first century in Rome.

[6]Arnold Meyer, *Das Rätsel des Jakobusbriefes* (BZNW, 10; Giessen: Töpelmann, 1930).

[7]Gerhard Hartmann, "Der Aufbau des Jakobusbriefes," *ZKT* 66 (1942): 63-70; and B. S. Easton, "The Epistle of James: Introduction and Exegesis," *IB* 12:3-18.

of allegorical interpretations of the names of the sons of Jacob. Gertner[8] proposed that the Epistle was a midrash on Hos 10:2 utilizing the pattern of Ps 12:1-5. Hartwig Thyen,[9] and later Peter Forbes,[10] attempted to isolate the structure by considering the demands of oral presentation within the rhetorical setting of a homily.

Yet each of these studies agreed with the essentially 'atomizing' approach of form criticism. These scholars accepted that the reader of the Epistle was confronted with a collection of traditional sayings; their concern was with how the sayings could be related to one another. The peculiarly anachronistic analogy drawn by Forbes clearly shows these sayings were still viewed, however, in more or less isolated fashion:

> Suppose James had been writing this Epistle to read it, or have it read, into a microphone, to go out on the air. I imagine, in the ignorance of my complete inexperience, that he would write it so that it could be divided up into convenient little sections, each fairly intelligible by itself and nicely typed, as it were, on its own separate sheet, but all adding up to a coherent and integrated whole. Could I do this for you with the Epistle of James? It ought to be possible, for, in principle, that is precisely what James was aiming at.[11]

Thus for Forbes and others, each "little section" remained "fairly intelligible by itself" and contributed to a perception of an overall "coherent and integrated whole."

The first proposal regarding an overall framework for the Epistle of James to gain fairly wide acceptance was set forward in 1970 by Fred Francis.[12] Drawing upon a study of the structure of public and private letters, Francis argued that the Epistle has a double opening in which the themes of the letter are stated and then repeated with slight modification. The letter closes by playing on the expectations within the epistolary genre for an oath formula and health wish (in the Epistle of James one finds instruction about oaths and prayers for the sick). Francis's model

---

[8]M. Gertner, "Midrashim in the New Testament," *JSS* 7 (1962): 267-292.

[9]Hartwig Thyen, *Der Stil der Jüdisch-Hellinistischen Homilie* (FRLANT, NF 47; Göttingen: Vandenhoeck und Ruprecht, 1955), 14-16.

[10]Peter B. R. Forbes, "The Structure of the Epistle of James," *EvQ* 44 (1972): 147-153.

[11]Ibid., 149.

[12]Fred O. Francis, "The Form and Function of the Opening and Closing Paragraphs of James and I John," *ZNW* 61 (1970): 110-126. The abrupt dismissal of Francis's proposal by Kümmel (*Introduction*, 408, nn. 15 and 17) is out-of-step with the assessment of it by more recent commentators; see the discussion which follows.

was utilized by Peter Davids[13] who sought to complete the analysis for the whole of the Epistle by arguing that the themes of the two-fold introduction are expanded in inverse order within the body of the letter. Both François Vouga and Ralph Martin[14] have also used modifications of Francis's proposal in their treatments of the organization of the Epistle. Thus, Francis's proposal for relating the structure of the Epistle of James to known epistolary conventions, coupled with the methodological advances of redaction criticism (see below), provided the basis for the growing challenge to the entrenched form-critical consensus.

Consequently, if we attempt to answer our questions of "how could someone have written such an apparently disorganized text as the Epistle of James" and "why would someone have written such a text, i.e. what are the 'purposes' or 'goals' of the Epistle," utilizing an historical paradigm, we can proceed along either a form-critical or a redaction-critical path. In order to assess the strengths and weaknesses of the historical paradigm for explaining the relationship between the organization and purposes of the Epistle, we need to examine both of these approaches more fully. Let us begin with form criticism, and then turn to redaction criticism as a development arising from it.

Dibelius and the Form Critics

The Structure of the Epistle

I have already noted that Dibelius contended that one of the characteristic features of paraenetic literature was the "stringing together" of sayings without any general pattern of organization. Nevertheless, he did argue that there were some sequences within the Epistle of James where each saying was related to a similar topic or topics and so might be considered "sections" of the book. Our present concern will be to review the limits set for these "sections" by Dibelius, to summarize his arguments in support of these divisions, and to compare his analysis with that of the form critics who followed him.

Dibelius treated Jas 1:1 as a standard epistolary prescript, though he did not allow that the book as a whole was a genuine epistle.[15]

---

[13]Davids, *James*, 24-28, and 29.

[14]François Vouga, *L'Epître de Saint Jacques* (CNT, 2nd ser., XIIIa; Genève: Labor et Fides, 1984), 18-23 and Martin, *James*, xcviii-civ. Cf. also Reese, "Exegete as Sage," 82-85 (especially 84) and Hartin, *James and Q*, 25-34.

[15]There is virtually complete agreement among form critics of the Epistle on both these points. Only Mayor (*St. James*, 31) and Mußner (*Jakobusbrief*, 11)

Noting that epistolary forms were widely used as a "literary veneer" by ancient authors, Dibelius argued that the Epistle was not an "actual letter" since it lacked an "epistolary situation," any "epistolary remarks" (e.g. news, messages, personal greetings), and a formal "epistolary introduction" or "conclusion." He concluded that "the prescript in 1:1 is the only epistolary element in the entire document."[16] Unlike many of his successors, however, Dibelius did offer a theory as to why such a prescript might have been included: "the vagueness of the address could have been the means by which the author left the origin and nature of the document surrounded with intentional ambiguity."[17]

Dibelius set the limits for the first section of the Epistle as Jas 1:2-18, referring to it as "A Series of Sayings Concerning Temptations."[18] In support of his contention that these sayings comprised "a complete unit," he pointed to "the visible effort in 1:2-8 and 1:12-15 to establish a connection (if only a *superficial* one) between one saying and another, and ... the *obviously not accidental* resumption in 1:12ff of the term 'trial/temptation' (πειρασμός) from 1:2."[19] Dibelius is at pains to stress, however, that "this unity is nevertheless only superficial" as was indicated by the appearance of 1:9-11 which seemed out of context to Dibelius, and more importantly by the semantic shift of πειρασμός from referring to "persecutions of Christians or similar tests of 'endurance' (ὑπομονή)" in 1:2 to a reference to "temptation to sin" in 1:13-15.[20]

Dibelius identified the first individual saying within this "series" as Jas 1:2-4 ("Concerning persecutions"). It is followed by 1:5-8 ("A saying about praying in faith"), which is connected to the preceding saying only by the "catchword" link between "lacking" (1:4) and "lacks"

---

suggest it may have been an actual encyclical letter circulated among churches.

[16]Dibelius, *James*, 1-2.

[17]Ibid., 65. Ropes (*St. James*, 9) explained the prescript by arguing that it was "altogether natural and appropriate for a tract" in this period to have such epistolary trappings; cf. also Reicke (*James, Peter and Jude*, xxix-xxxii) and Sidebottom (*James, Jude, 2 Peter*, 1-3).

[18]On Jas 1:2-18 as a unit, see also Reicke (*James, Peter and Jude*, 13-18), Ropes (*St. James*, 4), and Mußner (*Jakobusbrief*, 62-63). Laws dissents slightly; she takes 1:2-8, 1:9-11, and 1:12-18 each as separate units (*James*, 49-50, 62, and 66). Thus she places more emphasis on the discontinuity of 1:9-11 than is found in Dibelius (see below).

[19]Dibelius, *James*, 69; emphasis mine.

[20]Ibid., 69-70. He goes on to state that any "exegesis which in spite of this observation attempts to bring both sayings together under one common denominator ... must be categorically denied ...."

(1:5). Jas 1:9-11 ("the rich man and his downfall") marks the third saying within the series, and it "appears to [have] no connection at all" with 1:8. Likewise, Dibelius argued "1:12 is an isolated saying separated from what precedes it," but resuming the connection with 1:2-4. This connection only highlights, however, the contrast between 1:12 and 1:13-18 ("The source of temptations"), in that 1:2 and 1:12 deal with "trials" whereas 1:13-15 is concerned with "temptations." Thus, once again there is only a catchword link between 1:12 and 1:13. A final saying (1:16-18) is offered in support of the position that temptation cannot come from God since "all good comes from God."[21]

Dibelius next treated Jas 1:19-27 under the heading "A Series of Sayings About Hearing and Doing."[22] He regarded this section as "far more unified" than 1:2-18. The organization of this section is drawn from the three-part admonition of 1:19b: "be quick to hear" is connected with 1:21-25, "an elaboration about hearing and doing;" "slow to speak" is related to 1:26 ('bridling one's tongue'); and "slow to anger" is expanded by the contrast between "human anger" and "divine righteousness" in 1:20. Dibelius argued that James inherited the saying of 1:19b, possibly with 1:20 already attached, and used it to introduce his main theme expressed in 1:21-25. The saying regarding "true religion" in 1:27 is connected to 1:26 by the catchword link with "religious," and also carries forward the main theme of "hearing and doing" in 1:21-25.[23]

The central portion of the Epistle was the most structured according to Dibelius, consisting of three independent "treatises:" "A Treatise on Partiality" (Jas 2:1-13), "A Treatise on Faith and Works" (Jas 2:14-26), and "A Treatise on the Tongue" (Jas 3:1-12).[24] Each

---

[21]Ibid., 70-71. Reicke (*James, Peter and Jude*, 8) divides the text in exactly the same way as Dibelius. So also Ropes (*St. James*, 4), Cantinat (*Jacques et Jude*, 10) and Easton (*IB* 12:3), although the latter two do not group any of the isolated sayings into longer sections. Mußner (*Jakobusbrief*, 63-97) differs only in taking 1:12 together with 1:13-18.

[22]Cf. also Reicke, *James, Peter and Jude*, 19-25; Laws, *James*, 79; and Mußner, *Jakobusbrief*, 98.

[23]Dibelius, *James*, 108. Ropes (*St. James*, 4) saw more continuity between 1:19-27 and 2:1-26 than Dibelius allowed, taking all of 1:19 - 2:26 as a unit on the theme of "the need of reality and sincerity in religious instruction and public worship" (ibid., 168). Ropes divided this unit into five divisions, the first two of which were 1:19-25 and 1:26-27; for his divisions in chapter 2, see below.

[24]So also Easton (*IB* 12:34), Reicke (*James, Peter and Jude*, 8), Mußner (*Jakobusbrief*, 114, 127-28 and 157-158), and Cantinat (*Jacques et Jude*, 119, 138-

of these treatises is opened "by an admonition or (in 2:14) a rhetorical question which contains an admonition ... [that] states the leading interest in that section." He argued that each of these treatises derived "a certain consistency" from their stylistic structuring in the diatribe form.[25] In addition to the introductory admonition, each of these "treatises" utilize vivid illustrations (2:2-4, 2:15-16, 3:3-8), rhetorical questions and/or dialogues with an imagined interlocutor (2:5-7, 2:18-21, 3:9-12), and a summarizing conclusion (2:12, 2:24-26, 3:9-12).[26]

Dibelius maintained, in keeping with the paraenetic quality of the work as a whole, that no connection can be established between these three treatises.[27] Indeed, 2:13 is connected to the treatise proper of 2:1-12 only by the catchword "κρίνεσθαι/κρίσις,"[28] and the third of these treatises lacks the "neat arrangement" of the other two because its "ideas bump against or even clash with one another—evidence that the author is transmitting school material."[29] Thus, even this more structured portion of the Epistle is organized in the same fashion as its first chapter; it differs only in the length of the "treatises" as compared to the shorter "sayings" found elsewhere in the Epistle.

Dibelius argued that following this sequence of "treatises" the Epistle reverts to merely 'grouping' sayings together according to a very general theme. It is at this point that the greatest disparity emerges among the outlines of the Epistle proposed by the different form critics. This disparity is a consequence of their struggles to isolate any connections between the independent sayings garnered from the tradition by the author, as is evidenced by such unit headings as "Worldliness and Christian Life Contrasted,"[30] "Further General Exhortations,"[31] "Denunciations and Encouragements" and "Miscellaneous Precepts."[32]

---

139 and 161-162). Ropes (*St. James*, 4-5 and 185) dissents slightly by dividing the text of chapter 2 as 2:1-7, 8-13, and 14-26). Similar is Laws (*James*, 93, 110-111 and 118-119) who divides chapter 2 as 2:1-9, 10-13, and 14-26.

[25]Dibelius, *James*, 124.

[26]Cf. ibid. 125, 149-151, and 182-206. For a summary of the formal characteristics of the diatribe, see Stanley K. Stowers, "The Diatribe," in *Greco-Roman Literature and the New Testament*, ed. David E. Aune, SBLSBS 21 (Atlanta: Scholars Press, 1988), 74-76.

[27]Cf. Dibelius, *James*, 149 and 181.

[28]Ibid., 125-126. Easton (*IB* 12:3) likewise designates 2:13 as an isolated saying appended to the diatribe of 2:1-12.

[29]Dibelius, *James*, 182.

[30]Ropes (*St. James*, 5) for Jas 4:1 - 5:20.

[31]Sidebottom, (*James, Jude, 2 Peter*, 46) for 3:1 - 5:12.

[32]Mayor (*St. James*, cxxx-cxxxi) for Jas 5:1-11 and 12-20 respectively. Some

In that the majority of form critics accept Dibelius's analysis of individual sayings (if not his 'groupings'), we will utilize him in what follows as representative of one possible way the text can be ordered from a form critical perspective.

For Dibelius, the first "group of sayings" extends from Jas 3:13 - 4:12 and consists of admonitions "against contentiousness." The component sayings within this group can be isolated as the "warnings against jealousy and strife" in 3:13-17 and 4:1-6, "between which stand the isolated saying 3:18 [joined to 3:17 by the catchword καρπῶν/καρπός], and to which is joined the series of imperatives in 4:7-12."[33] A new "group of sayings against worldly-minded merchants and rich people" commences in 4:13 and continues to 5:6. The two major sayings within this group (4:13-16 and 5:1-6) share a common mood, content (denunciation of certain social groups), and form (Ἄγε νῦν in 4:13 and 5:1). These similarities suggested to Dibelius that this section "is not a series of sayings in which one saying is loosely appended to another, but rather a group of sayings which gives the impression of being unified because the beginnings are identical in form and the ideas are parallel."[34] Yet again the sayings are interrupted by the interpolation of an isolated saying (4:17), concerning which Dibelius was driven to admit that "[i]t is difficult to say what the author's reason was for inserting the saying here."[35]

At this point in the Epistle, any pretense to organization is completely lost so far as Dibelius is concerned. He described Jas 5:7-20 as "a series of sayings on various themes" and commented that "[t]his section does not hold together as a unit, for 5:12 stands in the middle as a totally isolated saying, and 5:7-11 and 5:13-20 have no relation in thought either to this saying or to one another."[36] He analyzed the component sayings as 5:7-11 ("sayings on patience" with a complex compositional history), 5:12 ("prohibition against swearing"), 5:13-15 ("precepts for particular situations"), 5:16-18 ("prayer"), and 5:19-20 (correction of members of the community who have sinned).

---

commentators ultimately conceded it was impossible to form any groupings among the sayings in chapters 4 and 5. Cf. Cantinat (*Jacques et Jude*, 11) and Mußner (*Jakobusbrief*, VIII), who does, however, gather three very brief sayings in Jas 5:13-15 under the heading "Anweisungen für verschiedene Lebenslagen" (216-217).

[33]Dibelius, *James*, 208.

[34]Ibid., 230.

[35]Ibid., 231.

[36]Ibid., 241.

The Purpose of the Epistle

For Dibelius, the answer to the question "why" someone would have written a text composed simply by stringing together independent sayings is inherent to the formal characteristics of the paraenetic genre. He provides three dominant features of paraenesis in this regard. First, paraenetic literature is marked by a "pervasive *eclecticism*" arising from its chief concern for "the transmission of an ethical tradition that does not require a radical revision." Secondly, the "stringing together of saying after saying is the most common form of paraenesis" which leads to the "*lack of continuity*" characteristic of all paraenetic literature. Finally, paraenetic literature served as a kind of repository of traditional ethical admonitions. As a result, these admonitions "do not apply to a single audience and a single set of circumstances; *it is not possible to construct a single frame into which they will all fit.*"[37]

The paraenetic literary genre as understood by Dibelius, then, is closely tied to a deontological approach to ethics. Such ethical systems focus "on the clarity, consistency, publicness, and universality of moral principles ... [and] seek to identify and formulate the duties, both negative and positive, which are requisite to human social existence."[38] These 'universal moral principles' must be preserved, and therein lies the purpose or goal of any paraenetic writing. It is sufficient to collect them in any fashion that will aid their retention (such as the "catchword" links) because people would immediately sense their value and appropriateness to a variety of life situations.

This universalizing characteristic of paraenetic literature is at odds, however, with the dominant understanding held by historical critics of the "purpose" of biblical writings. Historico-critical exegetes usually conceive of the purpose of a such texts as being to respond to certain historical circumstances which "occasioned" their composition; e.g., the purpose of Galatians might be described as an attempt to defend Paul's apostleship and preaching against attacks by Judaizers who had infiltrated the churches of central Asia Minor. But the fact that the admonitions of paraenetic literature do not reflect any particular situations, and indeed are expressions of 'universal moral principles,'

---

[37]Ibid., 5-11, emphases his.

[38]Thomas W. Ogletree, *The Use of the Bible in Christian Ethics* (Philadelphia: Fortress Press, 1983), 16. See further his discussion of deontological approaches to ethics on 23-28.

precludes the possibility of finding any certain clues regarding the historical situation of paraenetic writings.

Dibelius was acutely aware of this problem relative to the Epistle of James. He argued that the book showed clear signs of a post-Pauline setting,[39] and was apparently known by the author of the Epistle of Jude. He thus dated the Epistle of James between 80 - 130 CE, and then immediately stated "[a]ll further judgments regarding the circumstances of the origin of Jas must take their departure from the paraenetic character of the writing."[40] He cautioned that "historical conclusions based upon these admonitions [within the Epistle] may be made only with regard to the overall state of affairs [regarding increasing 'secularization' within the churches] and may not be extended to individual cases."[41] Thus for Dibelius, the purpose of the Epistle is to preserve paraenetic instruction in the hope that it will serve as warning about and correction for the increasing secularization of the churches in the late first century.

But not every commentator so assiduously respected the implications of the 'universal' character of paraenetic traditions for historical reconstruction as Dibelius had done. These scholars believed that there must have been some historical situation(s) which prompted the selection of the particular sayings within the Epistle of James from the extensive paraenetic tradition available to the compiler. Mayor had drawn a fairly detailed picture of the recipient community by assuming that *every* admonition within the Epistle reflected a present situation within the social life of the churches.[42] In similar fashion, Reicke argued that the selection and

> order of the material is ... dependent on the conditions current in the communities which stir and trouble the author. If the reader fails to recognize how concrete and disturbing the evils are, against which the author is fighting, then he [or she] will misjudge the text ....[43]

He argued more specifically that "[t]he different factors by which the recipients of the epistle of James appear to be influenced seem to fit especially well with social and spiritual conditions in the Roman empire

---

[39]"[I]t does not presuppose the preaching of Paul himself, but only the repetition of the Pauline watchwords as half-understood slogans" (Dibelius, *James*, 45).

[40]Ibid., 46.

[41]Ibid., 47.

[42]See Mayor, *St. James*, cxxxvii-cxxxviii.

[43]Reicke, *James, Peter and Jude*, 7.

during the reign of Domitian."[44]   For others, the images utilized within the sayings and the issues which they address point to a historical setting in the continuing dispute between Jewish Christians in Palestine and Pauline enthusiasts in the middle years of the first century.[45]

The reason these 'dissenting' form critics felt it necessary to establish at least a relatively clear picture of the historical setting of the Epistle goes beyond the dominant definition of the purpose of a writing for historical critics, however.   At least in part, they were reacting against the deontological ethic which Dibelius had isolated as an inherent element of ancient paraenetic literature.   Their own understanding of the nature of ethics would have been more in keeping with what Ogletree termed a "historical-contextual ethic":

> Historical contextualism accents the fact that the possibilities of moral understanding given with the constitutive structures of human being always appear in historically determinate forms.   They reflect a common culture shared by the members of a particular social group.   This culture articulates in specific ways the value realm that is latent in the human way of being in the world.   ... In short, the culture historializes the possibilities of moral understanding which belong to human being.[46]

Interestingly, Ogletree credits the "most comprehensive and forceful treatment" of this particular ethical model to Ernst Troeltsch,[47] a leading figure in both the elaboration and articulation of the historical paradigm of meaning and its implications for biblical interpretation.[48]

To understand the paraenesis—the ethic and moral instruction—contained within the Epistle of James, given the presuppositions regarding the nature of moral understanding within a historical-contextual ethic, required that the exegetes know what socio-historical factors shaped those concrete expressions of moral beliefs.   Thus, reconstruction of the *Sitz im Leben der Jakobus* became an essential factor for properly

---

[44]Ibid., 6.

[45]So both Cantinat (*Jacques et Jude*, 44-54) and Mußner (*Jakobusbrief*, 1-23). Similar is Kittel's argument for the Epistle being an authentic work by James the Just, but written prior to the "Jerusalem Council;" see Gerhard Kittel, "Die geschichtliche Ort des Jakobusbriefes," *ZNW* 41 (1942): 71-105.

[46]Ogletree, *Use of the Bible*, 35.   For his discussion of historical-contextual ethics, see 34-41.

[47]Ibid., 17.

[48]See Van A. Harvey, *The Historian and the Believer: The Morality of Historical Knowledge and Christian Belief* (New York: Macmillan, 1966), 3-9 et passim.

understanding both the purpose of the Epistle (in terms of the historical situation it sought to address) and its paraenetic content. Additionally, a historical-contextual reading of the Epistle's ethical demands was one way of reclaiming the text of the Epistle for a modern audience which resisted the universal, ahistorical nature of its admonitions as perceived by Dibelius.

Summary: Forms and Historical
Reconstruction

The nature of the dissenting views among form critics regarding the possibility of establishing a particular historical context for the Epistle of James highlights the fact that the conclusions reached by a study of the forms within the text are ultimately at cross-purposes with the historical concerns which first prompted the inquiry. The study of the traditional forms employed in the letter led Dibelius to assert the essentially ahistorical character of the sayings. This ahistorical characteristic of paraenetic sayings foreclosed the question of establishing the *Sitz im Leben der Jakobus*. It did, however, find a simple answer to the question of the relationship between the structure and purpose of the Epistle: both the loose organizational structure and the lack of a particular historical setting and corresponding purpose are characteristic features of the paraenetic genre. The goal of such a writing is preservation of received tradition, and any organizational pattern with mnemonic value would suffice.

Many historical critics, however, could not be satisfied with the limits imposed on historical reconstruction by the ahistorical character of paraenetic forms, either because they defined historical reconstruction as an essential part of their task or because they worked from a historical-contextual ethic rather than a deontological one. They sought to circumvent the problem by assuming that any pattern of concerns discernable from the selection of isolated, ahistorical sayings might provide clues regarding the historical situation of the collection proper. Nevertheless, they continued to accept the characteristic of loose organization as being typical of paraenesis, even though this view of the structure of the Epistle exacerbated the problems of determining any pattern of concerns which might then have been used for historical reconstruction. The neat answer to the problem of the relationship between the structure and purposes of the Epistle of James provided by Dibelius began to unravel; the lack of structure within the Epistle became an impediment to a conclusive answer regarding its purpose.

What was needed was a tool that would allow exegetes to discern a pattern of concerns within an otherwise disorganized text. Just such a tool was found in redaction criticism, which is "concerned with the interaction between an inherited tradition and a later interpretive point of view" and seeks

> to understand why the items from the tradition were modified and connected as they were, to identify the theological motifs that were at work in composing a finished [text], and to elucidate the theological point of view which is expressed in and through the composition.[49]

Noting that among these concerns of redaction critics is understanding "why the items from the tradition were modified and *connected* as they were," we should not be surprised if we also find that redaction critics of the Epistle of James discerned more organizational structure between the component sayings than their form critical predecessors.

Davids and the Redaction Critics

The Structure of the Epistle

It was in fact the desire to understand better the organizational structure of the Epistle of James, more so than concerns of historical reconstruction, that led Peter Davids to employ redaction criticism in his commentary on the Epistle. Having been convinced by Francis's proposal regarding the presence of epistolary forms in James and 1 John, Davids argued the Epistle "is far from a random collection of thoughts and sayings, but is a carefully constructed work. ... [S]cholarship must move beyond Dibelius's form-critical view of James, valuable as that is, and discover the redactional level."[50] For Davids, the cipher which reveals this "redactional level" is the double introduction of the Epistle.

Francis had shown that a typical feature of Hellenistic public and private letters, as well as "secondary letters" (i.e., letters embedded in narratives or 'literary letters') which "lack situational immediacy," was a two-fold introduction in which the second part paralleled and added to the themes contained in the first part. It was the theme(s) common to both parts of the two-fold introduction that identify the major emphases of the letter.[51] Moreover, he had argued that this same formal struc-

---

[49]Via, Forward to *What is Redaction Criticism?*, vi-vii.
[50]Davids, *James*, 25.
[51]Francis, "Form and Function," 111-117. Francis characterized his own study

ture was found within the epistles of James and 1 John. His isolation of
the individual sayings in Jas 1:2-27 essentially followed the divisions
proposed by Dibelius,[52] but he took 1:2-11 and 1:12-27 as the two
parts of the introduction. He described their relationship as follows:

> In the one paragraph and then the other, the same three elements are
> introduced in identical order and with complementary effect. The compo-
> nents are testing/steadfastness (1:2-4, 12-18), wisdom-words/reproaching
> (1:5-8, 19-21), rich-poor/doers (1:9-11, 22-25).[53]

Francis argued that these themes were then treated in the body of the
letter in inverse order relative to their occurrence within the introduction, but he divided the body of the Epistle into only two sections (2:1-
26 and 3:1 - 5:6).

Davids accepted Francis's proposal regarding the structure of the
two-fold introduction in its entirety. However, he was more consistent
in applying the principle of inverse development within the body of the
Epistle (2:1 - 5:6) in that he divided it into three sections, each
corresponding to one of the themes of the introduction. His proposal
regarding the overall structure of the Epistle can be presented as in
Table 1.[54]   David's suggested parallelism between the third theme of
the introduction ("Poverty Excels Wealth" // "Obedience Requires
Generosity") is a marked improvement over Francis's "rich-poor/doers,"
but both their statements of the parallel in the second theme of the
introduction are less than obvious.

Two full-length scholarly commentaries on the Epistle have
appeared since the publication of David's "New International Greek
Testament Commentary," namely Vouga's volume in the "Commentaire
du Nouveau Testament" and Martin's "Word Biblical Commentary."
While both are appreciative of the work by Francis and Davids,[55]
neither of them adopts the major divisions proposed by their predeces-

---

as an extension of the form-critical analysis of the Hellenistic epistolary genre (110).
I have chosen to save the discussion of whether or not "the Epistle of James" is a
letter, whether 'real' or 'literary,' for the conclusion of this study. Consequently,
I will reserve the full discussion of the particulars of Francis's argument until that
time.   See the section "An Overarching Figure: the 'Epistle' of James" in the
concluding chapter of this study.

[52]See Francis, "Form and Function," 121.

[53]Ibid., 118.

[54]The table is adapted from Davids, *James*, 29.

[55]For Vouga, see *Jacques*, 18-20; and for Martin, see *James*, xcix-ci.

Table 1:
STRUCTURE OF THE EPISTLE OF JAMES

I. Double Opening Statement (1:2-27)

A.	Testing Produces Joy (1:2-4)	Wisdom through Prayer (1:5-8)	Poverty Excels Wealth (1:9-11)
B.	Testing Produces Blessedness (1:12-18)	Pure Speech Contains No Anger (1:19-21)	Obedience Requires Generosity (1:22-25)

[Summary and Transition (1:26-27)]

II. Body (2:1 - 5:6)

The Excellence of
Poverty and
Generosity (2:1-26)

The Demand for
Pure Speech
(3:1 - 4:12)

Testing through
Wealth (4:13 - 5:6)

III. Closing (5:7-20): Endurance in the Test (Theme Summary, 5:7-11)
Rejection of Oaths (5:12)
Helping One Another through Prayer (5:13-18)
Closing Encouragement (5:19-20)

sors. They do, however, agree that certain themes introduced within the opening chapter provide the basis for the coherence of what follows within the Epistle. In that Martin follows Vouga with only minor alterations, I will use Vouga as the basis for the discussion that follows.

Vouga began by correctly observing that "the division of the text implies and determines its interpretation."[56] He described the bases

---

[56]Vouga, *Jacques*, 18: "Le découpage du texte implique et détermine son interprétation." Martin (*James*, ci) was overly influenced by the English cognate when he strangely characterizes Vouga's use of "découpage" as "suggest[ing] that the letter is a collection of illustrations mounted on a surface in decorative arrangement (a découpage)."

for his divisions as being drawn from the historical-critical study of the theological traditions within the Epistle, its provenance (which he suggested was a cosmopolitan city like Alexandria or Antioch), and a rhetorical analysis of the debate with its recipients. He thereby proposed three main themes were developed within the Epistle: the testing of faith (1:2-19a), the obedience of faith (1:19b - 3:18), and the fidelity of faith (4:1 - 5:20).[57] Somewhat surprisingly, however, "faith" does not play a direct role in his statement of the "fundamental question" of the letter: how can human existence accomplish its vocation and find dignity?[58]

Vouga noted several parallels between the opening and closing of the Epistle as he isolated the different parts of his first unit. He identified Jas 1:2-4 as the statement of the central theme of this section, the testing of faith. This "testing" is specified in three ways. First, there is opposition to diversion and opportunism (1:5-8 // 4:13-17). The second test is the opposition to riches (1:9-11 // 5:1-6). The sequence of tests is then interrupted by the beatitude upon those who endure trial (1:12 // 5:7-11), but completed by the opposition to determinism (1:13-19a // 5:12-20).[59]

The central part of the Epistle, for Vouga, extends from 1:19b - 3:18. He identified 1:19b-27 as the introduction to this unit and proposed that each of its five major themes were developed later within the unit:

> the indicative of free justification is manifested by the imperative of love (1:27a // 2:1-13); the Word is spoken in order to be observed and not so as to only be heard (1:22-24 // 2:14-26). The tongue is a destructive force, over which it is important to stand guard (1:19-20, 26 // 3:1-13), and it is necessary to be wary of wisdom that serves to assume power rather than to listen to and to live the Cross (1:19 // 3:14-18). The responsibility of Christians is in effect not only within the ecclesiastical community, but even more a dissent within the world (1:27b // 4:1 - 5:20, third part of the epistle).[60]

---

[57]Vouga, *Jacques*, 20. Martin (*James*, ciii-civ) accepted these divisions and also adopted Vouga's section headings: Enduring Trials, Applying the Word, and Witnessing to Divine Providence.

[58]"L'interrogation fondamentale qui traverse toute l'épître est: comment l'être humain accomplit-il sa vocation et où trouve-t-il en définitive sa dignité?" (Vouga, *Jacques*, 21).

[59]Vouga, *Jacques*, 21. Martin (*James*, cii-civ) simplified the division into three sections by taking 1:2-4 and 5-8 together ("Trials, Wisdom, Faith"), maintaining 1:9-11 ("The Reversal of Fortunes"), and combining 1:12 with 13-19a ("Testing: Its Source and Mischief—and Rationale").

[60]Vouga, *Jacques*, 21, translation mine.

Thus, his major divisions in the body of the Epistle, if not his opinion regarding their interrelatedness, correspond essentially to those presented by Dibelius.

The final section of the Epistle brings the argument to its climax by showing that "fidelity to the faith" is demonstrated by fulfilling the Christian vocation within the world. "They are not called to speak by self-importance, but by humility and submission (Jas 4:1-10). They are not to prophesy either by resentment or judging (4:11-12)."[61]   The final admonitions of the Epistle return once again to the ideas of the opening section (see above) and round out James's message. It is in this section that Martin differs most from Vouga. He tended to fragment the text more, referring to his divisions in 4:11 - 5:20 as "separate panels"[62] and only generally acknowledging Vouga's parallels between the opening and closing sections of the Epistle.

Martin's chief complaint with Vouga, however, is that he did not feel Vouga gave enough emphasis to the socio-historical matrix from which the Epistle emerged.   He commented that "[a]ny idea of the immediate context (so far as it may be recovered) of James's teaching and the readers' situation tends to get lost" in the midst of "Vouga's desire to give an 'existentialist' application to James's admonitions." But despite these objections, Martin ultimately "borrow[ed] his divisions and use[d] his work as a basis for [Martin's own] summary."[63]

The Purpose of the Epistle

Although the combination of form and redaction criticism had proven powerful tools in Gospel research for distinguishing between the *Sitz-im-Leben Jesu*, *Sitz-im-Leben alte Kirche*, and *Sitz-im-Leben Evangelium*, their application to the traditional materials contained in the Epistle of James provided less than overwhelming results for isolating the historical situation of the Epistle itself.   While both Davids and Vouga discussed the historical circumstances of the recipients of the Epistle, neither advanced significantly beyond the proposals of the 'dissenting form critics.'[64]   In fact, Davids admits that his research

---

[61]Ibid., 22, translation mine.

[62]Martin, *James*, ciii.

[63]Ibid., cii.

[64]For Davids, see *James*, 28-34; for Vouga, see *Jacques*, 17-18 and 24-27. Davids indeed admitted (*James*, 30) that he was forced to use the same method suggested above with reference to the 'dissenting form critics': "it is hard to understand how the choice of this material could not reflect the *Sitz im Leben* of the

failed to "find a clear and specific historical situation," and ultimately concludes that "one can never be sure of the setting of James."[65]

Only Martin offered with some confidence a proposal regarding the purpose of the Epistle in response to particular historical circumstances. He proposed a two-stage development of the letter. The first stage was a collection of the teachings of James the Just which was then carried by his disciples to Antioch on the Orontes. It was there that the extant Epistle was edited:

> [A]n enterprising editor ... published his master's work in epistolary form as a plan to gain for it credibility as an apostolic letter. And in doing so, he aimed to address a situation of critical pastoral significance in his region. The nub of the problem was a challenge to the authority of teachers in a congregation whose listeners' roots went back to the early days when "prophets and teachers" were the chief leaders (Acts 13:1).[66]

Martin went on to theorize that this editor also sought to champion the "underprivileged and disadvantaged" within a congregation which was "sufficiently socially stratified to have poor and rich together."[67]

Martin's proposal does have the benefit of trying to re-establish the link between the structure and purpose of the Epistle: the editor chose an epistolary structure to give the impression of authority perceived by the early church in the apostolic letters. Thus, Martin attempted to establish the link between structure and purpose by implicitly granting Francis's and Davids's contentions that the Epistle of James has the structural elements of an epistle. By utilizing a literary form and structure associated with authoritative discourse by the recipients, the editor contributes to his or her purpose of reasserting "the authority of teachers in [the] congregation" for which the Epistle was written.

The difficulty is that this 'purpose' for choosing an epistolary form does not contribute materially to the more fundamental question of the

---

author, his readers, or both. ... [H]is selection of the units will be limited to those which are relevant to his own time."

[65]Ibid., 28 and 34.

[66]Martin, *James*, lxxvii.

[67]For Martin's full discussion of the relationship of James the Just to the Epistle, see lxi-lxxvii. His conclusions are stated on lxxvi-lxxvii. The views presented in the commentary differ from his earlier proposal in "The Life-setting of the Epistle of James in the Light of Jewish History," in *Biblical and Near Eastern Studies*, W. S. LaSor Festschrift (Grand Rapids: William B. Eerdmans Publishing Company, 1978), 97-103, which placed the writing of the Epistle in Jerusalem prior to 70 CE.

actual situations the editor sought to address. That is to say, there are no clear connections between the purposes which the editor hoped to achieve in the Syrian church (re-establishing the authority of teachers, championing the disadvantaged) and the controlling themes which Martin had borrowed from Vouga in discussing the organization and structure of the letter (namely the testing, obedience and fidelity of faith). This disparity arises from the fact that Vouga chose more modern, "existentialist" categories for his analysis of the organization of the Epistle,[68] rather than relying upon a reconstructed *Sitz im Leben* (either his own or someone else's).

Summary: Redaction and Ethical Discourse

We have seen that a major focus of concern in Davids's commentary on the Epistle is to make it more literarily acceptable to modern readers by isolating a definite organizational structure. He maintains his association with the historical critics by implicitly asserting that the organizational structure must be one which was available in the first century of the common era. He found an answer to this problem in the earlier work of Francis, which he then expanded and refined. However, Davids's more conservative theological position did not lead him to the conclusion reached by the form critics that a deontological ethic would itself be problematic for modern readers of the Epistle. If ultimately the admonitions contained within the letter are the word and commands of God and not simply the theological and ethical musings of James the Just or one of his disciples, then of course they are 'universal moral principles' applicable across both time and space.

Martin's commentary on the Epistle, however, shows that an easy acceptance of a deontological ethic is not inherent to a conservative theological position which views this text as an expression of the word of God. Martin, too, sensed that modern readers might wince at the universal claims of a deontological ethic. Thus, he sought to make the Epistle more palatable by incorporating the existentialist strains of Vouga's interpretation. In so doing, he also moved the interpretation of the paraenetic materials toward a "perfectionist" ethic, which draws both on "Aristotle's interest in the cultivation of those excellencies (virtues) which actualize human potential" and on "Nietzsche's vision of *Übermensch*, an ecstatic celebration of human powers of self-transcendence."

---

[68]So Martin (*James*, cii) assesses Vouga's analysis. For the relevant discussion in Vouga, see *Jacques*, 21-23.

Perfectionist ethical theories center "on perfecting human powers and on creating social conditions which facilitate such perfection."[69]

By expounding James's admonitions in terms of the question of 'how human existence can accomplish its vocation and find dignity,' both Martin and Vouga began to move toward redefining both the structure and purpose of the Epistle within twentieth century terms rather than first century terms. But both Martin and Vouga also attempted to keep one foot in each century, as it were, by mixing their existentialist readings with an interest in the historical setting of the Epistle and by adopting certain aspects of Francis's proposals regarding first century epistolary forms.

Conclusion: Reading the Epistle of James through Historical Lenses

What then are the results of reading the Epistle of James "from the outside in," looking through historical-critical lenses across the wide expanse of time and distance that separates us from it in an attempt to understand "how some one could have written such an apparently disorganized text" and "why some one would have written such a text"? The most consistent picture of the relationship between these two issues is provided by a thorough-going form criticism such as is found in Dibelius. The paraenetic genre within Greco-Roman literature was characterized by a stringing together of traditional materials by mnemonic devices such as catchwords, even if the sayings so joined were only ever so loosely related by topic. Further, the sole purpose of such writings was the preservation of universal moral principles. The history of the form "paraenesis" leads inexorably to the conclusion that there is no structured argument or specific purpose for the Epistle.

By bracketing out of the field of vision certain aspects of one or the other of our questions, these historical lenses can bring a little more focus to either our concern to know the purpose or the organization of the Epistle. Thus, if we grant that there is no development of thought from one saying to another (no "real" organization), it may be possible to find a repetition of certain concerns that will show us the historical circumstances that led to the selection of these particular traditions—and thus "why" some one wrote *this* text. Conversely, we can look at "how" ancient writers organized letters and thereby see an overall

---

[69]Ogletree, *Use of the Bible*, 16-17. For his fuller discussion of perfectionist ethical theories, see 31-34.

organizational pattern in the Epistle; but in the end we will have to admit that the structure so isolated does not truly bear on the question of "why" some one wrote *this* text.

The lenses of form and redaction criticism have limited our vision to historical concerns. The only organizational patterns they perceive are the genres made available by the historical study of texts from the Greco-Roman period, in this case paraenesis and epistolary literature. The only purposes they allow are likewise historical: either prevention of the loss of traditions with the passing of time or attempting to respond to particular historical circumstances. And the only consistent relationship they can perceive between the structure and purpose of the Epistle—Dibelius's 'no' structure and 'no' purpose—has proven increasingly unsatisfactory for commentators, since it cannot satisfy modern desires for literary organization nor assuage concerns about deontological ethical systems.

Is there another way of viewing the relationship between the structure and purposes of the Epistle of James?

CHAPTER TWO

READING THE EPISTLE FROM THE INSIDE OUT: GREIMASIAN STRUCTURAL SEMIOTICS

Our review of historico-critical studies of the Epistle of James has supported the contention that the adoption of an historical paradigm for investigating the relationship between the text's structure and purpose leads to reading the text "from the outside in." It is thus incumbent upon us to investigate my contention that investigations grounded in a linguistic paradigm which study the text as an example of the communication process read the text "from the inside out." But what does it mean to read a text in this way?

We can gain an initial entry into this way of reading texts by considering some comments by Johannes Louw regarding how one such linguistic method, namely "discourse analysis," understands the role of the "structure" of a text:

> Whenever a person has something to say on a given subject, he is faced with the problem of how to say it, for it is by no means a matter of merely "throwing together"[1] a number of randomly selected utterances. The material must be put in some order, and language normally offers a multiplicity of arrangements, all of which would serve differently to effect the purpose. ... Therefore, the way or the manner, i.e. the structure, in which a notion is communicated, is the heart of its effectiveness. Although the structural pattern may not be obtrusive (and effective communication

---

[1]This phrase reminds me of the title of an essay on the structure of James 2: G. M. Burge, "'And Threw Them Thus on Paper': Rediscovering the Poetic Form of James 2:14-26," *StBTh* 7 (1977): 31-45.

usually *does not* reveal its structure obtrusively) it is a necessary prerequisite for any sensible discourse that it should be based on an underlying structural pattern.

Although it is through analysis of the surface structure that the receptor is able to retrace what the author actually had in mind, we should beware of seeing this procedure as an end in itself, because the author never starts with a surface structure. ... [O]ur task is not actually that of going from surface structure to deep structure, but of reconstructing the path from the original deep structure to the surface structure conveyed by our text. ... This procedure is more informative ... for it reveals the selections, orderings and arrangements made by the author in moving from the deep to surface structure.[2]

But it is not enough to simply note the possibility of reading a text "from the inside out" (i.e., from its "deep structures" to its "surface structures"); we need also to understand what strengths and weaknesses such an approach has relative to the problem at hand—how one can relate the structure and purposes of the Epistle of James.

This chapter will examine how a methodological approach grounded in a communication paradigm provides significant advantages for an analysis of the Epistle which sets as its goal discerning an organizational structure that will contribute to an understanding of James's purposes in writing. Secondly, it will set forward a thesis regarding one way that the discursive structure and purposes of the Epistle can be related. The chapter will conclude with an outline of the procedure to be used in testing this thesis in the exegetical chapters to follow. Let us begin by reviewing some linguistically based methodologies which have previously been utilized in studying the Epistle.

Early Linguistic Studies of the Epistle of James

The rather lengthy quote from Louw regarding discourse analysis in the introduction to this chapter is fitting since the first linguistic studies of the Epistle were based on a discourse analysis approach. In a series of papers written at the "Summer Institute of Linguistics" of the International Linguistics Center between 1974 and 1978,[3] five students

---

[2]Johannes Louw, "Discourse Analysis and the Greek New Testament," *BT* 24 (1973): 101-102, emphasis his.

[3]The International Linguistics Center is the training division of Wycliffe Bible Translators located in Dallas, Texas. I wish to thank their staff for providing me with copies of these unpublished papers.

performed analyses of the Epistle, each building on the previous work. Consequently, the different studies are of mixed value, and occasionally only serve to compound the weaknesses of their predecessors.

The first study completed seems to owe less to the particularities of discourse analysis theory than to the methodology of James Thayer who wrote it. To be fair, it should be noted that discourse analysis theory was still in its very early stages of development. The problem was that Thayer simply made a summary of previous divisions of the text from the paragraphing of modern translations and outlines of commentators and then sought to isolate the "various grammatical forms which are found at the beginning of a section or paragraph."[4] As a result, imperative-vocative structures and rhetorical questions were identified as the "grammatical forms" that mark the onset of new sections/paragraphs. Although other criteria were later introduced (lexical evidence and topics),[5] these criteria were simply correlated to the grammatical forms rather than used as a check on the initial findings (themselves not based on a fresh reading of the text of the Epistle itself). Thayer's imperative-vocative introductory structure was then taken as established, without further investigation, by those who followed him and used as a criteria for isolating units.[6]

Without question the best analysis of the Epistle among these papers is that presented by Ralph Hill and Kiyoko Torakawa.[7] Yet Hill

---

[4]James Thayer, "On James," TMs [photocopy], 1974, International Linguistics Center, Dallas, 6. That Thayer relied too heavily on previous analyses rather than making a fresh reading of the Epistle is a criticism which could also be made of a more recent discourse analysis performed by Patrick J. Hartin ("James: A New Testament Wisdom Writing and its Relationship to Q," [D.Th. thesis, University of South Africa, 1988], summarized in Hartin, *James and Q*, 23-34 and 245-246). His overall pattern of organization is drawn from Francis (cf. "Form and Function," 121) and his chiastic ordering of the body of the letter had already been suggested by Catherine Rountree (see "Further Thoughts on the Discourse Structure of James," TMs [photocopy], 1976, International Linguistics Center, Dallas).

[5]Thayer, "On James," 9-14.

[6]See J. O. Ekstrom, "The Discourse Structure of the Book of James," TMs [photocopy], 1975, International Linguistics Center, Dallas, 1; Rountree, "Further Thoughts," 30; and Ralph Hill, "An Overview of the Discourse Structure of James," TMs [photocopy], 1978, International Linguistics Center, Dallas, ii, though Hill and his collaborator Kiyoko Torakawa were apparently unaware of Thayer's study and were drawing on Ekstrom and Rountree.

[7]In addition to Hill's "Overview," see Kiyoko Torakawa, "Literary-Semantic Analysis of James 1-2," TMs [photocopy], 1978, International Linguistics Center, Dallas; and Ralph Hill, "An Analysis of James 3-5 to the Paragraph Constituent

conceded that their study was still hindered by two factors long since emphasized by Dibelius:

> First, the predominance of asyndeton on all levels of structure make it difficult to assign communication roles between the units. Second, the presence of close to 60 imperatives gives rise to many multiheaded paragraphs from which theme statements must be abstracted.[8]

Thus, these particular discourse analysis studies of the Epistle failed to offer any major advances in understanding the relationship between the organization and purposes of the Epistle as a whole.

Just before Hill and Torakawa began their work, Wilhelm Wuellner published an excellent study of the Epistle of James in the spring of 1978 which sought to combine the insights of modern linguistic theory and the categories of classical rhetoric.[9] In the opening sections of his essay, Wuellner critiqued the approach of Dibelius and his followers for having adopted a "static" view of texts with regard to the relationship between the text and reader. Drawing upon reader response criticism, Wuellner argued in favor of a "Textpragmatic" approach that would conceive of texts as a process of communication. Among the elements of this process, Wuellner emphasized the choice of media ("Medienwahl," i.e. direct or indirect, dialogue or monologue, private or public communication), the choice of genre ("Gattungswahl"), the choice of arguments ("Argumentationswahl," drawing heavily on the categories of classical rhetoric), and the choice of linguistic and stylistic features ("die Wahl der sprachligen und stilistischen Wirkmittel"). But while Wuellner provides a detailed reading of the Epistle, he still begins somewhat "outside" of the text by prefacing his analysis with a discussion of "die argumentative Situation" in terms of the ecclesial and social circumstances of the recipients.[10]

In 1979-80, one year after the appearance of Wuellner's study, an early stage of Greimas's structural semiotic model was applied to the study of the Epistle by a group at the Centre pour l'analyse du discours religieux (CADIR).[11] This group offered an analysis of the structure

---

Level," TMs [photocopy], 1978, International Linguistics Center, Dallas.

[8]Hill, "Overview," ii.

[9]Wilhelm H. Wuellner, "Der Jakobusbrief im Licht der Rhetorik und Textpragmatic," *LB* 43 (1978): 5-66.

[10]See ibid., 21-22.

[11]See F. Genuyt, "Le chapitre 1 de l'Epître de Jacques. Compte-rendu d'une séance du séminaire 'Littérature Biblique' du C.A.D.I.R. (1979-1980)", *SemiotBib*

of the Epistle ("organisation narrative") and some notes on the development of the discourse ("observations discursives") by utilizing certain discrete aspects of structural semiotic theory. For example, most of the structure of James 1 is presented in terms of the "Sender—Object—Receiver" structure, and the metaphor about 'the poor and the rich' in Jas 1:9-11 is analyzed by application of the "semiotic square." But this somewhat piecemeal approach has hindered its effectiveness in addressing our particular concern of relating an overall structure of the Epistle to the purposes of its author.

This observation, however, points up an important issue relative to each of these early linguistic studies of the Epistle of James. At least in part, Genuyt and his colleagues were restricted to using a piecemeal approach because Greimas had only that year offered an integrative framework for the discrete aspects of his semiotic theory.[12] Indeed, each of these different linguistic studies has become quite dated by theoretical advances in the methodologies on which they are based.[13] I would suggest that three particular advances in structural semiotics make it especially well suited for studying the relationship between the structure and purposes of the Epistle of James.[14]

---

17 (1980): 38-45; "Epître de Saint Jacques—Chapitre 2," *SemiotBib* 19 (1980): 25-31; "Epître de Jacques—Chapitre 3," *SemiotBib* 22 (1981): 55-59; "Epître de Jacques 4,1 - 5,6," *SemiotBib* 23 (1981): 44-56; and "Epître de Saint-Jacques, ch. 5,6-20," *SemiotBib* 24 (1981): 28-36.

[12]See A. J. Greimas and Joseph Courtés, *Sémiotique: dictionaire raisonné de la théorie du langage* (Paris: Hachette, 1979); ET *Semiotics and Language: An Analytical Dictionary*, trans. Larry Crist and Daniel Patte, *et al.* (Bloomington: Indiana University Press, 1982).

[13]For discourse analysis, see Johannes P. Louw, *Semantics of New Testament Greek* (SBLSS; Atlanta: Scholars Press, 1982). For Wuellner's "Rhetorik und Textpragmatic" approach, see Wilhelm Wuellner, "Hermeneutics and Rhetorics: From 'Truth and Method' to 'Truth and Power'," *Scriptura: Journal of Bible and Theology in South Africa* S 3 (1989): 1-54; and cf. Hubert Frankemölle, "Gespalten oder ganz: Zur Pragmatik der theologischen Anthropologie des Jakobusbriefes," in *Kommunikation und Solidarität*, ed. Hans-Ulrich v. Brachel and Norbert Mette (Freiburg and Münster: Edition Exodus, 1985), 160-178; and idem, "Das semantische Netz des Jakobusbriefes: Zur Einheit eines umstrittenen Briefes," *BZ*, NF 34 (1990): 161-197. For advances in structural semiotics, see below.

[14]It is perhaps illustrative of how different the historical and communications paradigms truly are that there is virtually no mention of any of these studies in historico-critical studies of the Epistle published in the past decade. Perhaps ironically, the least available works (the discourse analysis papers) are cited by Davids (*James*, 24) as having "reconfirmed" his own analysis of the text. Elsewhere

Advantages of a Structural Semiotic Model

Three basic theoretical insights gained by Greimasian structural semiotics provide methodological advantages for attempting to relate the discursive structures and purposes of the Epistle. First, structural semiotic research has shown that a text may be primarily ordered (i.e., find a "coherence") in multiple ways depending on the levels of the discourse (e.g., its discursive syntax or its discursive semantics) being considered. Secondly, the application of these models to the study of biblical texts has shown that one of the major goals, or purposes, of religious discourse *qua* "religious" discourse is the communication of a new micro-semantic universe to the reader. Finally, structural semiotics posits the possibilities of semantic organizations fundamentally based either on issues of ontology (the dominant pattern in Euro-American cultures) or on issues of value (a characteristic feature of early Palestinian Jewish texts, for example). Let us consider each of these insights so as to understand their particular methodological advantages.

Syntactic vs. Semantic Organization

Greimasian structural semiotic research has shown that all discourses have multiple coherences, each deriving from the different levels of the discourse.[15] Every text has a (potential) coherence in terms of

---

Davids notes the existence of Genuyt's work in a *forschungsgeschichtliche* article (Peter H. Davids, "The Epistle of James in Modern Discussion," *ANRW* II.25.5 [1988]: 3639, n. 70), but I have found no other references to them. Similarly, the only such citations of Wuellner's essay that I have found are mentions within two surveys of research (Birger A. Pearson, "James, 1-2 Peter, Jude," in *The New Testament and Its Modern Interpreters*, ed. Eldon Jay Epp and George W. MacRae, SBLBMI [Atlanta: Scholars Press, 1989], 375; and Wiard Popkes, *Adressaten, Situation und Form des Jakobusbriefes*, SBS 125/126 [Stuttgart: Verlag Katholisches Bibelwerk GmbH, 1986], 16-17) and passing references in a few articles (cf. John G. Lodge, "James and Paul at Cross-Purposes? James 2,22," *Bib* 62 [1981]: 197, n. 7; 201, n. 15; and 204; and Robert W. Wall, "James as Apocalyptic Paraenesis," *ResQ* 32 [1990]: 12, n. 7; and 19).

[15]A similar point is made by Mieke Bal, who draws on the work of the Italian semiotician Umberto Eco. She uses the term "code" rather than "coherence," and discusses four "disciplinary codes" (historical, theological, anthropological, and literary codes) within contemporary biblical studies and two "transdisciplinary codes" (thematic and gender). For her description of "codes," see *Murder and Difference: Gender, Genre, and Scholarship on Sisera's Death*, Indiana Studies in Biblical Literature (Bloomington: University of Indiana Press, 1988), 3-7. For its theoretical base, see Umberto Eco, *A Theory of Semiotics*, Advances in Semiotics

such areas as its discursive syntax (the expressions relating issues of time, space and actants, or what might more generally be called a 'logical sequence'), its discursive semantics (the thematization and figurativization used to express meaningful relationships), or its narrative semantics (the micro-semantic universe created in the discourse).

However, not every text will necessarily be fully coherent at all levels of the discourse.[16] For example, the distinction between the two types of primary organization[17] provided by discursive syntax and discursive semantics can be illustrated by considering the different organizing principles governing the formulation of a syllogism as compared to a poem. Whereas the legitimacy of a syllogism depends on the consistency of its terms (e.g. the actants within the major and minor premise must be the same or comparable), the appropriateness of the themes and figures of a poem are determined by the meanings that they evoke and not, for instance, by the 'logical relations' between the elements of its metaphors. While one cannot logically "compare apples and oranges," it is not difficult to imagine them meaningfully following one another as figures in a poem.[18] A syllogism is organized primari-

---

(Bloomington: University of Indiana Press, 1976), and idem, *Semiotics and the Philosophy of Language*, Advances in Semiotics (Bloomington: University of Indiana Press, 1984).

[16]It is in fact the breakdowns in the coherence of a text that provide both its interest and, perhaps ironically, its believability. On the role of inconsistencies in creating the verisimilitude of narratives, cf. Mary Ann Tolbert, *Sowing the Gospel: Mark's World in Literary-Historical Perspective* (Minneapolis: Augsburg Fortress, 1989), 30-31 and the references cited there.

[17]All discourses are of course organized to a degree both syntactically and semantically. The issue is whether the dominant organizing features are syntactic or semantic and thus whether the particular discourse is primarily organized in terms of its syntax or semantics.

[18]The differences between 'logical' and 'poetic' argumentation have also been noted by Lodge ("James and Paul," 209-210) in commenting on the use of chiasmus within the argumentation of the Epistle:

Truth here is perceived by poetic expression, not only by reasoned logic. ... [T]he author of our epistle has borrowed the forms common to the tradition of Hebrew Wisdom literature. As with that body of writing, the literary devices cannot be considered merely external or ornamental. As von Rad says, the poetry of a wise man's teaching

cannot be separated from the intellectual process as if it were something added later; rather, perception takes place precisely in and with the poetic conception (*Wisdom in Israel*, 24).

The first clue, then, is the manner of perceiving a truth through poetic form.

ly in terms of its discursive syntax, whereas a poem is primarily structured by its discursive semantics.

According to the semiotic model developed by Greimas and others, the limits of all discursive units are marked by the parallels between the "inverted" and "posited contents" of their 'introductions' and 'conclusions' respectively.[19] Delimiting discursive units by this means involves the tentative isolation of themes expressed by these inverted parallelisms. These parallels may themselves be either primarily syntactic or semantic parallels.

In the case of inverted parallelisms constructed by the discursive syntax, the themes of a discourse unit are frequently posited by the author[20] at the close of a division as the "solution" or "resolution" to a "problem" set forth earlier in the discourse. It is the raising of this "problem" in terms which are acceptable or meaningful to the reader[21] that marks the beginning of the division. Within narrative discourses, this "problem—solution" pattern can take on a variety of particular expressions such as "wrong—wrong punished," "difficulty—difficulty removed," "task—task achieved."[22] In didactic discourses,[23] the "problem" might be a philosophical or theological question to be answered or error to be corrected.[24]

---

[19]For a brief explanation of these principles and their application to the isolation of discursive units, cf. Daniel Patte, "A Structural Exegesis of 2 Corinthians 2:14-3:6 and 6:11-7:4," SBLASP 26 (Atlanta: Scholars Press, 1987), 25 n. 6 and the references cited there, and idem, *Structural Exegesis for New Testament Critics* (GBS, NT series; Minneapolis: Augsburg Fortress, 1990), 10-16.

[20]From a semiotic vantage point, technically one should speak of the "enunciator," that is the "author" constructed as a component in the production of the discourse, similar to the "implied author" in other literary models. See Greimas and Courtés, *Semiotics and Language*, 105.

[21]Again, technically one should speak of the "enunciatee," that is the "recipient" constructed as a component in the production of the discourse, similar to the "implied reader" of other models. See Greimas and Courtés, *Semiotics and Language*, 105.

[22]See Robert C. Culley, "Action Sequences in Genesis 2-3," *Semeia* 18 (1980): 25-33.

[23]For a semiotic definition of "didactic discourse" in terms of the functions of "causing to know," "causing to do," and "causing to believe," see Daniel Patte, "Method for a Structural Exegesis of Didactic Discourses: Analysis of 1 Thessalonians," *Semeia* 26 (1983): 87-88.

[24]So that, for example, in 1 Thess 4:13-18 Paul provides the "solution" to the "problem" of the Thessalonians' grief caused by their "ignoran[ce] concerning those who are asleep" by brief instruction regarding the Parousia and its consequences

Inverted parallelisms can also be constructed from primarily semantic features. Thus, a figure can be invested with new meanings and nuances by being set in new relations of meaning, or conversely a theme can be invested with additional nuances by finding expression through new figures. The parallels might be between semantic values such as "life"—"death", "holy"—"profane", "love"—"hatred." And of course there is no requirement that the "positive" value must always be the "posited content" toward which the unit moves, or even that both the "positive" and the "negative" values must be developed within the same discourse unit.

Thus, the "inverted" and "posited" content are often presented discursively by means of the literary device of "closure,"[25] whether the parallels are between syntactic or semantic features. This fact provides the first advantage of a structural semiotic model for dealing with the problem of the discursive structures of the Epistle. Since the limits of discursive units are marked by parallels of "inverted" and "posited content" regardless of whether the primary organization is in terms of the discursive syntax or discursive semantics, it should be possible to isolate an organizational structure for the Epistle by this means even if that structure might differ from a 'logical sequence' traditionally sought by Western critical exegetes.

The recent history of research on the Epistle of James, as we have seen, has clearly shown that it is not possible to present a consistently coherent structure of the Epistle in terms of its discursive syntax. Even those interpreters who have argued for some overall organizational structure and argument are ultimately forced to classify at least certain sections of the Epistle as a 'collection of sayings on various topics.'[26] Therefore, at least the possibility exists that the Epistle is primarily organized in terms of its discursive semantics. Indeed all "religious" discourses have a coherence in terms of their discursive semantics in that they utilize the progression of themes and figures to accomplish the

---

both for the living and the dead believers.

[25]On this rhetorical device, cf. George Kennedy, *New Testament Interpretation through Rhetorical Criticism*, Studies in Religion (Chapel Hill and London: University of North Carolina, 1984), 33-34.

[26]So James B. Adamson (*The Epistle of James*, NICNT [Grand Rapids: William B. Eerdmans Publishing Company, 1976] 45) treats all of James 5 as "Conclusion," but does not relate the issues raised there to what has come previously. For Martin (*James*, civ) the problematic section is all of chapters 4 and 5 in which Martin gathers a variety of topics (several redundant) under the general heading "Witnessing to Divine Providence."

purposes for writing of their authors. How, then, does structural
semiotics conceive of the purposes of religious discourse?

A Major Goal of Religious Discourse

Traditionally, historical critics have identified an author's purpose
in writing with the circumstances which "occasioned" the work. Such
definite historical markers have been notoriously difficult to isolate
within the Epistle of James. Dibelius held, largely on the basis of his
classification of the Epistle as paraenesis, that no specific circumstances
prompted the work, and thus the book had no specific "purpose" as the
term is usually understood.[27] Other scholars, however, have argued
for allusions to historical circumstances that might have led, to a greater[28] or lesser[29] degree, to the composition of the Epistle; but none
of these scholars posits a truly unifying purpose for the Epistle.[30]

But a structural semiotic model allows us to envision discourses
with other kinds of goals. Thus, religious discourses have as one purpose or goal the attempt by the author to convince the implied reader to
adopt a certain "system of convictions," or in more technical terms a
"micro-semantic universe," regarding how to perceive and order the
realm of human experience. It is the communication of such a "faith-
pattern," rather than the specific content of the individual convictions
used to express it, that is the ultimate goal of "religious" discourse as
opposed to other types of discourse.[31]

This theoretical insight was initially set forward by Daniel and
Aline Patte who posited a distinction between "profane" and "sacred"
texts. They argued that "profane" texts seek to validate a new "semantic
universe" in such a way as to supplant the old vision of reality held by
the readers. "Sacred" texts, however, operate within the semantic universe of the readers and thus serve to reinforce the readers' perception
that such a vision of reality indeed corresponds to their experiences and

---

[27]Cf. Dibelius, *James*, 46-47. Cf. also Ropes's comment (*St. James*, 28) that
the Epistle was "not sent to meet the needs of any particular moment or crisis in a
definite church, but aiming at the edification of any Christians into whose hands it
might fall."

[28]Cf. Mayor, *St. James*, cxxxvii-cxxxviii; Reicke, *James, Peter and Jude*, 5-7;
and Mußner, *Jakobusbrief*, 14-22.

[29]Cf. Laws, *James*, 6-10; and Martin, *James*, lxxix-lxxvii.

[30]All of this, of course, has already been treated more fully in chapter one.

[31]Such as the "informational" discourse of scientific treatises. Cf. Patte,
Structural Exegesis for New Testament Critics, 63.

thereby strengthens their "faith" or "convictions."[32] The terminologi-
cal choice was unfortunate,[33] but more pertinent at this later stage of
theoretical reflection is that this distinction between "sacred" and "profane" seems more applicable to "dimensions" of religious texts than to
"types" of religious texts.[34]

That both "sacred" and "profane" dimensions can simultaneously
be at work within a single text is evidenced by Patte's later distinction
among three types of didactic discourse.[35] His first type of didactic
discourse "presuppose[s] that the addressees have already the 'right'
semantic universe (i.e., the addresser's semantic universe)" so that
"'causing to know' and 'causing to do' are the dominant functions."
This type corresponds to what had been termed "sacred" texts because
the semantic universe of the reader could be affirmed. The third type
have as their "only objective ... 'causing to believe.' They aim at
communicating a different semantic universe to the addressees," and thus
correspond to "profane" texts. It is the second type of didactic discourse
which evidences both "sacred" and "profane" dimensions:

> Didactic discourses which presuppose that the addressees might not
> perceive the relationship between the proposed action and their own semantic
> universe (which is too narrow in scope, or weak, but not contradictory to that
> of the addressees [*sic*, "addresser"]). ... In other words, "causing to
> believe" becomes the dominant function, but "causing to do" remains the
> ultimate objective of the discourse.[36]

Most examples of religious paraenesis in general and, as the exegesis
below will demonstrate, the Epistle of James in particular belong to this
second type of didactic discourse.

This intra-textual "micro-semantic universe" communicated to the
implied reader provides the basis, or "reason," for the actions proscribed

---

[32]See Daniel and Aline Patte, *Structural Exegesis: From Theory to Practice*
(Philadelphia: Fortress Press, 1978), Chapter 4, especially 97-99.

[33]As Patte himself acknowledged. See Patte, "Method for Didactic Discourses,"
92, and idem, *Paul's Faith and the Power of the Gospel: A Structural Introduction
to the Pauline Letters* (Philadelphia: Fortress Press, 1983), 379, n. 19.

[34]A point made by Elizabeth Struthers Malbon ("The Theory and Practice of
Structural Exegesis. A Review Article," *Perspectives in Religious Studies* 11
[1984]: 274-75). She speaks of the role of "religious symbols serv[ing] not only to
'establish world' but also to 'subvert world'" (275). The former she associates with
the Pattes' use of "sacred" and the latter with "profane."

[35]Patte, "Method for Didactic Discourses," 91.

[36]Ibid.

or admonished by the paraenetic materials[37] and has striking similarities with the "social world constructs" in the "sociology of knowledge" theories of Peter Berger and Thomas Luckmann,[38] as well as the
work of Victor Turner.[39]   Indeed, this description of one of the
purposes of religious discourse relates well to the social functions of
paraenesis proposed by Leo Perdue[40] on the basis of Berger's and
Turner's work.

Perdue described the social function of paraenesis as being to
provide concrete examples of the "social world" to individuals who have
recently entered a new social group or new level within the social
structure. Perdue defined paraenesis as

> a means by which an individual is *introduced to the group's or role's social
> knowledge*, including especially norms and values pertaining to group or role
> behavior, *internalizes this knowledge*, and *makes it the basis for both
> behavior and the meaning system by which he interprets and orders his
> world.*[41]

This definition of paraenesis has far more in common with a semiotic
understanding of the purpose of religious discourse than with Dibelius's
view of paraenesis as the preservation of a received ethical tradition.

Perdue described four particular social occasions where paraenesis
is typically found: (1) testamentary settings and literature, (2) periods
of separation of teacher and student, (3) during "rites of passage," and
(4) periods of reflection upon earlier "incorporation" into a group.[42]

---

[37]In terms of Patte's most recent discussion of the religious dimensions of texts,
the "micro-semantic universe" is related to the phenomenon of "believing self-
evident truths" which underlies the possibilities of "believing a truth on authority"
and "believing as thinking that something is true." See Patte, *Religious Dimensions*,
Part III, "Insights into the Religious Character of Biblical Texts: The Interface of
Semiotics and Faith," 103-215, where each of these dimensions of belief is discussed
in a separate chapter.

[38]Peter L. Berger and Thomas Luckmann, *The Social Construction of Reality:
A Treatise in the Sociology of Knowledge* (New York: Anchor Doubleday, 1967).

[39]Victor Turner, *The Forest of Symbols* (Ithaca: Cornell University Press,
1967), and idem, *The Ritual Process* (Ithaca: Cornell University Press, 1967).

[40]Leo G. Perdue, "Paraenesis and the Epistle of James," *ZNW* 72 (1981): 241-
256, and idem, "The Social Character of Paraenesis and Paraenetic Literature,"
Semeia 50 (1990): 5-39.

[41]Perdue, "Paraenesis and James," 251, emphases mine.

[42]Ibid., 247. Perdue elaborated on these social settings and the social roles of
the participants in his later article; see "Social Character of Paraenesis," 19-26.

But having accepted Dibelius's characterizations of the general and universal nature of paraenesis, Perdue encountered difficulties in trying to determine which of these social settings prompted the composition of the Epistle of James. Ultimately he admitted that the Epistle is largely "silent about the social settings in which [it was] used,"[43] and could only "suggest" that the Epistle is "an instruction given by a teacher when he is either separated from his audience (a paraenetic letter) or is about to leave them because of increasing age and approaching death (an address, later modified into an epistle)"[44] without giving any real bases for his proposal.

However, since the "system of convictions" elucidated by a structural exegesis is intra-textual, this semiotic model does not confront us with the methodological problems of determining an extra-textual social setting for the particular example of paraenesis as a prerequisite for further investigation. Additionally, since the first step in studying the "system of convictions" of a discourse involves the identification and analysis of the discursive semantic units,[45] this model necessarily maintains a relationship between discursive structures and purposes in a text.

Veridictory vs. Thymic Semiotics

The third advantage of this structural semiotic model is that it posits the possibility of quite different semantic organizations of the figures and themes of discourses, including semantic organizations that are quite foreign to the ontologically based semiotics found in most Euro-American cultures.[46] Interestingly, Cantinat has already suggested (without development) that perhaps the organization of the Epistle is not in keeping with the expectations of "our Western logic."[47] This

---

[43]Perdue, "Paraenesis and James," 247. He had earlier suggested that while Dibelius's conclusions may apply to particular paraenetic precepts they do not necessarily apply to "entire paraenetic texts themselves." But as we have seen in chapter one, Dibelius made his argument regarding the whole of the Epistle, and not just its individual pieces of paraenetic tradition.

[44]Perdue, "Paraenesis and James," 250.

[45]Cf. the sequence of "steps" for performing a "structural exegesis" outlined by Patte, *Structural Exegesis for New Testament Critics*, 26.

[46]This is not to say that only such Euro-American cultures utilize a veridictory semiotics. Certainly other and very different cultural systems and expressions prioritize ontological categories over valuative ones and so construct systems of meaning within a veridictory semiotics.

[47]Cantinat, *Jacques et Jude*, 11: "Remarquons que notre logique occidentale eût demandé de grouper entre plusieurs de ces thèmes. ... Mais nous n'avons pas à

theoretical research has shown that the semantic organization of discourses can be based on values rather than ontological issues.[48] Such semantic organization was referred to as "organic thinking" in Max Kadushin's studies on rabbinic thought,[49] and termed "holistic thinking" in E. P. Sanders's study of Paul which drew on Kadushin.[50]

What might such a value based semantic organization (a "thymic semiotic system") be like? Within a thymic semiotics, the different realms of human experience would be perceived in terms of the values (such as "holiness" or "uncleanness") with which they are associated rather than the particular circumstances of their mode of existence (or even their "non-existence"). For example, within a thymic semiotics "Temple worship" and "family life" might be "organically" related within a single realm of human experience by the "sacred" value ascribed to the act of "eating clean food." For those of us who order our experiences within a veridictory semiotics (one founded on ontological issues), we might perceive "Temple worship" as in some ways analogous to "family life," but we assign them to different realms of experience because they entail different "beings" (the Divine is involved directly in "Temple worship," but "family life" is an exclusively human involvement).[51] As a consequence of these distinct types of semantic organization, a series of figures that might appear disjointed or unrelated when assessed from a veridictory semiotics because they are too ontologically disparate could flow from and develop one another when assessed from a corresponding thymic semiotics that recognized the common value within the different figurativizations.

Thus, a methodological approach based on this structural semiotic model can help to mitigate not only our own cultural predilection to search for "logical sequences" of discursive structure but also our tendency to seek an ontological ground for semantic organization in a document which may have a quite different semantic structure.

---

substituer notre logique à celle de l'auteur ...."

[48]See Timothy B. Cargal, "The Generative Trajectory in Certain non-Western Cultures," in Patte, *Religious Dimensions*, 265-75.

[49]Max Kadushin, *Organic Thinking: A Study in Rabbinic Thought* (New York: Bloch, 1938) and *The Rabbinic Mind* (3rd ed; New York: Bloch, 1972).

[50]E. P. Sanders, *Paul and Palestinian Judaism: A Comparison of Patterns of Religion* (Philadelphia: Fortress, 1977), cf. especially 72-75.

[51]This example is abbreviated from my earlier essay on thymic semiotic systems ("Generative Trajectory," 270-71).

A Thesis for Relating Structure and
Purpose in the Epistle of James

It is the thesis of this study that the Epistle of James is in fact a discourse that has been organized primarily on the basis of its "discursive semantics" (thematization and figurativization) rather than its "discursive syntax." Thus, James would have used the progression of themes and figures to accomplish his purposes for writing the letter. Additionally, the semantic organization of these themes and figures in the Epistle is ultimately grounded in issues of value rather than ontology.[52] It is for these reasons that modern critical exegetes, who were looking for a "logical" progression of themes and an ontological connection among the figures, have been unable to relate the organizational structure and purposes of the letter.

It is the parallels between the inverted and posited content of each discursive (sub-)unit that provide the key for how the progression of themes and figures accomplish the purposes of the author, for these parallelisms are both thematic and figurative. The parallels are initially perceived and isolated by readers on the basis of the commonalities between the figures at the beginning and end of each unit. But it is not the particularities of these figures which express the purposes of the author; rather, the purposes of the author are related to the far more general themes that express the "inverted" and "posited" nature of the contents of the introduction and conclusion. That is to say, while the parallelisms are perceived because of the figures, their significance can only be unpacked in terms of the themes. This relationship should be clarified by the example which follows.

Inverted Parallelisms between the Opening
and Closing of the Epistle

Since our concern is with the purposes of the discourse as a whole, a preliminary statement of the major purposes of the Epistle can be set forth by considering the "inverted parallelisms" between the opening (Jas 1:1) and closing (5:19-20) of the letter. As we noted above,[53] it is the posited content of a discourse (or discourse unit) that expresses the goals of the author.[54] And so, we begin at the end.

---

[52]I.e., the semantic organization is founded on a thymic semiotics rather than a veridictory semiotics typical of many Euro-American societies.

[53]See 38.

[54]Or as Daniel and Aline Patte phrased it, "a study of the end of a text allows

The final verses of the Epistle read as follows:[55]

> My brothers [and sisters], if anyone among you should wander from the truth and someone should restore him [or her], let that one know that the one who restores sinners[56] from the error of their way will save their[57] souls from death and will cover a multitude of sins.

Notice that the implied reader is clearly associated with those who need restoration ("if *anyone among you* should wander from the truth"). Rather than simply a general admonition for the readers to be the "someone" who would restore others, the verses seem to relate the self-conception of the author as one who has restored errant brothers and sisters to the "truth" and so "saved their souls from death."[58]

How might this conclusion be related to Jas 1:1? With the language about "wandering" and "restoration" fresh in one's mind, the figure of the addressees as the "twelve tribes of the Diaspora" (ταῖς δώδεκα φυλαῖς ἐν τῇ διασπορᾷ) takes on immediate prominence. I will return shortly to a more detailed look at the process of figurativization and the exegetical moves necessary for its elaboration, but it is important to note here that all figures have a "two-fold semantic investment." That is to say, a figure is invested with certain meanings by both the author and the implied reader, and these investments of meaning may be consonant or dissonant to varying degrees. An author might choose a figure whose meanings she or he fully shares with the implied reader, or may choose a figure with well-established and acceptable meanings for

---

the exegete to identify without ambiguity the ultimate program of the text" (*Theory to Practice*, 39).

[55]Unless otherwise indicated, all translations of the Greek text of the Epistle are my own.

[56]The Greek here and in the related terms which follow is masculine singular.

[57]The pronoun αὐτοῦ is ambiguous (and in fact, textually problematic; cf. *TCGNT*, 686). It may take as its antecedent either the noun ἁμαρτωλόν (as in the translation given here) or the participle ἐπιστρέψας (and thus it is the one who restores another whose "soul is saved from death;" so Cantinat, *Jacques et Jude*, 261-62, and Adamson, *James*, 202-204). This ambiguity will be explored further in the exegetical treatment of these verses in chapter six.

[58]Davids (*James*, 26 and 201) has also taken the position that these verses express the purpose of the author in writing the book. Martin (*James*, 221) states that Jas 5:19-20 "drive home the main contentions the letter has emphasized throughout." Reicke (*James, Peter and Jude*, 62) is less direct by taking the position that these verses provide an admonition for others to do as the author has done.

reader precisely so she or he can reinterpret the figure and invest it with new meanings.

In the case of figures occurring at the outset of a discourse, the particular figures must be carefully selected by the author so that they will be acceptable and meaningful to the implied reader. It is in this way that the author attempts to capture the attention and interest of the reader, as well as to establish her or his trustworthiness as a person to be heard and heeded by the reader.[59] For example, the figure "Yahweh is a warrior" might be effective as part of an opening for a discourse aimed at people who view the Christian life in terms of "spiritual warfare" (*à la* "Onward Christian Soldiers"), but would most likely fail to draw in strict pacifists regardless of how the figure was interpreted or reinterpreted by the discourse as a whole. Why, then, might James have chosen the figure "the twelve tribes of the Diaspora" to refer to his envisioned readers?

Semantic Investments in the "Diaspora" Figure

The Implied Reader's Investment

The question "why this figure?" is really, as we have just seen, two questions: (1) what meanings did the author anticipate it would have invoked for the readers (the enunciatee's investment), and (2) with what meanings does the author hope to (re-)invest it (the enunciator's investment). I choose to begin with the implied reader's possible understandings, in part, because it more closely corresponds to the question normally put to such figures by critical biblical exegetes—how might a first century reader have understood this reference to the "Diaspora"?

Marxsen[60] has proposed three possible interpretations for the designation of the addressees of the Epistle as "the twelve tribes of the Diaspora:" (1) Jews who are living outside of Palestine (the technical sense of the word);[61] (2) Jewish Christians who are living among the

---

[59]Cf. Patte's discussion of the selection of topics for academic writing assignments (*Structural Exegesis for New Testament Critics*, 13-14) and his discussion of the "fiduciary-contract" between author and reader (ibid., 63).

[60]Marxsen, *Introduction*, 228-29.

[61]Mayor seems to accept this position when describing the Epistle as a missionary tract directed toward Jews (*St. James*, cxlviii), but at other times he seems to favor a predominately Christian audience (cxliii). It is rejected explicitly by Marxsen (*Introduction*, 228), Kümmel (*Introduction*, 407), and Vouga (*Jacques*, 37) precisely on the grounds that the Epistle is not a "missionary document."

Dispersion of Jews outside Palestine;[62] or (3) all Christians "thought of as 'the true Israel.'"[63] Since our purpose does not entail formulating a detailed socio-historical description of the recipients' *Sitz im Leben*, it is not incumbent upon us to make a final choice among these options.[64] Indeed, each of these interpretations in fact contributes something to the implied reader's semantic investment in the figure.

Any Christian reader[65] of the Epistle, whether of Jewish or Gentile ethnicity, could be expected to see within the figure "the twelve tribes of the Diaspora" not only a reference to Christians as a new 'people of God' and 'spiritual Israel.' The historical experiences of Diaspora Judaism as a people scattered as aliens in a hostile world would also have been appropriated as part of the "semantic investment" of the figure as applied to their own experiences as Christians who experienced persecution as "exiles" within the world (cf. 1 Pet 1:1, 1:17, and 2:11).[66] That the implied reader does in fact bring such meanings to the figure is evidenced by the discussion of "trials" (πειρασμοί) and "testings" (δοκίμια) in the immediately following verses.[67] The implied reader invests the figure with not only the significance of the Christians as the 'people of God,' but also as a people living in an

---

[62]Supported by Adamson (*James*, 20), Davids (*James*, 64), Martin (*James*, 8-10), and Brevard S. Childs (*The New Testament as Canon: An Introduction* [Philadelphia: Fortress Press, 1984], 435), though he stresses the "canonical" function of James as "the representative figure of Jewish Christianity" more than the geographical issue. Rejected explicitly by Kümmel (*Introduction*, 408).

[63]The position adopted by Marxsen (*Introduction*, 229), Kümmel (*Introduction*, 408), Dibelius (*James*, 67), Mußner (*Jakobusbrief*, 61-62), Ropes (*St. James*, 118-127), and Vouga (*Jacques*, 37). This option is rejected by Childs (*New Testament as Canon*, 435), although he accepts that this was the understanding of the church concerning the figure from shortly after the time the book was written.

[64]In fact, several historical critics are compelled to "leave the question open" as to whether the Christian recipients of the Epistle are Jewish or Gentile. See Cantinat, *Jacques et Jude*, 58-59; and Laws, *James*, 47-49 as examples.

[65]Siding with most scholars that there are few indications that the Epistle is a "missionary document," and therefore that the enunciatee constructed within the discourse is a Christian believer. At this point it is sufficient to note the language of 5:19-20 about "restoring" those who have "wandered from the truth" as evidence that the enunciatee shares (or shared) the Christian beliefs of the enunciator.

[66]Perhaps the most extensive discussion of this development of the use of "Diaspora" language is in Ropes, *St. James*, 118-127. Cf. also Karl Ludwig Schmidt, "διασπορά," *TDNT* 2:99-104.

[67]Cf. the comment of Vouga (*Jacques*, 37) that the term "Diaspora" was chosen "pour préparer l'appel à la persévérance par lequel s'ouvre ensuite l'épître (1,2-4)."

'unnatural' state of persecution awaiting their "restoration" by an act of divine deliverance.

The Implied Author's Investment

When we turn to the question of what meanings James hopes to invest in the figure of "the twelve tribes of the Diaspora," we must give priority to the relationships of meaning constructed by this particular discourse, the Epistle of James, rather than to the broader relationships of meaning that might be drawn from the "cultural dictionary" of Greek-speaking Jews and Christians of the first century.[68] But the use of the word "priority" should not be interpreted to mean that James invests certain meanings in the figure to the exclusion of meanings invested by the readers.[69] James may in fact share a "pilgrim" mentality regarding the Christian life. What we want to focus our attention on at this point, however, is whether there are indications that within the particularity of the Epistle there are other nuances of "Diaspora."

The language of the conclusion of the Epistle regarding "restoring" those who "wander from the truth" opens the possibility of performing a "backreading" of the figure applied to the addressees in the opening salutation of the book. James may perceive in the address "to the twelve tribes of the Diaspora" (the base meaning of "Diaspora" being "to scatter" or "to be led away") a reference to his desire "to restore those who have wandered away from the truth." Although he expects the readers to initially understand the figure as applying to testings and trials they may be experiencing, by the end of the book James challenges them to accept the view that they are (also) the "Diaspora" because they have "wandered from the truth." But James has brought them back to the "truth" through the course of the letter, "saving their souls from death and covering a multitude of sins" (5:20). The act of "restoring" Christian brothers and sisters may also figure prominently in the nuances of his self-designation as a "servant (δοῦλος) of God and of the Lord Jesus Christ" (1:1).

---

[68]Or, to use the language from the discussion of the implied reader's investment, we are not so much concerned with "how any first century reader might have understood this reference to the 'Diaspora'" but with how James, the author, might have wanted the figure to be understood within the specific context of this writing.

[69]Or even with concern for the hermeneutical appropriation of the text that the author's investments are "superior" or the only "legitimate" meanings that the figure can have.

Formulating Two Major Purposes
of the Epistle of James

By considering these inverted parallelisms, we see that one major purpose of the Epistle is to convince the readers that they are a "Diaspora" not only because of their status as "exiles" in an evil and hostile world, but also because they have become a "Diaspora" by "wandering from the truth." In light of this finding, let us consider J. B. Mayor's statement of the 'purpose' of the Epistle:

> The design of the Epistle is on the one hand to encourage those to whom it is addressed to bear their trials patiently, and on the other hand to warn them against certain errors of doctrine and practice.[70]

The first part of Mayor's description accurately reflects the views of the implied reader:[71] trials must be patiently endured until God restores the fullness of justice to the world at the dawn of the eschaton. As a consequence, many commentaries and monographs on the Epistle provide an extended treatment of the early Palestinian Jewish and Christian beliefs regarding "testings and trials" and the "piety of the poor" since this is perceived as a dominant theological motif of the Epistle.[72] The second part of Mayor's statement accurately reflects the emphases of

---

[70]Mayor, *St. James*, cxxviii. Cf. also the similar comment by Vouga (*Jacques*, 37): "Jc choisirait alors ce terme ["Diaspora"] pour rappeler l'enracinement juif du christianisme et pour préparer l'appel à la persévérance par lequel s'ouvre ensuite l'épître (1,2-4)."

[71]It is useful at this point to remind ourselves that the "implied reader" (the enunciatee) is purely a construct of the production of the discourse. That it is to say, the author of the Epistle imagines the readers for whom this discourse is written to hold this view and so crafts the book accordingly. But the possibility exists that the author has completely misunderstood the actual beliefs of the "flesh and blood" readers who will read the text and for whom it was in fact written. Thus, to assert that the "implied reader" holds a certain belief does not guarantee that the actual first readers of the Epistle of James shared that belief.

[72]Cf. Davids, *James*, 35-39 and 41-47; Martin, *James*, lxxxiv-lxxxvi and xciii-xcviii; Dibelius, *James*, 39-45; and Pedrito U. Maynard-Reid, *Poverty and Wealth in James* (Maryknoll, New York: Orbis Books, 1987), especially 24-37. Robert L. Williams ("Piety and Poverty in James," *Wesleyan Theological Journal* 22 [Fall 1987]: 37-55) wants to argue against this opinion; "[n]o special piety is attributed to the poor man, only special treatment from God to compensate for the rich man's exploitative 'inhumanity to man.'" But it is precisely such a "special treatment from God" that is meant by the phrase "piety of the poor," and not that poverty itself is in some sense meritorious.

James himself, "restoring" the readers to the "truth" from which they have "wandered." The problem, however, with his summary is that it projects both these concerns upon the intention of the author. While "warn[ings] ... against certain errors of doctrine and practice" is a major theme (or goal) for James, we can only be certain that "bear[ing] trials patiently," at least within the theological context of a doctrine of the "piety of the poor," is a major concern for the implied reader.

But what is this "truth" from which James believes his readers have "wandered" and so find themselves in need of "restoration"? Indeed, one can ask how is it that they have "wandered"—do their difficulties stem from failures to maintain "orthodoxy" or "orthopraxis"?[73] And what is the nature of the "restoration" that they should receive, both in terms of its means and its effects? We should expect to find sub-themes related to each of these issues in the unfolding of the discourse the Epistle of James.

Procedure for Testing the Hypothesis

Since the goal of this study is discerning an organizational structure that will contribute to an understanding of James's purposes in writing, the structural exegesis of the Epistle in the chapters that follow will necessarily proceed in two distinct stages. First, we must identify the limits of the discursive units that make up the internal structure of the Epistle. For this purpose, we will refer to the Epistle as a whole as the "discourse." The major divisions of the discourse will be called "discursive units" which will be broken down into "(discursive) subunits." For the sake of convenience in dealing with the thematic and figurative development of these "sub-units," we will further divide them into "sections."[74] We must also determine whether the respective

---

[73]To borrow the terms from Martin's discussion of the 'wanderer' in Jas 5:19 (*James*, 219).

[74]It is important to note that these "sections" are not the same type of segments of the discourse as the "discursive units" and "sub-units" in that they do not reflect "characteristics of the discourse as a whole" by giving full expression to a particular "theme," nor are their limits marked by parallels of "inverted and posited content." Rather, these "sections" will be designated mainly to facilitate the handling of the text in smaller divisions, although they will seek to be sensitive to the progressive development of the themes of their respective "discursive units" and "sub-units." On the distinction between the "discursive units" studied by a structural exegesis and other exegetical methods for dividing a text and the implications of the different approaches, see Patte, *Structural Exegesis for New Testament Critics*, 9-16.

themes of these units and sub-units contribute to the development of the proposed themes for the Epistle as a whole. Secondly, we will want to consider how James uses these discursive structures to accomplish this purpose; that is, how does the author "transform" the opinions of the readers so that they accept his analysis of their condition and recognize their need for "restoration"?

Inverted Parallelisms and Thematization

On the basis of an isolation of parallels between "inverted" and "posited" content, I would propose that the Epistle of James may be divided into four major discursive units.

(1) The first discursive unit would be Jas 1:1-21, marked by the parallelism between the admonition to "be complete and whole, lacking in nothing" (1:4) and the means for fulfilling this admonition, namely, "having put aside all filth and abundance of wickedness, by meekness, [to] receive the implanted word" (1:21). The theme of this unit may be summarized as "'receiving the implanted word' in order to 'be perfect.'"

(2) The second unit is delimited by the parallel between the admonition "be doers of the word and not only hearers" (1:22) and the dictum "faith separated from works is dead" (2:26), a parallelism which suggests that James understands "works" to be "doing the (implanted [1:21]) word." It thus extends from 1:22 - 2:26, and its theme can be summarized as "'works' of the 'word.'"

(3) The theme of the third unit, extending from 3:1 -4:12, relates to having a proper attitude about oneself by "humbling oneself" in the light of the impending "judgment." It is marked by the admonitions that "not many of you ... should desire to become teachers" (3:1) and to "humble yourselves in the presence of the Lord and (the Lord) will exalt you" (4:10), as well as the theme of "judgment" that awaits "teachers" (3:1) and the role of the "one Lawgiver and Judge" as compared to those who "judge their neighbor" (4:11-12).

(4) The fourth and final unit is bracketed by the 'inverted content' of "speak[ing] against one another" (4:11)[75] and the 'posited content' of "restor[ing]" "anyone among you [who] should wander from the

---

[75]Thus 4:11-12 serves as part of both the conclusion of the third unit and the introduction of the fourth unit. The presence of such "hinge" verses marking the transition from one discourse unit to another, particularly a concluding discourse unit that one can anticipate will recall many of the major sub-themes of the discourse as a whole, is not unusual.

truth" (5:19). The theme of this final discursive unit, then, would be "'bringing back' one's 'neighbor.'"

Each of these units will be further analyzed in the exegetical chapters that follow to confirm that these divisions are correct and to isolate their sub-units. But notice that even at this very preliminary stage some of our questions regarding the theme of the Epistle as a whole are finding general answers. It would appear that the "truth" from which they have "wandered" is related to the "implanted word" (unit 1). They have "wandered" from this "truth" by being ones who "hear" it, but are not "doing" the "works" of this "word" (unit 2), and by not having a "proper understanding about themselves" that would lead them to "humble themselves" before the coming "judgment" (unit 3). Their "restoration" is to be accomplished both by being "perfected" by this "implanted word" (unit 1), and by the efforts of those who "restore" rather than "condemn" these wayward "neighbors" (unit 4), thereby "saving their souls" (1:21 and 5:20). But we are still far from understanding these themes in terms of the "system of convictions" that James wants the readers to adopt and share with him.

Transforming the Opinions of the Implied Reader

In examining the discursive processes whereby the readers come to accept the "posited content" toward which the author wants to move them, we have two primary concerns. First, we need to be certain that we have properly identified the "theme" of the discursive unit, the "goal" or "purpose" toward which it moves, by verifying that the "convictions" expressed within that unit actually contribute to that "theme." Secondly, we need to discern what beliefs of the readers were in need of "transformation," in the view of author, so that we do not confuse the "semantic investments" in the discourse by the author, i.e. her or his "purposes" in writing, with the "semantic investments" by the implied reader that may or may not even be shared by the author.

Oppositions of Actions

The first of these concerns is addressed by a study of the "oppositions of actions" within each discursive unit. I will not attempt here to review either the theoretical basis for the assertion that "oppositions of actions" directly express the convictions of an author[76] or to outline

---

[76]For a simplified explanation with minimal technical language, see Patte,

the formal procedures for identifying and analyzing the explicit "oppositions of actions" within a discourse.[77] Let it suffice to say that since the author's convictions find direct expression within these oppositions, the conclusions reached by their analysis provide both an important check for statements of the theme of discourse units and invaluable information for understanding the author's "semantic investment" in the figurative dimensions of the text.

Figurativization

By figurativization, we are not limiting our concerns to what are generally referred to as "figurative" forms of language (such as metaphors, similes, symbols, etc.), but are rather considering all those "specific features of a discourse unit"[78] whereby the author attempts to persuade the reader to accept the new view of human experience that comprises the author's system of convictions. These "specific features" are chosen by the author both because they are already meaningful, and thus convincing, for the readers and because they are capable of being invested with new meanings that the author wants the readers to accept. For example, the "Diaspora" figure of the salutation of the Epistle has meaning in terms of both the "experiences"/convictions of the readers (the "persecuted people of God" living as "aliens in a hostile world" awaiting "divine deliverance") and the "experiences"/convictions James wants to communicate to the readers (people can "wander" from the "truth" and must be "restored"). But it is important to keep the semantic investments of the author and the readers distinct.

To ascertain what "semantic investments" the readers bring to the discourse, i.e. their "old knowledge" presupposed by the author, we must ask what are the 'possible' meanings of the text. We will gain significant assistance in this area from the work of historico-critical exegetes who have studied the language and philosophical/theological systems of the first century. However, not all the 'possible meanings' within the broader "cultural dictionary" of first century life and thought can be expected to apply to the use of a "figure" within the text of the Epistle. To determine which of the 'possible' meanings are 'pertinent' to the context of the Epistle, we must try to adopt the vantage of first-

---

Matthew, 5-8. A far more thorough treatment of the total theoretical base provided by Greimasian structural semiotics is provided in Patte, *Religious Dimensions*.

[77]See Patte, *Structural Exegesis for New Testament Critics*, 23-45.

[78]So Patte, *Structural Exegesis for New Testament Critics*, 61-65.

time readers who follow the unfolding of the text; we can only draw on
material previously presented in the discourse without recourse to what
will come later.[79]

For the author's understanding of the "figure," however, we want
to rely primarily upon the theme which the unit is developing and the
convictions expressed by the oppositions of actions. Here we are concerned above all else with the meanings of the "figure" within the
system of meaningful relations created by the discourse the Epistle of
James. This fact allows somewhat more freedom to make recourse to
what comes later in the text (particularly the 'posited content' expressed
by the conclusion of the discourse unit or sub-unit), but we must not
abuse this privilege. Too quickly making reference to later sections of
the discourse will prevent us from sensing how the reader is manipulated
by the text to adopt the "new knowledge" presented by the author to
supplant the "old knowledge" of the readers. As a consequence, we
would miss how the discursive structures of the text contribute to
accomplishing James's purposes in writing.

The Reading Strategy of this Study

In light of these theoretical and methodological considerations, I
will adopt the following procedure in the exegetical chapters which
follow. First, I will discuss the discursive structure of the unit in terms
of the parallels of inverted and posited content, including establishing the
limits of any discursive sub-units contained within the unit. I will also
map out the "sections" (see note 74) that will be used to facilitate tracing
the progressive development of the theme of the discursive (sub-)unit.

Secondly, proceeding by sections, I will perform an analysis of the
oppositions of actions. This formal analysis will serve both as a check
on the statements of the themes of the discourse (sub-)units and as a
primary means for isolating the convictions that James wants to communicate to his readers. Additionally, the results of this analysis will
provide the foundation for a systematic presentation of the "system of
convictions" operative in the discourse as a whole presented in the
conclusion of this study.

Finally, I will trace the progressive development of the themes
through the figurativization of each section. I will seek to make explicit
any tensions between the semantic investments of the figures by the
implied reader and the author, with particular reference to how the

---

[79]Cf. Patte, *Matthew*, 11.

author seeks to convince the reader to adopt the "new" system of convictions. I will give attention to indications that the semantic organization of these figures is ultimately grounded in issues of value rather than ontology (i.e., that a "thymic semiotic system" is at work in the Epistle). And lastly, we must continually take care to respect the ambiguities of the text and to resist the temptation to find "the one" meaning of the Epistle—a meaning which would undoubtedly owe more to our own "convictions" than those of James.

CHAPTER THREE

"PERFECTION" THROUGH THE "IMPLANTED WORD": JAMES 1:2-21

Reading through the opening verses of the Epistle of James, one cannot avoid feeling tensions between certain elements of the text. Already in the second verse, we are confronted with the problem of how the experience of "diverse trials" can be considered a cause for "complete joy." There is a sense of contradiction between the assertion on the one hand that "patient endurance" makes one "complete and whole, lacking in nothing" (1:3-4), and the statement on the other hand that if someone "lacks wisdom" it must be obtained from "the God who gives to everyone generously" (1:5). And what is one to make of the fluctuation of meanings of the nouns and verbs of the πειράζω word group which sometimes have the sense of "trial" and sometimes the sense of "temptation" (1:2 and 12-14)?

I will not try to 'resolve' these tensions in what follows. Rather, I will attempt to understand them in terms of the competing investments of the implied reader and the implied author. How are the traditions known to the implied reader (the focus of form critics) adopted and adapted by the implied author (the focus of redaction critics) in order to manipulate that reader into accepting the perception of the world held by the implied author (one goal of a structural exegesis)? In other words, how does the recognition of these tensions assist us in understanding the relationship between the discursive structures and purposes of the Epistle of James?

Discursive Semantic Structure
and Thematization

In chapter two I proposed that the first discursive unit of the Epistle extended from Jas 1:2-21, and was marked by the inverted parallelisms between "be complete (τέλειος) and whole, lacking in nothing" (1:4) and the means for obtaining that perfection, namely, "having put away all filth and abundance of wickedness, by meekness, [to] receive the implanted word" (1:21). As we shall see, the 'problem' for James is that the readers perceive the patient endurance of trials as the means to achieving this "perfection" (cf. Jas 1:2-4). However, he believes that such can only be achieved by the gift from God of the "implanted word." Thus, this unit develops the theme "'receiving the implanted word' in order to 'be perfect'" as a corrective to the beliefs of the implied readers.

As we begin to read carefully through this first discursive unit of the Epistle, we notice certain inverted parallels which suggest that the unit is composed of two sub-units. The first of these sub-units is marked by a series of three parallels between Jas 1:2-4 and 1:12.[1] There is the parallel between the juxtaposition of "complete joy" (πᾶσαν χαράν) and "trials" (πειρασμοῖς)[2] in 1:2 that parallels the beatitude pronounced upon the person "who endures trial" (πειρασμόν) in 1:12. The second parallelism is between the assertion that "testing (δοκίμιον) ... produces patience (ὑπομονήν)" in 1:3 and the reference to the one "who endures (ὑπομένει) trial" in 1:12 as "one who has become approved" (δόκιμος). The third parallel is not quite as obvious in that it does not involve repetition of related key words; it is established between the goal of the initial admonitions, "that you might be complete and whole, lacking in nothing" (1:4), and the reward of the "crown of life" promised to the one who endures in 1:12. We may therefore summarize the theme of this first sub-unit as "The Blessing of Trials."

Additional evidence that 1:12 marks the conclusion of a sub-unit can be found in the semantic shift in the πειρασμός/πειράζω word

---

[1] Jas 1:1-12 is taken as a unit by Alexander Ross (*The Epistles of James and John*, NICNT [Grand Rapids: William B. Eerdmans Publishing Company, 1954], 23), Rountree ("Further Thoughts," 1) and Hill and Torakawa (see Torakawa, "Literary-Semantic Analysis," 4 and 36). Vouga (*Jacques*, 49) refers to Jas 1:2-12 as "le première période de sa parénèse."

[2] I have chosen here to refer to the simple juxtaposition of the terms regarding "joy" and "trials" because the actual nature of their syntactic relationship is somewhat ambiguous. See the discussion of the figurativization of this verse below.

group. The noun πειρασμός appears in 1:2 as roughly synonymous with δοκίμιον, and thus refers to a "trial" or "test." The appearance of δόκιμος in 1:12 supports the position that the same semantic range functions for the occurrence of the noun πειρασμός within that verse. But the appearance of the verb πειράζω in 1:13 marks a sudden shift to the semantic domain of "temptation."[3]

In considering how this theme is developed, it is possible to distinguish three sections[4] within this opening sub-unit. The first section, following the epistolary greeting of 1:1, sets forth the major topic of this sub-unit, namely "trials" and "testings" and includes 1:2-4. The second section extends from 1:5 to 1:8 and develops the idea of "wisdom" as a "gift of God."[5] The final section of the sub-unit runs from 1:9-12. It is often argued that the beatitude of 1:12 is distinct from the "great reversal"[6] of 1:9-11.[7] However, they can be viewed as a single section: the "exaltation" of the "humble/poor (ταπεινός) brother [and sister]" in 1:9 parallels the awarding of the "crown of life" in 1:12.[8]

As we shall see below in summarizing the discursive maneuvers in this section, James disagrees with the readers' conception as to why "trials" may be considered a "blessing." The beatitude of Jas 1:12 expresses the relationship between the two as perceived by the readers; the one who endures "trials" is promised the "blessing" of the crown of life. But for James, "trials" prove to be a "blessing" because they drive

---

[3]Dibelius (*James*, 69-70) likewise locates the semantic shift at 1:13, as do the majority of commentators. The attempt by Davids (*James*, 80-83) to link 1:12 and 13 by arguing that the meaning "test" is maintained within both verses is, in effect, overly consistent. The opposite approach is taken by Martin, who argues that 1:12 and 13 belong to a different division than 1:2-4 precisely because πειρασμός already means "temptation" in 1:12 (*James*, 13 and 32). See the discussion of the figurativization of these verses below.

[4]Remember that the "sections" isolated within the sub-units of the Epistle will not be identified using specifically structural semiotic principles; see note 74 in chapter 2. As a consequence, one can expect to find greater continuity between divisions proposed at this level within this study and the divisions reached by exegetes using other methodologies.

[5]The isolation of 1:2-4 and 1:5-8 as distinct sections/sayings within the Epistle is widely acknowledged by commentators.

[6]To borrow Maynard-Reid's colorful designation of the saying in 1:9-11 (*Poverty and Wealth*, 38).

[7]So Dibelius, *James*, 71; Sidebottom, *James, Jude, 2 Peter*, 29-30; Ropes, *St. James*, 4; Easton, *IB* 12:26; and Vouga, *Jacques*, 49.

[8]Cf. Richard Kugelman, *James and Jude*, New Testament Message, 19 (Wilmington, Delaware: Michael Glazier, 1980), 16.

the believer to the realization of her or his dependence upon "the God who gives to everyone generously" (1:5).

As was the case with the first discursive sub-unit, the second sub-unit is likewise marked by three inverted parallelisms and extends from 1:13-21. The assertion in 1:13 that "God tempts no one" finds its parallel in 1:20 where the author states that "human anger does not accomplish godly righteousness;" i.e., the 'inverted content' expressing the readers' belief that God can be a source of "temptation," and so at least indirectly also of sin, is paralleled by the 'posited content' of James's contention that God is typified only by "righteousness." Thus, this inverted parallelism is very closely related to the parallel between James's statement that it is human "desire" (ἐπιθυμία) that tempts a person (1:14), so that what is needed to correct this proclivity to sin is to "receive the implanted word" (1:21).[9] The final parallel is between the consequences of "desire," namely "death" (1:15), and the ability of the "implanted word ... to save the soul/life (ψυχάς)" (1:21). Therefore, we will summarize the theme of this second discursive sub-unit as "Saving the Soul from Death."

What 'old' and 'new knowledge' are contrasted by the theme of this discursive sub-unit? The readers have identified their problems with external forces. They are experiencing "trials" and even being "tested" by God (1:13). For James, however, the real problems a person faces are internal; it is one's own "desire" that ultimately produces "death." Since the problem confronting believers is internal, so must be the solution—"the *implanted* word."

Also as was the case with the first sub-unit, this second sub-unit can be divided into three sections. Verses 13-16 comprise the first section which treats the origin and consequences of temptations. The second section includes 1:17-19a and links the "perfect gift of God" to the "word of truth" by which the believers were "birthed" by God. The δέ of 1:19b, then, has true adversative force ("but") and introduces a final section (1:19b-21) containing an admonition to "receive the implanted word" which brings to a close both the sub-unit and the unit as a whole.[10]

It is interesting to note the parallel development of topics between the two sub-units of this opening discursive unit:

---

[9]Could it be that it must be an "implanted" (ἔμφυτον) word so that it will be capable of transforming human 'nature' (φύσις) and "desire"?

[10]Martin (*James*, 44) also takes 1:19b as the introduction of a new division within the text. Cf. also Vouga, *Jacques*, 59-60.

1:2-4 — trials (πειρασμοί) and tests	1:13-16 — temptation (πει- ράζω)
1:5-8 — the gift of God is wisdom	1:17-19a — the "perfect gift" of God is the "word of truth"
1:9-12 — culminates with a "crown of life"	1:19b-21 — culminates with the salvation of the soul

The demonstration of such a parallel development within the opening division of the Epistle is a major aspect of Francis's argument that the Epistle of James follows an established epistolary form.[11] However, since the other major component of his argument concerns conventions for closing letters, we will reserve the question regarding to what extent, if any, James has drawn on epistolary conventions for the conclusion of this study.[12]

Exegesis and Commentary

The Blessing of Trials (Jas 1:2-12)

Jas 1:2-4 — Trials and Testings

Figurativization in Jas 1:2-4

The first saying of the Epistle of James consists of a thematic[13] admonition to "Consider it complete[14] joy when you encounter diverse trials." Or at least it is usually considered an admonition since this is a paraenetic writing that is replete with imperatives.[15] However, there

---

[11]See Francis, "Form and Function," 111-117.

[12]The treatment of the "Epistolary Prescript" (Jas 1:1) will be taken up as part of this discussion of epistolary conventions in the conclusion of this study.

[13]I.e., it occurs in a section which draws on the 'old knowledge' of the readers and does not directly express 'new' convictions of the author by means of oppositions of actions. Such "thematic" sections (defined as sections not containing oppositions) are more indirect expressions of the author's convictions.

[14]The use of the adjective "all" in this context "denote[s] the highest degree [of], *full, greatest*" joy that one can have (BAGD, "πᾶς," 1aδ, 631). One might paraphrase the expression as "all that joy means" (BDF §275[3], 143).

[15]The precise number given by commentators varies to some degree, as one might expect, but the figure of 54 imperatives within 108 verses adopted by Marxsen (*Introduction*, 226) is typical and sufficient to make the point.

is no morphological reason why the verb ἡγήσασθε could not be rendered in the indicative mood; thus James would be commenting on the readers' normal response to affliction: "You considered it complete joy when you encountered diverse trials." Since we are endeavoring to distinguish between the views of the readers and that of the author, the question of whether one finds here an admonition (imperative mood) or an observation (indicative mood) is significant.

Let us assume that most exegetes, being highly-trained readers, have tended to identify with the role prescribed for the reader by the text. In such a case, we can anticipate that the implied reader was expected to hear in the phrase πᾶσαν χαρὰν ἡγήσασθε a charge to respond to "trials" with "joy." They were encouraged to fulfill this charge because they "know that the testing[16] of [their] faith produces patient endurance." Additionally, they were encouraged to permit that resultant "patience" to have its "complete work, in order that [they] might be complete and whole lacking in nothing." Since these charges are warranted by beliefs already held by the readers (γινώσκοντες ὅτι ...),[17] it might be better to interpret them as exhortations rather than harsh admonitions.[18]

However, the fact that the statements of 1:2 and 4 are warranted by beliefs already held by the readers can also be used to support rendering ἡγήσασθε in the indicative mood: "You considered it complete joy, my brothers [and sisters], when you fell into diverse trials because you knew that the testing of your faith produces patience."[19]

---

[16]Or perhaps more specifically "trials as a means of testing" following Dibelius (*James*, 72-73). He correctly rejects the proposal that δοκίμιον is to be taken as a substantive neuter adjective (thus, "the genuineness of your faith;" see *TCGNT*, 679) in that such a rendering fails to relate to either the "trials" which precede or the resulting "endurance" that follows (cf. also Davids, *James*, 68).

[17]A point also emphasized by Dibelius (*James*, 72), although he interprets it as evidence of the traditional nature of the contents of the Epistle against any creativity by its author.

[18]A tone supported by the possible jussive force of the third person imperative in 1:4a (ἐχέτω; but notice that this verb has a genuine third person subject, ἡ ὑπομονή). Contra the opinion of Douglas J. Moo (*James*, Tyndale New Testament Commentaries [Grand Rapids: William B. Eerdmans Publishing Company, 1985], 59): "The command is categorical, suggesting the need for a definitive decision to take up a joyful attitude."

[19]Reicke's opposing view that "[t]he readers of the epistle have exhibited dissatisfaction and impatience because of the afflictions to which they have been exposed" (*James, Peter, Jude*, 13) arises from a purely mimetic view of literature. If James charges his readers to do one thing, it must be because they were doing the

We will see in considering Jas 1:5-8 that such a relationship between "trials" and "patience/endurance" was part of the beliefs of the implied readers, and it is not unlikely that such a belief—held in a broader context of the "piety of the poor"—might even provide the basis for the experience of "joy."[20] This understanding of Jas 1:2-3 seems to call for reading 1:4 with a harsher tone—"But let endurance have its complete work!" Then these words mark the beginning of an indictment of his readers by James: "Do you think that your 'patient endurance' is a sign that you have arrived at 'perfection'?[21] You must let 'endurance' have its 'complete' work if you are going to be 'perfected' by it."

Jas 1:5-8 — The Gift of Wisdom

Convictions Emphasized in Jas 1:5-8

As discussed in the preceding chapter, the study of the author's convictions emphasized by "oppositions of actions" serves two important functions relative to our concerns regarding the structure and purposes of the Epistle of James. First, these convictions provide us with an important check on whether we have properly articulated the theme of the discourse (sub-)unit on the basis of identification and analysis of the inverted parallelisms. Secondly, the results of our study of the convictions underscored by oppositions and the interrelationships among them provide the foundation for a systematic presentation of the overall "system of convictions" operative in the discourse as a whole. As the pattern of those interrelationships begins to emerge, I will present those findings somewhat schematically by means of a developing chart of convictions (see for example page 69) which will provide the basis for a narrativizing of James's convictions regarding the process of becoming a believer ("how does one receive blessedness?") that will be presented in the final chapter of this study.

---

opposite of what he admonishes.

[20]Granted, such "joy" in the face of persecution and trial strikes many in our day and age as at best disingenuous, and at worst perverse. Cf. Moo's comment that "[w]hat is remarkable about this command is that it applies to a situation in which a joyful reaction would be most unnatural" (*James*, 59). But we need only consider certain sectarian groups within our own society to recognize that people can, and do, view "persecution by the world" as evidence of "divine vindication" and thus a cause for celebration.

[21]As Dibelius (*James*, 74) notes, "it is the perfection of the Christians which Jas expresses with the term 'perfect work.'" Cf. also Mayor, *St. James*, 36-37; Laws, *James*, 53-55; and Davids, *James*, 69.

OPP 1:5[22] — *The Generosity of God.* The first opposition of actions within the Epistle of James is found at 1:5. It opposes the positive action of "giving to everyone generously" (διδόντος ... πᾶσιν ἁπλῶς) to the negative action of "reproaching/reprimanding" (ὀνειδίζοντος).[23] Since the injunction is for "anyone among you" (τις ὑμῶν) to make the request for "wisdom" to this generous God, we can identify the receivers of both positive and negative actions as "believers."[24] The subject who performs the positive action is the true God[25] who is qualified by the will to give "generously" (ἁπλῶς),[26] while the subject who performs the negative action is a 'hypothetical' God (a false god, according to James's convictions) who is qualified by a will to "reprimand" those believers who lack wisdom.

In the present case, this negative "hypothetical God" is not just some randomly selected "straw divinity" chosen for the sake of argument;[27] the "hypothetical God" within James's system of convictions

---

[22]Each opposition of actions will be designated by the chapter and verse designation(s) in which the positive and negative actions are found. A complete listing of oppositions of actions within the Epistle is provided in Appendix B.

[23]On the use of ὀνειδίζω to refer to "reproach" in the sense of correction, see Johannes Schneider, "ὄνειδος, ὀνειδίζω, ὀνειδισμός," *TDNT* 5:238-39. Cf. also LSJ, "ὀνειδίζω II," 1230; and Johannes P. Louw and Eugene A. Nida, eds., *Greek-English Lexicon of the New Testament based on Semantic Domains*, 2 vols. (New York: United Bible Societies, 1988), §33.422 (1:437). A different use of ὀνειδίζω lies behind the NRSV's translation of the participle by "grudgingly," apparently following BAGD's reference to a "special kind of reproach [that] is the manifestation of displeasure or regret which too often accompanies the giving of a gift" (BAGD, "ὀνειδίζω" 1, 570). Related to this special use of ὀνειδίζω is the view that ἁπλῶς should be rendered here by "without hesitation" (so Dibelius, *James*, 77-79; and Harald Riesenfeld, "ΑΠΛΩΣ: Zu Jak. 1,5," ConNT 9 [1944]: 41).

[24]The antecedent of ὑμῶν appears in Jas 1:2 as "my brothers [and sisters]" (ἀδελφοί μου). It will be remembered from the previous chapter that we have identified the enunciatee as a Christian believer who, at one time at least, shared the beliefs of the enunciator.

[25]I.e., the "true" God according to the system of convictions about the Divine held by James and which he wants the readers to adopt.

[26]The understanding of ἁπλῶς as a term expressing "without hesitation or reservation" is also consistent with this view that God's "generosity" is a qualification of the will. In addition to the references at the end of note 23, see Davids, *James*, 72-73; Martin, *James*, 18; and Vouga, *Jacques*, 43.

[27]The normal pattern, of course, is that the "negative action" and its "subject" are selected 'simply for the sake of argument' and are not to be identified with the convictions of the implied readers. Only when there are clear textual markers indicating that the "negative action" is perceived positively within the system of

is in fact the "true God" within the system of convictions held by the readers. As part of their self-conception as "the people of God scattered in a hostile world" (figurativized in the opening salutation by "the twelve tribes of the Diaspora") and their theological beliefs relative to the "piety of the poor," they believe that God does in fact "reproach" or "reprimand" believers relative to their lack of "wisdom." The concept of the "piety of the poor" emerged from within the Wisdom traditions of ancient Judaism,[28] and a key part of that tradition was that God used adversity as a form of "rebuke" and "discipline" (Job 5:17)[29] to instruct the righteous.[30] Indeed, many adherents of the Wisdom school believed that "trials" (πειρασμοί) produced wisdom.[31]

That James construes his readers as believing that God uses "trials" as a means of "instructing the righteous" to produce wisdom in them is clear from the thematic materials of Jas 1:2-4. Why do they respond to "trials" with "complete joy"? Because they can positively value "trials" as the process whereby God teaches them "wisdom" and ultimately brings them to "perfection." As a corollary then, if people ask God for "wisdom," they should expect God to respond by sending adversity and "trial" so they may gain the "wisdom" they "lack." Within such a pattern of beliefs, God does not "reprimand" people because they ask for "wisdom;" rather, God "reprimands/instructs" people as the means of answering their request for "wisdom."

To this belief, James counters that the "true God" does not desire to "reproach believers," but rather wants "to give to everyone generously." Moreover, James seeks to mollify their resistance to changing their belief about God by relating it to something they do believe about God (or at least might be expected to want to believe about God), namely that God grants "wisdom" to those who ask. Wisdom thought figured prominently in the religious beliefs of the readers,[32] and their desire

---

convictions of the readers (as is the case here in Jas 1:5) should such an assignment of "negative actions" to the beliefs of the readers be made.

[28]See Gerhard von Rad, *Wisdom in Israel* (Nashville and New York: Abingdon Press, 1972), 195-206.

[29]It is not insignificant in this regard that Job is chosen as an example of "endurance" familiar to the readers (Jas 5:11).

[30]Cf. von Rad, *Wisdom*, 200-203.

[31]Ulrich Luck, "'Weisheit' und Leiden: zum Problem Paulus und Jakobus," *TLZ* 92 (1967): 253-55.

[32]On the importance of the Wisdom tradition as a background to the Epistle, see Davids, *James*, 51-56; Hartin, *James and Q*, 44-115; Hoppe, *Hintergrund*, 18-71; Martin, *James*, lxxii-lxxxiv and lxxxvii-xciii; and Ernst Baasland, "Der Jakobusbrief

for wisdom—and James's concern that it be "the wisdom from above"—is treated directly in Jas 3:13-18.

What are the effects upon believers as receivers of the respective actions of the 'true God' and the 'false/hypothetical God'? Clearly the receivers of the positive action of the 'true God' are given the "wisdom" they "lack" (δοθήσεται αὐτῷ), whereas those who would have received "reproach" would still lack "wisdom." This distinction is of no slight significance. Whereas the readers, in keeping with the theological tendencies of the Wisdom tradition, believed they gained "wisdom" as a result of their experiences of suffering (again, see Jas 1:2-4), James counters that "wisdom" is a "generous" gift from God. God does not "reprimand" believers in the hope that they will learn "wisdom;" God desires to *give* believers the "wisdom" that they lack.[33]

But just what kind of qualification "wisdom" is remains somewhat vague. "Wisdom" is most 'naturally'—at least by modern, Western readers—associated with knowledge, especially in its practical applications (i.e., knowledge that grants an ability, a "knowing how to do").[34] However, it is best at this point to leave open the question of whether "wisdom" within James's system of convictions is a qualification that brings an ability or a willingness to act.

OPP 1:6 — "Faith" vs. "Doubting". A second opposition of actions located within this section carries forward the development begun with OPP 1:5. In Jas 1:6, we have the rather elliptical opposition between making a request to God with faith (αἰτείτω δὲ ἐν πίστει) and making a request to God with doubt (διακρινόμενος). Here the syntactic roles of the Divine and believers are reversed from what we found in OPP 1:5; i.e., it is (true and false) believers who perform the action ("let him [or her] ask"), and God is the receiver of these requests.

---

als Neutestamentliche Weisheitsschrift," *ST* 36 (1982): 119-139.

[33]It should be emphasized that the idea of "wisdom" as a divine gift was not alien to the early Jewish and Christian wisdom traditions (cf. Davids, *James*, 51-56; Laws, *James*, 54; and Martin, *James*, 17). But this opposition of actions and the figurativization of this discourse unit clearly suggest that the readers stressed the other side of this tradition, namely the human search and quest for wisdom within the struggles of life.

[34]Cf. the comments of Davids (*James*, 52): "Wisdom in the OT is very closely tied on the one hand to practical action and on the other to God. ... [W]isdom relates one to God, not by an increase of theoretical knowledge, but by producing obedience to his commands ...." See further the discussion below of "wisdom" as a figure within these verses.

The positive subject is obviously the same as the receiver of OPP 1:5: believers are to "ask with faith" in order to receive the "wisdom" that they "lack" from the God who will give it to them "generously." Thus, they are qualified to ask on the basis of their "faith." Conversely, the negative subject is qualified by "doubt" rather than "faith," and is to be identified with the "double-minded person" (ἀνὴρ δίψυχος)[35] who "should not expect to receive anything from the Lord" (Jas 1:7-8). The question is whether "faith" and "doubt" are qualifications of will, ability or knowledge.

It has been widely argued (usually on the basis of Jas 2:18-19) that "faith" in the Epistle is nothing more than knowing and assenting to certain doctrines.[36] But this sense cannot easily account for the use of "faith" here in 1:6, and is particularly difficult in its connection to prayer in Jas 5:14-15 and 18. This inconsistency led Cyril Powell to distinguish between two concepts of "faith" within the Epistle—an "intellectual strain" and a "dynamic attitude."[37] From a semiotic

---

[35]I have rendered ἀνήρ by the more generic translation "person," realizing that it is usually understood in the more exclusively male sense in contrast to the more generic ἄνθρωπος. Notice, however, that these terms occur in synonymous parallelism within Jas 1:7-8; ὁ ἄνθρωπος ἐκεῖνος = ἀνὴρ δίψυχος. The problem of gendered language is particularly acute within the Epistle. While James clearly recognizes both male and female members within the community (note the explicit mention of "brother or sister" [ἀδελφὸς ἢ ἀδελφή] in Jas 2:15), we frequently find the more exclusive ἀνήρ where we might have expected, even by first century standards, the more generic ἄνθρωπος (cf. Jas 1:12, 20, 23; 2:2; 3:2). In light of this, I will follow contemporary standards of inclusive language in my translations where I judge that the referent is any member of the community or that gender is not essential to the point at hand. Nevertheless, I will also try to consistently note where these translations do not reflect the Greek text in an effort not to occult completely the clear androcentric bias of the language of the Epistle.

[36]See as examples of this interpretation Marxsen, *Introduction*, 229-30; Perrin, *Introduction*, 255-56; Rudolf Bultmann, *Theology of the New Testament*, 2 vols., Scribner Studies in Contemporary Theology (New York: Charles Scribner's Sons, 1951-55), 2:163; George E. Ladd, *A Theology of the New Testament* (Grand Rapids: William B. Eerdmans Publishing Company, 1974), 592; and Dan O. Via, "The Right Strawy Epistle Reconsidered: A Study in Biblical Ethics and Hermeneutics," *JR* 49 (1969): 256.

[37]Cyril H. Powell, "'Faith' in James and its Bearings on the Problem of the Date of the Epistle," *ExpTim* 62 (1951): 311. Just exactly what Powell intends by "dynamic attitude" is difficult to isolate. He relates it to the request for wisdom in Jas 1:5-6 and the passages about prayer in chapter 5. But by way of definition, he simply states, "This kind of faith is, in the nature of the case, not divorced from works. To exercise it involves an inward dynamism, and the appropriate action,

vantage point, however, the key to understanding James's use of "faith," at least here in Jas 1:6, is its opposition to "doubt." Now an opposition to "doubt" could be in keeping with an "intellectual strain" of faith within the Epistle ("doubt" = "intellectual uncertainty"), but this overlooks the identification of the doubter as a "double-minded person."

The fact that the word δίψυχος apparently occurs for the first time in extant Greek literature in the Epistle of James has made it the focus of considerable attention. Most scholars agree that the word derives from Jewish ideas of the "divided/two heart(s)" (בְּלֵב וָלֵב) and the "two inclinations" (יֵצֶר).[38] This background points more toward "doubt" (and thus also "faith") being a qualification of will.[39] Seitz describes the influence of this background on Jas 1:8 and 4:4-5 as follows:

> When the double-minded man approaches God in prayer he wavers or hesitates; his heart is in need of purification because his motives are mixed; his mind is not wholly turned to God because of his desire for other things, especially the wealth and pleasures of the world.[40]

Thus, "to ask with faith" would be to ask with consistent and proper desire, but "to ask with doubt" is to have improper desire and mixed motivations for making the request. But how is it one comes to have "faith" rather than "doubt"? OPP 1:5 suggests that "faith" may be the product of knowing/believing something about God, specifically that God

---

whenever called for, would naturally follow."

[38]See Oscar J. F. Seitz, "Antecedents and Signification of the Term ΔΙΨΥΧΟΣ," *JBL* 66 (1947): 211-19, for a discussion of Hebrew Bible and rabbinic backgrounds. For additional evidence derived from the Qumran literature, see Wallace I. Wolverton, "The Double-minded Man in the Light of Essene Psychology," *ATR* 38 (1956): 166-175, and Oscar J. F. Seitz, "Afterthoughts on the Term 'Dipsychos,'" *NTS* 4 (1957/58): 327-334. Seitz posits that James did not coin the word, but rather the uses within the Epistle of James, Shepherd of Hermas, 1 Clement and Didache were all independently derived from a common, no longer extant, source (Oscar J. F. Seitz, "Relationship of The Shepherd of Hermas to the Epistle of James," *JBL* 63 [1944]: 131-140).

[39]Nevertheless, it could still have an element of knowledge in the sense of a knowledge that establishes one's will. That it is to say, it is a "knowing-how-to-be" ("knowledge of the value") as opposed to a "knowing-how-to-do" ("knowledge as means") which establishes one's ability to act. See Greimas and Courtés, *Semiotics and Language*, "knowledge," 167-68; Patte, *Structural Exegesis for New Testament Critics*, 34-36; and idem, *Religious Dimensions*, 182-95, especially paragraph 5.15 on 192.

[40]Seitz, "Antecedents," 214.

"gives generously" rather than "reproaching." However, we will need to look for confirmation of this suggestion by oppositions of actions elsewhere in the Epistle.

The relationship between "faith" or "doubt" and the will is also evidenced by the effect each has on God as the receiver. In the case of the positive action, the presence of "faith" with the request establishes God's will to grant "wisdom" to the believer "generously."[41] Conversely, the presence of "doubt" in the request fails to establish God's will to give "anything" to the doubter, who is a "double-minded person, unstable in all his [or her] ways."

When we consider these two oppositions together, we can already begin to see something of the pattern of James's system of convictions. Believers are qualified by a lack of "wisdom." Whereas the readers of the Epistle have emphasized that they must gain this "wisdom" by "enduring" certain unspecified "trials" which God uses as a means of "reprimand" and instruction (Jas 1:2-4), James stresses that the solution to this dilemma is for God to "give" this "wisdom" to believers. Although God will give this wisdom "generously," it is not given automatically. Rather, one must "ask with faith, without doubting" before God's will is established to grant the wisdom one lacks. This pattern can be presented as follows:

Positive	Negative
1. Having "faith."	1. Having "doubt."
2. Asking for "wisdom" from God.	2. Not asking for "wisdom" from God, or asking with "doubt."
3. Receiving "wisdom" from God.	3. Receiving nothing from God.

Two major questions remain unanswered: (1) how does one come to have "faith" rather than "doubt," and (2) what effect does receiving "wisdom" have on the believer?

---

[41]Against the view of Martin (*James*, 18) that "there are no conditions to [God's] giving."

Figurativization in Jas 1:5-8

In discussing Jas 1:2-4, we noted that it is possible to hear within those verses an implicit critique of the readers perception of their maturity or "completeness." This critique becomes more explicit in Jas 1:5, in spite of the continued subtleness of the expression. James uses the grammatical construction of a 'simple condition'[42] ("If anyone among you lacks wisdom, let him [or her] ask ...") to suggest that there are some among the implied readers who do lack "wisdom."[43] Thus, despite their expectations to the contrary (see the discussion of OPP 1:5 above), their "patient endurance" of the "testing of [their] faith" has failed to make them "complete and whole, lacking in nothing."[44] Indeed, it has failed to provide for them the very thing they believed "testing" would produce in them—"wisdom."

But what is this "wisdom" that James believes his readers still lack?[45] There is virtually universal agreement among interpreters of the Epistle that the background for this term lies in the Wisdom traditions of early Judaism and Christianity rather than the philosophical speculations of the Stoics or Gnostics.[46] "Wisdom" is a "practical

---

[42]εἰ + the present indicative in the protasis, indicative mood or its equivalent in the apodosis. The Greek 'simple condition' is without temporal reference and expresses simple cause-effect relationships.

[43]Cf. Martin, *James*, 17: "The conditional clause opening with εἰ δὲ does not imply doubt or suggest contingency. Rather it presupposes 'a standing fact.'"

[44]Thus, we clearly have more than just a 'catchword' link between the "lacking nothing" in 1:4 and the "lacking wisdom" in 1:5. Dibelius (*James*, 77) misses this connection, at least in part, because he identifies the subject of 1:5-8 as "praying in faith" without relating it to the context which concerns prayer for a specific thing, namely "wisdom." Against Dibelius, see Davids, *James*, 71; and Mußner, *Jakobusbrief*, 68.

[45]In raising this question as part of the discussion of figurativization, we are not yet taking up the issue of what kind of "qualification" (will, ability, or knowledge) wisdom is within James's system of convictions. We are here concerned with what wisdom "is," what meanings the word evokes for readers and author. To ask what kind of qualification "wisdom" is, is to inquire as to its benefit for those who possess it—does it make them willing or able to perform certain positive actions or to not perform certain negative ones?

[46]A slight deviation from this pattern is the position taken by Ulrich Wilckens ("σοφία, σοφός, σοφίζω," *TDNT* 7:524-25) who argues that James counters the Gnostic speculations of his opponents by the concept of wisdom as "a morally upright walk." He identifies these adversaries as Gnostic on the basis of Jas 3:17-18 which "speaks of a heavenly wisdom which comes down from above, which contrasts with everything earthly, psychic and devilish, and which is thus heavenly,

righteousness," often characterized as a "quality of the soul" or "virtue." As Douglas Moo has described it, wisdom provides an "'[i]nsight' into the will of God and the way it is to be applied in life."[47]

One of the more intriguing possibilities is that a very specific strand of this broader Wisdom tradition contributes to the readers' investment in the term "wisdom," namely the link between Wisdom and the divine Spirit found within certain portions of the Hebrew Bible, Qumran literature and the New Testament[48] that led Davids to argue that "James has a wisdom pneumatology."[49] J. A. Kirk points to the similarity of language regarding the certainty of God's giving in response to one's request in Jas 1:5 to that of Matt 7:7-11 // Luke 11:9-13, and in Luke 11:13 this "gift" is specifically identified as the Holy Spirit. He finds additional similarities between the discussion of the influence of wisdom in Jas 3:13-18 and the "fruit of the Spirit" in Gal 5:16-25. Thus, he argued, "wisdom" in the Epistle is analogous to the Holy Spirit in other writings.[50]

While I would agree "that such an interchange of terminology is by no means outside the bounds of probability even if this certainty cannot be established," I cannot concur with Kirk's contention that "the internal evidence of the epistle seems to be the strongest" in support of this view.[51] I find nothing within the text of the Epistle itself that would have suggested an identification between the Holy Spirit and "wis-

---

spiritual and divine by nature. ... [Wisdom] is obviously a personal revealer" (7:525). But as we shall see in discussing Jas 1:17-18, there is little warrant for identifying the divine origins of wisdom, which James seeks to emphasize rather than to oppose, with Gnosticism.

[47]Moo, *James*, 62. Cf. also Ropes, *St. James*, 139 and Sidebottom, *James, Jude, 2 Peter*, 28.

[48]See J. A. Kirk, "The Meaning of Wisdom in James: Examination of a Hypothesis," *NTS* 16 (1969/70): 24-38.

[49]Davids, *James*, 56. In terms of the specific concerns of this study, we must take care to distinguish between the possible backgrounds of the figure "wisdom" brought to the text by the implied readers and the convictions of the implied author; i.e., the observation that a "wisdom pneumatology" may provide important information regarding the possible semantic investments in the term "wisdom" by the readers is not proof that James, the implied author, "has" and emphasizes these same investments.

[50]Kirk, "Meaning of Wisdom." Cf. also Davids, *James*, 51-56 and 65; Hartin, *James and Q*, 102-104 and 114-115; Hoppe, *Hintergrund*, 148; and W. Ralph Thompson, "The Epistle of James: A Document on Heavenly Wisdom," *Wesleyan Theological Journal* 13 (1978): 7-12.

[51]Kirk, "Meaning of Wisdom," 38.

dom."[52]   Thus, I would conclude that while such a "wisdom pneumatology" may have been part of the beliefs of the readers, it plays no significant role, either positively or negatively, in the semantic investment in the figure "wisdom" by the implied author of the Epistle.

Thus, we are left with our preliminary conclusion that "wisdom" for James is an insight into the application of the will of God in life. But we need to go further since the key to James's semantic investment in the term "wisdom" here lies in its parallel section within this discursive unit.   In Jas 1:17-19a there is also mention of a "perfect gift" from God, namely the "word of truth."[53]   Its importance to the believer resides in the fact that it is by means of this "word of truth" that God "gives birth" to the believers, and so this "word of truth" is probably to be identified with the "implanted word which is able to save [their] souls."   We will examine these relationships more fully below.

Jas 1:9-12 — The "Crown of Life"

Figurativization in Jas 1:9-12

The initial question one faces in addressing the figurativization of this section is how to interpret the description of the believer as ὁ ἀδελφὸς ὁ ταπεινός. If one focuses on the contrast between persons in Jas 1:9-11 (ὁ ἀδελφὸς ὁ ταπεινός contrasted with ὁ πλούσιος), then ταπεινός seems to be a socio-economic designation contrasting the "poor brother [or sister]" with "the rich."   However, if one focuses on the contrast between their respective states (the "exaltation" [ὕψος] of ὁ ἀδελφὸς ὁ ταπεινός as compared to the "humility" [ταπείνωσις] of ὁ πλούσιος), then ταπεινός would seem to be a moral or ethical term designating the "humble brother [or sister]."[54]   These options are

---

[52]Indeed, apart from a possible reference to the Spirit of God in Jas 4:5 there is no mention of the Spirit anywhere within the Epistle.   On the problems of interpreting the reference to "the spirit which God caused to dwell in us" in Jas 4:5, see the exegesis in chapter 5 below.

[53]Davids (*James*, 52 and 88) uses the parallel to argue in the opposite direction; in that Jas 1:17-18 parallels 1:5-8, both within the structure of the opening section of the Epistle and in language about gifts from God, the latter is a reference to wisdom even though the word "wisdom" is not found there.   Cf. also Kirk, "Meaning of Wisdom," 38, n. 5.

[54]For a discussion of whether ὁ ταπεινός is to be understood as an economic or an ethical/moral description with a listing of scholars for each view, see Maynard-Reid, *Poverty and Wealth*, 40-41 (notes on 113-114).   Both Maynard-Reid (ibid.) and Davids (*James*, 76) favor the socio-economic nuance.

further complicated by the fact that ταπείνωσις itself can designate either the moral "quality of unpretentious behavior, suggesting a total lack of arrogance or pride,"[55] or indicate a "state of low status" in a socio-economic sense.[56]

However, it is not incumbent upon the readers to decide between the socio-economic and the ethical/moral nuances of the words.[57] Indeed, they can simultaneously maintain both these nuances by virtue of the 'piety of the poor' that provides the eschatological hope of "exaltation" in which they, the "poor" and "humble," can "boast."[58] Further, this "exaltation" is the "crown of life," the "salvation of the final consummation,"[59] that has been promised to those who love God.

Actually, the more difficult question is what it means for "the rich person [to] boast in his [or her] humility." Dibelius offers two possibilities for resolving this problem.[60] The "boasting of the rich" can be perceived as an "heroic" response to the loss of great material wealth accepted with joy in the light of the dawning eschaton.[61] Alternatively, the elliptical construction of 1:10 can be understood ironically; whereas the poor can truly boast in that their exaltation is sure (having been promised by God, 1:12), the rich can only boast in an ironic sense

---

[55]Louw and Nida, *Greek-English Lexicon*, §88.51 (1:748). They cite Jas 1:10 as an example of this usage.

[56]Ibid., §87.60 (1:740). Yet another possibility is that it refers to the experience of humiliation "caused by severe external loss" (BAGD, "ταπείνωσις," 805). This option will be explored more fully below.

[57]As Maynard-Reid states, "[a]n absolute either/or position here ... seems to be a faulty option" (*Poverty and Wealth*, 40). Having said this, however, his own agenda seems to compel him to assert that James's "emphasis is on the social status of those classes" (ibid., 41).

[58]Cf. Dibelius, *James*, 85; and Davids, *James*, 76. I would agree with Martin (*James*, 24) that Maynard-Reid, in his desire to disallow a spiritualizing reading of "poor" over against true economic poverty, "unnecessarily downplays the motif of the 'piety of the poor.'"

[59]Dibelius, *James*, 89, though he did not link the "exaltation" of 1:9 with the "crown of life" in 1:12. Cf. also Davids, *James*, 80; Laws, *James*, 68; and Mußner, *Jakobusbrief*, 85-86. The connection between the "boasting" in 1:9 and the beatitude of 1:12 is drawn, however, by Maynard-Reid, *Poverty and Wealth*, 39.

[60]*James*, 84-85; cf. Maynard-Reid, *Poverty and Wealth*, 41-44.

[61]This position is argued at length by Ropes, *St. James*, 145-148. The position of Moo is similar. He argued that the poor are humbled in the sight of society but exalted in relation to God, whereas the rich are exalted by society but must humble themselves before God. "Both Christians, in other words, must look at their lives from a heavenly, not an earthly, perspective" (Moo, *James*, 68-69).

because the basis of their boasting (wealth) is to be taken away in the eschatological consummation.

Maynard-Reid contends that both these options suffer from a "presuppositional fault," namely that there were "rich" Christians within James's community:

> The heroic viewpoint ... artificially break[s] up the antithesis of vv. 9 and 10-11 and ... mak[es] the rich man a brother whose trial is the loss of his riches. ... The ironic viewpoint is able to assume there were rich Christians in James's community by spiritualizing the concept of poverty. Thus, a Christian in the early church could be rich and yet "poor," because he was "pious."[62]

But his objections are ultimately grounded in his opposite presupposition that there could have been no "rich Christians according to modern categories"[63] within the community. The ingrained antipathy against the "rich" because of their socio-economic oppression of the poor precludes such a possibility, according to Maynard-Reid. He further appeals to the 'Christian communism' of Acts 2:44 and 4:32 to argue that those who may have been wealthy would have lost their status as "the rich" when they gave up their property to the common use of the community.[64]

If we recall, however, that Jas 1:9-12 is a thematic section which draws primarily on the convictions of the readers, we can see that the issue is not so much who *James* identifies as the "poor" and the "rich," but rather with which group do the *readers* identify themselves. On that question there can be no doubt. The readers see themselves as the "poor" who can "boast" in their "exaltation." They have "endured" the "trials" of human experience and have become "complete and whole, lacking in nothing." Unlike the "rich" who are "humiliated" and will lose everything including their lives,[65] the readers will receive "the crown of life" promised them by God.

If there is any irony here in terms of the semantic investments in these figures from the side of the author, it is that the "poor," far from being "humble," are exceedingly status conscious. They "boast in [their] exaltation" and even conceive of eschatological salvation itself in terms

---

[62]Maynard-Reid, *Poverty and Wealth*, 43-44.

[63]Ibid., 43.

[64]Ibid., 114, n. 17.

[65]As is powerfully expressed by the images on the passing beauty of the flower in Jas 1:10-11.

of a social badge of honor, the στέφανος.[66] They profess to identify themselves as the "poor/humble brothers and sisters," but they actually identify themselves with the "rich" and strive for the trappings of power (as will become painfully clear in Jas 2:1-13). As Reicke said, "In these verses, the author expresses his concern over the readers' preoccupation with the question of wealth."[67] Perhaps James includes these images "to send a warning of impending judgment,"[68] not to the wealthy but in the hope that the readers will recognize their true allegiance.

Summary of Jas 1:2-12

We are now in a position to review the adequacy of the proposed statement of the theme of Jas 1:2-12, "The Blessing of Trials." We have seen that for the readers "trials" are a "blessing" because they, in and of themselves, produce "patient endurance" (1:3) which ultimately assures them of a "crown of life" (1:12). Moreover, they perceive themselves as being "complete and whole" (1:4), and so they "rejoice when [they] meet various trials" (1:2) and "boast in [their] exaltation" (1:9). But James conceives of the "blessing of trials" differently. For him, "trials" serve as a warning of the coming eschatological judgment; as Sidebottom has phrased it, "The drift, then, is not that trials produce steadfastness, but that they provide the opportunity for steadfastness to have its full effect, to lead to the prayer of faith (verses 4, 5) and thence to wholeness and completion."[69]

James leads the readers to accept this view by the convictions expressed in 1:5-8. They cannot achieve the "wisdom" they "lack" by being "patient" students of divine "reprimands" and instruction. Rather, "wisdom" is a "generous gift" given by God to those who "ask with faith" (1:5), with a singleness of desire and motivation. They "lack wisdom" because of their "double-mindedness" (1:8). And how are they "double-minded"? In part because they claim to identify with the poor, but actually are driven by a desire to "boast in [their] exaltation" and to possess the signs of power and prestige (1:9, 12). James warns them that if they continue in this way, they like the rich "will die in the midst of their pursuits" (1:11). Why this is so, and how one can escape such a fate, provide the themes for the next sub-unit.

---

[66]On the distinction between the στέφανος as an "ornament or badge of honour" and the διάδημα as a royal crown, see Ropes, *St. James*, 150-52.

[67]Reicke, *James, Peter and Jude*, 15.

[68]So Martin, *James*, 26; Mußner, *Jakobusbrief*, 73.

[69]Sidebottom, *James, 2 Peter, Jude*, 27.

Saving the Soul from Death
(Jas 1:13-21)

Jas 1:13-16 — The Origin of Temptation

Convictions Emphasized in Jas 1:13-16

As we again focus on the convictions being underscored by James, we should remind ourselves of the two questions with which we were left in analyzing the oppositions in Jas 1:5-8: (1) how does one come to have "faith" rather than "doubt," and (2) what effect does receiving "wisdom" have on the believer? Our analysis of the inverted parallelisms for this sub-unit suggested that James is here trying to persuade his readers that God is typified by "righteousness" rather than being a source of "temptation" and so also evil. Might such knowledge about God be in some way related to whether a person has "faith" or "doubt"? Moreover, by receiving an "implanted word" believers "save [their] soul/life" (ψυχάς) from the "death" which results from human "desire." Might this then be the effect of receiving wisdom? We need to look to the oppositions of actions within this sub-unit to find confirmation of both our statement of its theme and the suggestions which it offers regarding James's system of convictions.

OPP 1:13-14 — The Non-tempting God.[70] The final opposition of actions in this first discursive unit is found at Jas 1:13-14. It involves an elliptical polemical dialogue,[71] with the contents of the sayings themselves containing an opposition. The negative statement is expressed by what "no one who is being tempted [should] say," namely, "I am being tempted by God." The positive statement is what one who is being tempted should rather say, along with James: "God tempts no one. Rather, each one is tempted when he [or she] is dragged away and enticed by his [or her] own (evil) desire."[72]

---

[70]On the translation of the verb πειράζω in Jas 1:13-14 as "to tempt," see note 3 above and the discussion of the figurativization of these verses below.

[71]On the 'special' case of polemical dialogues as 'oppositions of cognitive actions,' see Patte, *Structural Exegesis for New Testament Critics*, 28.

[72]On the importance of the Jewish יֵצֶר theology discussed above as the background to Jas 1:13-16, see Joel Marcus, "The Evil Inclination in the Epistle of James," *CBQ* 44 (1982): 606-21. He is perhaps overly zealous in his reading of this theological motif into the bulk of the Epistle (cf. 620-21); nevertheless, he shows how prominently human volition (either for good or for evil) is woven into the convictional fabric of the Epistle.

The opposed actions within these opposed sayings are the positive action that God does not tempt people, and the negative action of a (hypothetical) God who does tempt people. But as in OPP 1:5, this "hypothetical" God is in fact the view of the divine within the system of convictions of the readers. James expects his readers to respond to temptation by saying, "I am being tempted/tested by God." This expectation is clearly evidenced by the fact that James concludes the section in which this opposition of actions occurs with the admonition, "Do not continue to be deceived, my beloved brothers [and sisters]" (Jas 1:16). But he wants them to change their beliefs about the Divine and about the origins of temptation so that they will respond to temptation by saying, "I am being tempted because I have been dragged away and enticed by my own (evil) desire." To understand how he manipulates the readers to accept this position, we will need to consider the figurativization of this sub-unit below.

There are two points that we should, however, note at this stage. First, since "temptation" is defined here in terms of one's will ("desire," ἐπιθυμία), the fact that God is "unable to be tempted to do evil"[73] tells us something about God's will, namely that it must always be a good or positive will. Secondly, it appears likely that the readers' incorrect knowledge ("I am being tempted by God") is to be related to the "double-mindedness" of 1:8.[74] The doubters make their request to God with uncertainty because they do not know God's will; they do not know whether God will desire to give them something good (the "wisdom" which they "lack"), or whether God will desire to give them something bad ("temptation"). As Mußner observes, they are torn by a simultaneous trust and distrust of God.[75] Moreover, they anticipate

---

[73]So Dibelius (*James*, 92) renders the construction ἀπείραστος κακῶν; similar renderings are favored by the vast majority of commentators. Peter Davids's objections to it ("The Meaning of ἀπείραστος in James i. 13," *NTS* 24 [1978]: 388) are ultimately unconvincing. His chief criticism is that the Torah contains traditions that "Israel did test God in the wilderness." But this de-emphasizes κακῶν in Jas 1:13; perhaps God's initial desire to judge Israel was not "evil," but warranted and justified. Even if one concedes that this desire was in fact "evil" (cf. Exod 32:12 and 14, though most modern translations render רָעָה by "disaster" rather than "evil"), God still remains "unable to be tempted to do evil" in that the judgment is ultimately not carried out ("Yahweh repented of the evil ..."). See the further discussion of Davids's article below.

[74]On the יֵצֶר theology behind Jas 1:8 and 1:13-16, see nn. 38 and 72 above.

[75]Mußner, *Jakobusbrief*, 70: "so ist für Jak auch der διακρινόμενος ein Mensch, der in einem innerin Widerstreit zwischen Vertrauen und Mißtrauen Gott

that God is more likely to desire to give them the bad ("temp-
tation/trial"), at least with regard to their acquisition of wisdom,[76] as
we have already seen in discussing OPP 1:5.

Thus, this opposition confirms what we suggested earlier regarding
James's system of convictions. "Faith" is a qualification of a person's
will, a "consistent and proper desire" that stems from a knowledge that
God is "good." Knowing that God "gives [wisdom] generously," is
"unable to be tempted to do evil," and "tempts no one" makes one willing to trust God completely. This knowledge provides people with the
"faith" to ask God for what they lack because they desire what God will
give them. However, those who say (i.e., know and believe) they are
"being tempted by God" can only request wisdom from God with
"doubt." They are "double-minded," simultaneously trusting and dis-
trusting God because they are uncertain whether God will give them
something desirable ("wisdom") or undesirable ("reproach," "a test").
Or worse, their distrust of God—their belief that God will tempt and try
them—leads them not to ask God for wisdom at all. Therefore, we can
expand the pattern of convictions as follows:[77]

	Positive	Negative
1.	*Knowing "God tempts no one."*	*Knowing "I am tempted by God."*
2.	Having "faith."	Having "doubt."
3.	Asking for "wisdom" from God.	Not asking for "wisdom" from God, or asking with "doubt."
4.	Receiving "wisdom" from God.	Receiving nothing from God.

---

gegenüber lebt." Cf. also Davids, *James*, 73.

[76]We will see that such is not their constant expectation when we turn to the
figurativization of Jas 1:17-19a.

[77]Each time some new conviction(s) or element(s) are added to the pattern of
James's convictions, we will highlight them within the schematic presentation of the
system of convictions.

The question of why one needs this "wisdom," however, remains unanswered, or at least unconfirmed, by an explicit opposition of actions.

Figurativization in Jas 1:13-16

In considering the semantic investments in the figures of Jas 1:13-16, the first issue is to sort out the semantic range assigned by the author and the readers to the words from the πειράζω word group. Commenting on the transition from 1:12 to 1:13-16, Laws has argued that "[t]he author reiterates the conventional blessing on those enduring *peirasmos*, but he will be conscious of the ambiguity of the word he uses, and this suggests to him a further theme of trial to be explored."[78] She seems to project both possibilities on James (who "*reiterates* the conventional blessing" which "suggests to *him* a further theme"), but the possibility that the ambiguity arises between competing investments by the author and readers must be considered.

If we assume the role of "first-time readers," it is only natural that we would continue investing the πειράζω verbs with the same meaning that has served the noun πειρασμός thus far in the Epistle: "Let no one who is being tested say, 'I am being tested by God.'" As Davids has shown, it is even possible to continue this semantic range into the clause ὁ θεὸς ἀπείραστός ἐστιν κακῶν by translating it "God ought not to be tested by evil people."[79] This rendering draws on the tradition from the Hebrew Bible "that the person in distress ought not to turn and accuse God, putting [God] to the test."[80]

However, James compels a "backreading" of 1:13 by the continuation of the argument in 1:14-15. His statement that "each one πειράζεται by his [or her] own desire," coupled with the progression 'desire—sin—death,' all but forces understanding the πειράζω words within the semantic range of "to tempt" rather than "to test." Thus, James wants the reader to see this meaning already in Jas 1:13: "Let no

---

[78]Laws, *James*, 69.

[79]Davids, "ἀπείραστος," 390-391. In addition to this rendering and the translation "God is unable to be tempted to do evil" discussed in n. 73 above, Davids cites a third possibility: "God is inexperienced in evil." This option is supported by F. J. A. Hort (*The Epistle of St. James* [London: Macmillan, 1909], 23) and Martin (*James*, 35), though he emphasizes that the "evil" is "the evil situations which the readers are facing." For the arguments against this translation, see Davids, "ἀπείραστος," 388-390.

[80]Ibid., 391. See Davids's n. 1 there for references where this tradition is employed in the Hebrew Bible.

one who is being tempted say, 'I am being tempted by God.'"[81] Additionally, ἀπείραστος would most likely be understood by James to mean that God is "unable to be tempted to do evil" (see note 73 above).

Nevertheless, Davids admirably reconstructs the manipulation of the reader within these verses, even to the point of himself backreading the meaning "temptation" into 1:13:

> ... one should not say, 'I am *tempted* by God'—that would be to test God and God ought not to be tested. This is a traditional answer, for it fits with the tradition of God's *testing* people. ... [T]he author continues with his second statement about God, which statement shifts away from the first in rejecting the idea that God *tests* people at all. The assertion that 'I am *tempted* by God' is factually wrong, for God never *tempts* anyone at all.[82]

But the real issue in terms of the system of convictions that James wants the readers to adopt is not tied up in the particularities of the meanings of πειράζω. What James stresses by the ambiguity of "testing/tempting" is that the problems the readers face are ultimately *internal*, and focusing on the *external* 'trials and tests' can only cause them to miss what is essential. Again citing Davids:

> This internalization of the demonic [i.e., realizing temptation comes from the evil יֵצֶר within, one's ἐπιθυμία] means that the person cannot externalize his failures; he cannot blame either the external divine or the external demonic. Rather the person must come to terms with himself as he is, as the one who wishes to fail but at the same time wishes to avoid the guilt by blaming God. The way is then paved for repentance and restoration, the author himself fulfilling the role of the restorer which he praises in chapter v.[83]

Thus Davids has admirably performed the role of the ideal reader. He not only initially 'misreads' the meaning that James invests in the πειράζω word group in 1:13-15, but ultimately 'backreads' the verses and recognizes the conviction that James wished to communicate. The

---

[81]As I stated in note 3 above, Martin presses the "backreading" too far by taking πειρασμόν in Jas 1:12 to mean "temptation." Despite his attempted appeal to Ropes in support of this position (Martin, *James*, 32), Ropes correctly argues that πειρασμόν must mean "trial" and not "temptation" in 1:12: "Inner enticement to evil would have to be *resisted*, not *endured*" (Ropes, *St. James*, 150; emphasis his).

[82]Davids, "ἀπείραστος," 391; emphasis mine. Vouga (*Jacques*, 53) likewise asserts that James rejects the theological traditions of God testing people.

[83]Davids, "ἀπείραστος," 392.

readers' problem, from James's point of view, is not *external* trials but *internal* temptations that will ultimately lead to death.[84]

In that James affirms certain aspects of the readers' יֵצֶר theology ("desire" leads to "sin" and ultimately "death") in order to make this point, there is confirmation here that James is not attempting to "convert" the readers by having them adopt an entirely new system of convictions.[85] Some of their beliefs need to be corrected, others do not. Nevertheless, James underscores the importance of this particular belief (their true problems are *internal*, not external) by the imperative which concludes this section (Jas 1:16): "Do not continue to be deceived, my beloved brothers [and sisters]!"[86]

Two additional sets of figures warrant attention before proceeding to the next section. The first of these are the metaphors used to describe the actions of one's "desire:" people are "tempted when [they] are dragged away and enticed by [their] own desire." These metaphors are apparently drawn from fishing, and refer to drawing a fish from the water on a line and luring fish with bait respectively.[87] Adamson observes that 'logically' it makes no sense for the 'baiting' to occur after the 'drawing out.' Therefore, he attempts to impose a logical order by emending the text to read ἐφελκόμενος καὶ δελεαζόμενος ("attracted and enticed").[88] However, there is little justification for such an emendation. It matters not whether they are first "dragged" or "enticed;" what

---

[84]In this respect then, perhaps both Davids and Vouga (see n. 82) overstate the case in arguing that James rejects the tradition that God "tests" people. James seems to be less intent on engaging this theological debate than on urging the readers to see their particular hardships as stemming less from "trials" than from "temptations" arising from their own "(evil) desire."

[85]See the discussion in the previous chapter regarding semiotic descriptions of paraenetic discourse.

[86]Cf. also Cantinat, *Jacques et Jude*, 89; and Martin, *James*, 31. The identification of an imperative as the *conclusion* of a section goes against the dominant tendency of the discourse analysis studies at the International Linguistics Center to utilize imperative-vocative structures as indicators of the inception of new sections. But that tendency seems to owe less to the particularities of discourse analysis theory than to the methodology of James Thayer who performed the first study there on the Epistle of James. See the discussion of Thayer's work in chapter 2 above.

[87]Cf. BAGD, "δελεάζω," 174. In Herodotus, *History*, 2.70, the terms are used in this way of capturing crocodiles.

[88]Adamson, *James*, 71-72. He cites in support a proverb found in Homer, *Odyssey*, 16.294, and Thucydides, *History*, 1.42.

is important is that they are "led away from the truth" and must be "restored" (5:19).

These angling metaphors are quickly dropped, however, in favor of a more powerful image. Ἐπιθυμία is personified in 1:15 as "a seductress who, having enticed the person to her bed, conceives a bastard child"[89]—ἁμαρτία, "sin." Once it "has matured," sin "gives birth to death."[90] The readers may hear in this figure the contrast between "Wisdom" and the "adulteress" in Proverbs 7-9,[91] but its forcefulness within the immediate context of James 1 derives from its contrast to the birth imagery of Jas 1:18. The close connection between 1:13-16 and 1:17-19a is well stated by Laws: "The impossibility of finding in God the origin of this sequence leading to death is further underlined by James in drawing attention to what in fact comes from him, both gifts in general and birth in particular."[92]

Jas 1:17-19a — Birth by the True Word

Figurativization in Jas 1:17-19a

The next section of this sub-unit contains no new convictions expressed by oppositions of actions. Rather, it is a thematic section that serves as a warrant for the readers to accept the convictions expressed in Jas 1:13-14 by relating it to beliefs the readers already hold about God.[93] Since the material in 1:17-18 is thematic and thus draws on the 'old knowledge' of the readers,[94] I have taken the ἴστε of 1:19a as indicative ("You know [this], my beloved brothers [and sisters].") rather than imperative ("Know [this] ...").[95]

---

[89]Davids, *James*, 84. Cf. Kugelman (*James and Jude*, 17) who refers to "desire" as "a prostitute."

[90]It is tempting to follow Hort (*St. James*, 27) in highlighting the nuance of ἀποκύω referring to 'monstrous births' since the child of "sin" is the 'still-born' "death." However, the use of this same word to refer to God "giving birth" to believers in Jas 1:18 militates against this nuance; see Laws, *James*, 71-72 and Martin, *James*, 36.

[91]So Davids, *James*, 84.

[92]Laws, *James*, 72.

[93]Its role as a warrant is clearly demonstrated by the statement that rounds out this section: "You know [this], my beloved brothers [and sisters]" (Jas 1:19a; cf. the discussion which follows). On the use of "thematic" to refer to sections of a discourse which do not contain oppositions of actions, see n. 13 above.

[94]And thus they should not need a warning about "deception" in this area in that James agrees with (or at least concedes) the position presented in 1:17-18.

[95]I favor this rendering despite the fact that BDF (§99.2, 50), A. T. Robertson

Why should the readers accept James's contention that their problem is related to "temptations" arising within themselves rather than "tests" originating with God? Because they already believe that "every good gift and every perfect present is from above, coming down from the Father of Lights." First notice that these gifts are "from above, coming down from the Father." Thus, James emphasizes the divine origins of the gifts as opposed to human attainment. What these "gifts" may refer to is left intentionally vague so as to further emphasize that *"every* good gift and *every* perfect present" comes from God.

Some commentators have criticized James's logic in formulating the argument: Would not a rebuttal of the position that "temptation/trial" comes from God require not simply that "every good gift" but rather *"only* good gifts" are given by God?[96] However, within a thymic semiotics, because of its prioritizing of "value" over "existence," the progression here still accomplishes its goal. If "every good gift and every perfect present" comes from God, who is valued as "pure good," then nothing bad or evil can come from God.[97]

That God is indeed valued as "pure good" is made clear by the figurativization of God as "the Father of lights with whom there is neither variation nor shadow cast by turning."[98] The difficulty of any

---

(*A Grammar of the Greek New Testament in the Light of Historical Research* [Nashville: Broadman Press, 1934], 329), and Wilbert F. Howard (James H. Moulton, Wilbert F. Howard, and Nigel Turner, *A Grammar of New Testament Greek*, 4 vols. [Edinburgh: T and T Clark, 1908-1963], 2:222) all state that the only indicative use of ἴστε in the New Testament is at Heb 12:17. The indicative rendering allows for a very plausible understanding of the text supported by the better textual witnesses (see also Reicke, *James, Peter and Jude*, 19-20, who, however, takes 1:19a as introducing a unit 1:19-27). On the textual variants introduced by scribes to deal with this seemingly awkward verse, see *TCGNT*, 680.

[96]E.g., Davids comments that "one notices that the argument could be more direct and clear" (*James*, 88). Some have tried to circumvent this difficulty by treating the occurrences of the adjective πᾶς as grammatically equivalent to the use in Jas 1:5 (cf. the discussion above, n. 14) in an attempt to impose the meaning "only" here in 1:17. However, as Ropes (*St. James*, 158) has indicated, this grammatical rendering is "almost, if not quite, impossible" in 1:17.

[97]If God gives both "good" and "evil," God could be perceived as "not judged non-good" (i.e. "not having not [to be] good," the relation of "implication" to "pure good") if the euphoric value of the divine exceeds the dysphoric, or "not judged good" (i.e. "not having [to be] good," the relation of "contradiction" to "pure good") if the dysphoric exceeds the euphoric. In neither case, however, could God be "pure good" (i.e. "having [to be] good") since both good and bad come from God. See Cargal, "Generative Trajectory," 267-269.

[98]Taking τροπῆς as "genitive of description" and following the translation

precise rendering of the Greek is manifestly evidenced by the number of textual variants for this verse.[99] I will not repeat the discussion of these variants here, in that "the general sense of the passage is not materially altered by any of them."[100] Nor do I wish to enter into detailed discussion over whether the mixture of general vocabulary with technical term(s) from astronomy indicates that specific astronomical phenomena or astrological forces are in view,[101] or that the phrase lacks any technical reference and simply asserts that God does not change.[102] Rather, I will focus on the issue of whether this description is an ontological metaphor or one which expresses how God is valued and experienced as either good or bad.

As is to be expected, most Western exegetes have heard within this metaphor a statement about the nature of God's existence. Consequently, one frequently finds phrases such as "the unchangeableness of God," "God's unvarying nature," and "in God's nature there is no wavering"[103] within the commentaries. They perceive the relation of the figure to James's argument as that the giving of evil by God would be inconsistent with God's nature and so impossible. But James has based his arguments not in the divine essence, but in God's will to provide good things for believers (Jas 1:5, 17a, and βουληθείς in 1:18). The point of the description "the Father of lights" is that God does not vacillate (as the astronomical bodies in their courses) or waver (as the "double-minded person" tossed about as waves by the wind, 1:6)

---

suggested by Robertson, *Greek Grammar*, 501.

[99]Cf. *TCGNT*, 679-680; Dibelius, *James*, 101-102; and Ropes, *St. James*, 162-164.

[100]Concurring with the judgment of Laws, *James*, 74.

[101]So Martin, *James*, 39; Mußner, *Jakobusbrief*, 91-92; and Vouga, *Jacques*, 57-58. Reicke (*James, Peter and Jude*, 16) provides a thoroughly astronomical translation: "since it comes down from the Father of the Luminaries with whom there is no change of position, nor any periodic concealment."

[102]So Davids, *James*, 87-88; Laws, *James*, 74; and Ropes, *St. James*, 174. As will appear from what follows, I prefer this 'general' reading to more cosmologically speculative ones. Dibelius (*James*, 102-103) seems to take a middle course; while he supports translating τροπή by "eclipse," he favors an interpretation of the phrase as a general assertion of God's "unchangeableness."

[103]So Dibelius, *James*, 103; Ropes, *St. James*, 161; and Martin, *James*, 39; respectively. Martin bases his statement on the Greek construction παρ᾽ ᾧ; likewise, Davids (*James*, 87) states that the use of the preposition "to express an *attribute*" (emphasis mine) is uncommon but evidenced.

between giving good and bad things to believers.[104] God is completely good and desires only good for believers.

It is the benefits of God's will toward believers as contrasted with
the effects of "[their] own desires" that is expressed in verse 18. There
is a direct contrasting parallelism between this verse and verse 15:
"desire" by an intermediary means leads to certain consequences. Both
the nature of the two desires and their results are set as direct antitheses:

1. God's desire (βουληθείς)

2. by means of the "word of
   truth" (λόγῳ ἀληθείας)

3. "gives birth" (ἀπεκύη-
   σεν) to believers as a
   "first fruit of [God's]
   creations."

1. Human (evil) desire (ἐπιθυμία)

2. gives birth to sin (ἁμαρτία) which matures and
   in turn

3. "gives birth" (ἀποκύει)
   to "death."

Thus, God "gives birth" to believers themselves by means of "the word
of truth;" God provides life (a 'good and perfect gift') rather than death.

This contrasting parallel between 1:15 and 18 strongly supports
reading James's investment in the figure "a kind of first fruit of [God's]
creation" as a reference to 'regeneration,'[105] against the opinion that
it refers to God's election of Israel,[106] and the position that it refers
to humanity in general over against the created order either in terms of
a Gnostic androgynous creator myth[107] or Hebrew Bible concepts of
creation.[108] It is indeed possible James has utilized a figure that his

---

[104]Among the commentators, Laws comes the closest to this non-ontological
interpretation of Jas 1:17b. She states "it is a further insistence upon the consistency
of God as only and always the giver of good (an idea complementary to that of God
as the single, i.e. ungrudging, giver of i.5)" (*James*, 73).

[105]So Laws, *James*, 75; Martin, *James*, 39; and Moo, *James*, 77, among others.

[106]So Meyer, *Rätsel des Jacobusbriefes*, 157-159.

[107]As in Carl-Martin Edsman, "Schöpferwille und Geburt. Jac 1, 18: Eine
Studie zur altchristlichen Kosmologie," *ZNW* 38 (1939): 11-44, later modified in
"Schöpfung und Wiedergeburt: Nochmals Jac. 1:18" in *Spiritus et Veritas*, Karl
Kundzin Festschrift (Eutin: Ozolin, 1953), 43-55.

[108]As in L. E. Elliott-Binns, "James I.18: Creation or Redemption?" *NTS* 3
(1956/57): 148-161. Perhaps ironically Elliott-Binns's interpretation would gain

readers would have either known or initially read as a reference to God's role as creator of the cosmos and humanity's special place within it. But James has re-invested this figure in terms of God's giving birth to a special people within humanity more generally.[109]

Most scholars who take this 'regeneration' reading of the birth imagery in 1:18 identify the "word of truth" by which God gives birth to believers as the Christian gospel.[110] While such an identification is indeed plausible (perhaps even probable), it should not be allowed to preclude an identification with other figurative elements within the text. I earlier proposed that the similarities between Jas 1:5-8 and 17-19a suggested that "wisdom" and "word of truth" might be related terms, and further that both were also to be identified with "the implanted word which is able to save your souls" (Jas 1:21). We will now examine how this adds to the meanings of Jas 1:19b-20.

Jas 1:19b-21 — The Implanted Word

Figurativization in Jas 1:19b-21

This final thematic section opens with three general admonitions, widely evidenced within the Wisdom traditions of early Judaism and Christianity:[111] "Let every person be quick to hear, slow to speak, slow to anger." Since the readers were well-versed in such Wisdom thought, we can be sure that they knew these traditional exhortations. Yet, as Davids observes, "[t]o point to this ample background, however, is not to give the meaning of this text."[112] One must go on to ask

---

support from C. B. Amphoux's suggestion that the name ὁ πατὴρ τῶν φώτων should be read "the Father of humanity" (i.e. ὁ φώς, "mortal, human") rather than "the Father of lights" (i.e. τὸ φῶς, "light"). But Amphoux argues that the former reading would support a Hellenistic background for the name, while the latter suggests a "syncretistic Hebraic" background influenced by Iranian dualism. See C. B. Amphoux, "A propos de Jacques 1,17," *RHPR* 50 (1970): 136.

[109]Consequently, Vouga (*Jacques*, 58-59) melds the election of Israel with Christians as the 'new Israel' as one option over against the "creation" reading. He states the figures are "marquées d'une certaine ambiguïté," and that "[l]es deux lectures ne s'excluent pas." Cf. also Laws, *James*, 83.

[110]Dibelius (*James*, 105) states it "doubtlessly refers to the gospel." Cf. also Cantinat, *Jacques et Jude*, 97, and Davids, *James*, 90. Mußner (*Jakobusbrief*, 95-96) has proposed that "the word of truth" may be a specific proclamation of the gospel, namely catechetical instruction and the baptismal liturgy.

[111]For parallel references from the Wisdom traditions, see Dibelius, *James*, 109-110, and Davids, *James*, 92-93.

[112]Davids, *James*, 92. Of course from a semiotic perspective we need to modify

how these admonitions relate to and contribute to the discourse in which they are found.

Dibelius argued, on the basis of their relationship to the Wisdom tradition, that the admonitions "quick to hear and slow to speak" could not be limited to hearing and speaking the "word of God."[113] But while the meaning effect of these admonitions cannot be *limited* to the "word of God," this fact alone does not preclude the possibility that they do *also* refer to a person's response to the "word of truth" by which God "gives birth" to believers as well as providing general truths for the moral life.[114] James admonishes his readers to be "quick to hear" this "word of truth," and perhaps "slow to speak" since they tend to speak rashly and incorrectly ("I am being tempted by God," 1:13).

But what of the admonition "slow to anger"? James has provided the reason for its inclusion ("for human anger does not accomplish godly righteousness," 1:20); yet the explanation itself is not entirely clear. Most commentators focus on the theologically laden δικαιοσύνη θεοῦ as the *crux interpretationis* of this verse.[115] However, given the parallel with "human anger" (ὀργὴ ἀνδρός), a reading that gives equal weight to both elements of this parallelism would be preferable. Both ἀνδρός and θεοῦ may be construed as descriptive genitives. Thus, "godly righteousness" (that righteousness that is characteristic of God) cannot be accomplished by "human anger" (that anger characteristic of human relationships).[116] The figures suggest for James a rough parallelism with the contrast between "human desire" that culminates in "death" and "God's

---

Davids's statement; it is not possible to give "the meaning" (a single meaning which precludes the legitimacy of all other meanings). It would be better to say that this background does not "exhaust the meanings of this text."

[113]Dibelius, *James*, 109-110.

[114]Contra Davids, *James*, 92, who writes: "to see a reference to 1:18 would appear to violate the structure and the break between 1:18 and 1:19; but to see this passage as introducing the theme to be dealt with in chap. 3 ... appears justified by the structure of the book." Even if one accepts a break between *sections* (not a unit or even a sub-unit) at 1:18 and 19 as Davids proposed (*James*, 27 and 29), it seems highly unlikely that a reader will sense a greater connection between 1:19 and 3:1-4:12 than with the immediately preceding verse.

[115]See Dibelius, *James*, 111; Laws, *James*, 81; and Martin, *James*, 47-48.

[116]Other possibilities exist. Dibelius (*James*, 111) emphasizes the parallel with "human anger" and concludes "what is involved is in fact a human attribute." He thus understands "godly righteousness" to mean "righteousness before God." Cf. Laws, *James*, 81. For Martin (*James*, 48), "godly righteousness" is "synonymous with God's salvation, based on the OT's understanding of Yahweh's 'saving deeds.'"

desire" to "give birth" and life to believers:　that which typifies
humanity is constantly at odds with that which typifies God.　This
parallelism opens yet another possibility for these figures; "human anger," like "human desire," cannot provide a person with the eschatological life that God desires to give to people.[117]

James describes the process by which one may receive this 'gift
of life' from God in the final verse of this unit: "Therefore, having put
aside all filth and abundance of wickedness, receive with meekness[118]
the implanted word which is able to save your souls." The prepositional
phrase ἐν πραΰτητι is ambiguous; it may be taken either with the
imperative of 1:21b as in the translation just given[119] or with the
participle of 1:21a ("having put aside by meekness all filth ...").[120]
It is best to respect this ambiguity rather than to assign the phrase exclusively to either of the verbal elements.[121]　"Meekness," as a counter-
point to "human anger," is necessary both to "put aside" evil and to be
willing to "receive the implanted word" as a "gift" from God rather than
trying to attain it by one's own efforts.

The ability of this "implanted word" to save the "lives" or
"souls" (ψυχή) of believers clearly indicates that, at least for James, it
is a parallel figure to the "word of truth" in 1:18 by which God "gives
birth" to believers.[122]　Further, it stands in semantic opposition to a
person's "own desire;" the "implanted word ... save[s] your lives," but
"desire ... gives birth to sin, and sin ... gives birth to death." The only
solution to the internal "desire" that will kill the believer is to "receive

---

[117]This meaning is similar to that proposed by Martin for these figures; see the
previous note.

[118]Here following Dibelius (*James*, 112) that ἐν πραΰτητι is to be taken with
δέξασθε and "refers to an accompanying circumstance."　He notes that the use of
"meekness" here in 1:21 "is no doubt an emphatic antithesis to 'anger'" in 1:19b
and 20. Cf. Vouga, *Jacques*, 63, who opposes it also to the "malice" of 1:21.

[119]In addition to Dibelius (see previous note), cf. Martin, *James*, 48 and Davids,
James, 94.

[120]So the punctuation of both *UBSGNT* and NA-26.

[121]So also Laws, *James*, 82.　Cf. also the translation by Vouga (*Jacques*, 60).

[122]Cf. Martin, *James*, 49: "The '[implanted] word' then ... is a virtual synonym
for the 'word of truth' (λόγος ἀληθείας) in v 18; and both refer to God's message
of new life and salvation ...."　See also Frédéric Manns, "Une tradition liturgique
juive sous-jacente à Jacques 1,21b," *RevScRel* 62 (1988): 87, who is at this point
drawing on Rinaldo Fabris (*Legge della libertà in Giacomo*, Supplementi alla Rivista
Biblica, 8 [Brescia:　Paideia Editrice, 1977], 133-146).

the implanted word which is able to save your souls" from the "death" that is born of "sin" and "desire."

By recognizing James emphasizes the internalized quality of the "implanted word" as the corrective to the internal problem of "desire," one avoids the "logical difficulty in a command to receive what is already within."[123] Whereas some commentators have attempted to resolve this "difficulty" by arguing that the command to "receive" in this context means "obey,"[124] James's point seems to be that believers must receive the word and internalize it. A close parallel would be the 'covenant written upon the heart' of Jer 31:33. Thus, the ἔμφυτος word is related to the human φύσις ("nature"), but as a corrective to the propensity for evil that is typical of human nature rather than an affirmation of its original goodness.[125]

Summary of Jas 1:13-21

The theme of this sub-unit was identified as "saving the soul from death," and it was further suggested that two sub-themes were developed within it: (1) why are the readers in danger of "death"?, and (2) how can "death" be avoided? The first of these sub-themes was addressed within the opening section (1:13-16). It alone contained an opposition of actions, because James sought to make it clear to the readers that the source of their problems was *internal* "desire," and not *external* "tests and trials." They did not recognize that their internal "desire" for the trappings of power and prestige would lead to sin and ultimately death. Their attention was too focused on the external indications of their status as the poor and oppressed.

James presents the solution to this imminent danger as "receiving the implanted word." Rather than utilizing an opposition of actions, James asserts this conviction by the semantic opposition expressed by the inverted parallelisms between the opening and closing of the sub-unit. Human desire can only lead to sin and death, but God's desire is to give

---

[123]Laws, *James*, 82.

[124]So Cantinat, *Jacques et Jude*, 104-105. Cf. Davids's proposal of "accepting and acting on it" (*James*, 95). Laws (*James*, 83) attempts to resolve the problem by diverting the focus to the "implanted word:" "the call to accept the word of the gospel is a call to man to be what he properly is, what he was created to be. A call to receive this word, already 'natural' to man, would not be a meaningless one." She then links this 'word that is "natural" to humanity' with the Stoic idea of the λόγος σπερματικός.

[125]Contra Laws, *James*, 83.

birth by the "word of truth" to believers as the preeminent work of creation. Since the threat of death is from an internal source, this "word of truth" is perceived as an "implanted word" capable of "saving [their] souls" by transforming their internal nature.

Discursive Structure and Purpose in Jas 1:2-21

Our semiotic reading of Jas 1:2-21 has isolated two sub-units within this discourse unit. The first of the sub-units (1:2-12) endeavored to persuade the readers that "enduring trials" was not an indication of their piety and status as "perfect and complete" before God, but rather "trials" provided an opportunity for the believer to ask God for the things that they lacked. The second sub-unit highlighted a particularly urgent lack: they needed the "implanted word" which would transform their nature so that their "desire" would not lead them to "death."

When we take these two sub-units together, we can perceive how each contributes to the broader theme of the unit as a whole. The readers, following the beliefs of the Wisdom tradition and the concept of the "piety of the poor," believed that the external forces of "trials" and divine instruction and "reprimands" would produce wisdom in them, making them "complete and whole" and earning them the "crown of life." James counters these beliefs by presenting a different system of convictions. The turmoils of life do not derive from external forces, either demonic or divine. Rather, they are the ultimately deadly effects of internal human "desire." The solution is indeed "wisdom," but this wisdom is not gained by "enduring" and learning from God's "reprimands." Wisdom is "generously" given by God to those who ask with "faith." It is a "good and perfect gift," "implanted" within them and "able to save [their] souls" from death.

We can thus expand and extend the schematic presentation of James's system of convictions:

Positive	Negative
1. Knowing "God tempts no one." *God is the source of* "every good and perfect gift" *and nothing bad or evil.*	1. Knowing "I am tempted by God." *Believing God gives both* "good and perfect gifts" *as well as bad or evil.*

2. Having "faith;" *being willing to ask because God is "good."*

2. Having "doubt." *Trusting and mistrusting God who is both good and bad.*

3. Asking for "wisdom" from God *as a gift.*

3. Not asking for "wisdom" from God, or asking with "doubt." *Believing one must learn "wisdom" by "enduring trials."*

4. Receiving "wisdom" from God. *Being changed internally by the "implanted word."*

4. Receiving nothing from God. *Having an internal "(evil) desire."*

5. *Being birthed by God through the "word of truth." Having one's "soul saved from death."*

5. *Having one's "desire" give birth to "sin" that gives birth to "death."*

Thus, "wisdom" appears to be a qualification of "ability;" it is "able to save your souls" from the "death" born of "sin" and "desire."

At this point, however, we can only say that "wisdom" *appears* to be a qualification of ability; it is possible that some as of yet unexpressed convictions come between 'receiving wisdom' and 'salvation' within the system of convictions of the implied author of the Epistle. We can note at this point that James exhorts his readers to be "doers of the word and not only hearers" (Jas 1:22) which implies that something more is necessary than simply passively "receiving the implanted word." But this observation takes us into the next discursive unit of the Epistle.

CHAPTER FOUR

"WORKS" OF THE "WORD":
JAMES 1:22 - 2:26

Our second discursive unit of the Epistle of James includes what is without question the most famous portion of the work—Jas 2:14-26. A thriving cottage industry has employed Protestant exegetes since the time of Luther's famous description of the book as 'an epistle of straw,' as scholars have argued about whether James was directly knowledgeable of Paul's writings or knew them only indirectly via slogans,[1] and whether James sought to correct Paul himself (whom, we are told, he probably misunderstood)[2] or Pauline enthusiasts who had misconstrued the teachings of the apostle.[3] What all these studies have in common,

---

[1]As Leonhard Goppelt suggested (*Theology of the New Testament* [Grand Rapids, Michigan: William B. Eerdmans Publishing Company, 1982], 2:209), the "polemic of James ... was not directed at the thesis of Paul, but a slogan derived from it." For Sidebottom (*James, Jude, 2 Peter*, 18), James knew Paul's teaching "only ... in an imprecise way" since the Epistle predates Paul's writings; cf. Mayor, *St. James*, xci-cii; and Laws, *James*, 131.

[2]So J. T. Sanders, *Ethics in the New Testament: Change and Development* (Philadelphia: Fortress Press, 1975), 115-128; Bultmann, *Theology*, 2:131; and Ropes, *St. James*, 48, though earlier he displaced the critique more to Paul's followers so that the actual concern is "the practical misuse which was made, or might be made, of Paul's doctrine ... to excuse moral laxity" (35).

[3]So Mußner (*Jakobusbrief*, 22): the Epistle refutes a "falsch ausgelegte Thesen der paulinischen Glaubenpredigt." See also Lohse, "Glaube und Werke," 291-292; and Dibelius, *James*, 179. For Trocmé, the focus is more on social issues than theological dissent. James was supporting the ideal of social egalitarianism, and so

even those that argue that James never read any of Paul's letters, is the belief that Jas 2:14-26 cannot be understood apart from the Pauline concept of justification by faith.

However, since we are employing a structural semiotic method within this study of the Epistle, we must take as our starting point the study of James's own convictions—not those of Paul. We want to isolate that pattern of beliefs James wanted to communicate to the readers, without being prejudiced by our own understandings of traditions which may have originated with Paul. Once we have a sense of what James believed and wanted his readers to believe, then it will be possible to consider the relationship between those convictions and the traditions which James drew on to figurativize them.[4]

Discursive Semantic Structure and Thematization

The limits of the second discursive unit of the Epistle of James are marked by the inverted parallelism between James's admonition in Jas 1:22 for the readers to "be doers of the word and not only hearers" and his dictum in Jas 2:26 that "faith separated from works is dead." This parallelism implies that James understands "works" to be "doing the (implanted [1:21]) word," an implication that will be borne out by the exegesis of this unit below. James introduces the unit with the imperative "be doers of the word" and concludes it by driving home the importance of fulfilling this imperative: if the readers have a "faith" (they are "only hearers") that is "separated from works" (they have not been "doers of the word"), then that "faith" is "dead" and will not be "able to save [their] souls/lives." The theme of this unit can be stated as "'works' of the 'word.'"[5]

The identification of the second discursive unit as 1:22 - 2:26 gains additional support from a second inverted parallelism between the

---

was critical of "les Eglises de tradition paulienne et leur tendance au conservatisme social." See Etienne Trocmé, "Les Eglises pauliniennes vues du dehors: Jacques 2,1 à 3,13," *SE* 2 (1964): 665-667.

[4]Yet, note that even this concern falls well short of the question of how one should understand the relationship between James's convictions and those of Paul. Such a question, as I noted in the preface, goes beyond the limits of this study.

[5]Among the historical critics, only Sidebottom (*James, Jude, 2 Peter*, 35) identified Jas 1:22 - 2:26 ("Doers, Not Hearers Only") as a unit of the Epistle. Moo (*James*, 77) comes close by identifying Jas 1:19 - 2:26 as a unit ("True Christianity Seen in its Works") as does Ropes (*St. James*, 168).

statement that those who profess religion but do not act upon it have a "religion (θρησκεία) [that] is useless (μάταιος)" (Jas 1:26) and James's contention that "faith (πίστις) separated from works is useless (ἀργή)" (2:20).[6] As will be seen in the discussion of the figurativization in Jas 1:26-27 below, the term "religion" utilized in the early verses of this unit is borrowed from the system of convictions of the readers. It is the readers who are preoccupied with "appropriate beliefs and devout practice of obligations" to the divine.[7] But James's chief concern is with "faith," which he perceives as a response to knowledge of God as pure good. Within this unit, James seeks to persuade his readers that both the 'devout practice' of "religion" and "faith separated from works" are useless; it is only when "faith" is joined with "works" arising from the "wisdom" received from the "implanted word" that there can be any "benefit" in terms of salvation (cf. Jas 2:14) for the believer.

As in the first discursive unit of the Epistle, other inverted parallelisms suggest that Jas 1:22 - 2:26 can be divided into two discursive sub-units. The repetition of 'hearing' and 'doing the word' in Jas 1:22-23[8] is paralleled in 2:12 by the admonition to "so speak and so act as ones who are about to be judged by the law of freedom." This figure of the "law of freedom" (νόμου ἐλευθερίας) in 2:12 itself forms a parallel with 1:25 (νόμον τέλειον τὸν τῆς ἐλευθερίας). A third parallel is formed by the description of one "who is not bridling his [or her] tongue" in 1:26 and James's statement of the pertinent limitations on speech, namely to "speak ... as ones who are about to be judged by the law of freedom" (2:12). These tightly interrelated parallelisms mark off Jas 1:22 - 2:13 as a sub-unit developing the theme of "consistency of word and deed."

This sub-unit unfolds in three stages. James introduces the discussion in 1:22-25[9] by exploring the cause of inconsistency in word and deed: the "word" has little impact upon those who "only hear" and do not "continue" in it by "doing the word." The body of this sub-unit,

---

[6]Cf. Martin's comments (*James*, 79) on the relationship between Jas 1:22-27 and 2:14-26.

[7]Louw-Nida, *Greek-English Lexicon*, "θρησκεία," §53.1 (1:531).

[8]The specific phrases are "be doers of the word, and not only hearers" in 1:22, and "if any one is a hearer of the word and not a doer" in 1:23.

[9]Davids (*James*, 96) likewise takes Jas 1:22-25 as a section, though for him it is the final section before the summary conclusion of the first unit of the Epistle (Jas 1:2-27). For Vouga (*Jacques*, 61-67), 1:22-25 is the middle of three sayings in the section 1:19b-27 which he states "ne se suivent pas dans un ordre immédiatement évident" (61). Cf. also Ropes, *St. James*, 174; and Mußner, *Jakobusbrief*, 103-104.

1:26 - 2:9, provides an extensive illustration of a particular inconsistency on the part of the implied readers. Although the readers claim to identify themselves with the poor (by means of their "piety of the poor"), they actually emulate and aspire to be the "rich."[10] We will need to examine carefully the oppositions of actions and the figurativization process in this section to see how James uses this material as a persuasive illustration of their inconsistency in word and deed. The final thematic section, 2:10-13, emphasizes why the need for consistency is so important.[11]

The second sub-unit of this discursive unit, then, is Jas 2:14-26. While these verses are almost universally acknowledged as forming a unit within the Epistle by form and redaction critics, within this structural semiotic study they can only be treated as a sub-unit because of the presence of inverted parallelisms between its opening and closing verses. In this regard, note that the posited content "faith separated from works is dead" (Jas 2:26) is paralleled by the inverted content of the rhetorical question in 2:14, "Is faith (unaccompanied by works) able to save him [or her]?", and by James's response to his own question in 2:17, "So faith by itself, if it does not have works, is dead."[12] This integral relationship between "faith" and "works" provides the point of focus for two illustrations that form a third inverted parallelism: the improper conduct of those who simply say "Go in peace" without providing for the needs of the destitute (2:15-16) is paralleled by the proper action of Rahab who "showed hospitality (ὑποδεξαμένη) to the spies" before sending them safely away (2:25).

The theme of this sub-unit can be summarized as "a 'living' faith." The inverted parallelisms clearly show, however, that there are two important aspects to this contrast between a "living faith" and a "faith that is dead." The parallelism between the rhetorical question in 2:14 ('can faith separated from works save?') and the assertion of 2:26 that "faith separated from works is dead" indicates that what is at stake is a "faith" that "is able to save your souls" from death (cf. Jas 1:21). The

---

[10]I alluded to this example in the previous chapter while discussing the figure about the "poor" and the "rich" in Jas 1:9-12.

[11]Laws (*James*, 93 and 110-111) comes close to this division, taking 2:1-9 and 2:10-13 as separate sections of the Epistle. Cf. also Easton (*IB* 12:38-39) who takes 2:10-13 as a sub-division in the section 2:1-13.

[12]Cf. Dibelius's comment (*James*, 149) that "the point of the section is expressed in the introductory rhetorical question in v 14: the section deals with faith and works and the relationship between the two." See his further comments on 151.

"living faith" is thus a 'faith which makes one alive' or 'can save one's soul/life.' The other aspect of this "living faith" is evidenced by the parallelism between the examples regarding hospitality in 2:15-16 and 2:25: a "living faith" is one which finds expression in a person's actions. That is to say, a "living faith" is one which a person lives by both what they say ("Go in peace," 2:16) and what they do ("having shown hospitality," 2:25).[13]

A review of the rhetorical pattern in Jas 2:14-26 suggests that this sub-unit should be divided into two major sections.[14] James raises a rhetorical question in 2:14 to which he responds in 2:15-19 by using two illustrations; this pattern is repeated by the rhetorical question of 2:20 and the two illustrations which follow in 2:21-25. Thus, James addresses the fact that a "living faith" must lead to action and not just profession (2:14-19) by the examples of provision for needy brothers and sisters (vv 15-17) and the response elucidated by one's beliefs about God (vv 18-19). He then turns to the relationship between a "living faith" and "works" for "justifying" (i.e., "saving") a person (2:20-25) by taking up the cases of Abraham (vv 21-24) and Rahab (v 25).[15] The major point of both this sub-unit and the discursive unit as a whole is then driven home by Jas 2:26—"For just as the body separated from the spirit is dead, even so also faith separated from works is dead."[16]

---

[13]Thus, Martin states (*James*, 82) that James "is advocating the need for a living faith in which belief and practice belong inextricably together. A faith without works is of no profit on two counts: it has no efficacy for the person claiming this kind of faith, for such self-delusion (cf. 1:22) can end only in eschatological disaster, and it does nothing to alleviate the suffering of the needy, who are not helped by pious words alone."

[14]This sub-unit is also divided into two sections by Ropes (*St. James*, 202-203 and 214-215) as Jas 2:14-18 and 2:19-26.

[15]Davids (*James*, 119-134) comes close to this rhetorical structure, dividing 2:14-26 into three sections: 2:14-17 ("Illustration"), 2:18-20 ("Rational Argument"), and 2:21-26 ("Biblical Argument"); cf. Ropes, *St. James*, 216. Although Davids included 2:20 in his middle section, he conceded that it introduces the examples of Abraham and Rahab in 2:21-26 more than it emphasizes the point of 2:18-19 (see *James*, 126).

[16]I find no evidence of a parallel structure between these two sub-units such as I suggested for Jas 1:2-21. Proposals for a parallel development between Jas 2:1-13 and 2:14-26 drawn from repetition of key words and rhetorical structures have been offered by Gilberto Marconi ("La struttura di Giacomo 2," *Bib* 68 [1987]: 250-257), and Martin (*James*, 78-79). For a possible chiastic ordering of the material in Jas 2:14-26, see Burge, "Threw Them Thus on Paper," 31-45.

Exegesis and Commentary

Consistency of Word and Deed
(Jas 1:22 - 2:13)

Jas 1:22-25 — The Cause of Inconsistency

Convictions Emphasized in Jas 1:22-25

We concluded the previous chapter by raising the question whether there was a conviction unexpressed in Jas 1:2-21 which might come between 'receiving wisdom' and 'salvation' within James's overall system of convictions. That suspicion arose at least in part from noting his exhortation in Jas 1:22 that the readers be "doers of the word and not only hearers." In point of fact, that exhortation contains an opposition of actions which should resolve our suspicions regarding an intermediary conviction between 'wisdom' and 'salvation.'

OPP 1:22 and OPP 1:25 — Doing and Hearing the Word.   The opening section of this discursive sub-unit is framed by two parallel oppositions. The positive actions are expressed as 'doing the word' (ποιηταὶ λόγου; 1:22) and 'doing the work' (ποιητὴς ἔργου; 1:25), and are opposed to the negative actions expressed somewhat elliptically as 'only hearing [the word]' (μόνον ἀκροαταὶ; 1:22) and 'forgetting [the law/word]'[17] (ἀκροατὴς ἐπιλησμονῆς ["forgetful hearer"]; 1:25). The repetition of the words ποιητής and ἀκροατής in the positive and negative portions of the oppositions respectively clearly establishes the parallelism between them, a parallel directly related to the theme of this sub-unit—"consistency of word and deed."

On the positive side then, we see that "doing (the) word" in 1:22 can be identified with "doing (the) work" in 1:25. That such actions result in the persons being "blessed" is clear whether the dative construction (ἐν τῇ ποιήσει αὐτοῦ; 1:25c) is taken as expressing advantage ('they will be blessed *for* what they do')[18] or attendant

---

[17]Within the immediate context of Jas 1:25, what is "forgotten" is most naturally associated with the "perfect law of freedom" into which the person has just looked, or more precisely the 'image' reflected there if one sustains the mirror simile. However, the shift back to auditory imagery ("forgetful *hearer*") of 1:22 from the visual imagery ("looking into a mirror/the law") of 1:23-24 clearly associates the "perfect law of freedom" with the "word" which one is to "do." See further the discussion of the figurativization of this section below.

[18]With eschatological overtones according to Davids (*James*, 100) and Mußner (*Jakobusbrief*, 110).

circumstances ('they will be blessed *in* all they do').[19] As Laws observed, "Very probably the author would consider both interpretations correct."[20] This effect of "doing the word/work" serves to relate the conviction expressed by OPP 1:22 and OPP 1:25 to the convictions expressed in the opening unit regarding the reception of the "implanted word which is able to save your souls" (1:21). On the basis of this relationship we can say that it is having proper knowledge (i.e., having "received the implanted word" [1:21]) that qualifies the positive subject to 'do the word/work.' James makes clear in the introduction to this (sub-)unit that what follows will be an explication of what it means to "receive the implanted word": "it means not simply to hear but to do, and anyone thinking it to be less than that deceives himself [παραλογι-ζόμενοι ἑαυτούς; 1:22] that he has received the word."[21]

The negative portions of these oppositions express a two-fold problem of knowledge. On the one hand (1:25), if one (only) "hears," then one "forgets" and thereby loses/lacks the knowledge gained by hearing/looking into the "law of freedom;" one does not truly "receive the word." On the other hand (1:22), this lack of knowledge ultimately becomes an improper knowledge which deceives the believer (παραλογι-ζόμενοι ἑαυτούς). Thus, the qualifications of the negative subject are also related to knowledge: an improper (i.e., 'deceitful') knowledge in 1:22 and a lack of (i.e., 'forgotten') knowledge in 1:25.

These insights clearly show that the conviction expressed by OPP 1:22 and OPP 1:25 represents an intermediary stage between "receiving wisdom" and being "birthed by God" in the system of convictions of the author as enumerated in the conclusion to the previous chapter:

---

[19]So Dibelius, *James*, 120; cf. Mayor, *St. James*, 204.

[20]Laws, *James*, 87-88. The reading of the prepositional phrase as dative of advantage seems more compatible with the convictions of the enunciatee, while a dative of attendant circumstances might better reflect the convictions of the enunciator. Since both nuances are consistent with the system of convictions of both readers and author, however, it is best not to make a rigid distinction at this point.

[21]Davids, *James*, 97; for Davids, this deception concerns one's very salvation (so also Dibelius, *James*, 114; and Reicke, *James, Peter and Jude*, 21-22). The interpretation by Mußner (*Jakobusbrief*, 104-105) is similar, though he restricts the deception to the "nature of true piety" ("über das Wesen wahrer Frömmigkeit [vgl. V 26 Beginn]").

Positive	Negative
4. Receiving "wisdom" from God. Being changed internally by the "implanted word."	4. Receiving nothing from God. Having an internal "(evil) desire."
5. *Being a "doer of the word/work."*	5. *Being "a forgetful hearer;" being "deceived [by] oneself;"* having one's "desire" give birth to "sin."
6. Being birthed by God; having one's "soul saved from death." Being "blessed for/in one's doing."	6. Having one's "sin" give birth to "death."

Thus, our suspicions have been confirmed that indeed there is a stage within James's system of convictions which comes between 'receiving wisdom' and 'salvation.' Believers must "do the word" which they have "received" if they are to have their "soul[s] saved from death."

Figurativization in Jas 1:22-25

One of the most striking features about the figurativization in Jas 1:22-25 is how easily James shifts between auditory and visual images. He begins by admonishing[22] his readers, "Be doers of the word and not only hearers," consistently utilizing oral/aural figures ("word," "hearer"). The simile regarding a person glancing into a mirror in 1:23-24 shifts to visual imagery, which is then 'muddled' in 1:25 with the earlier auditory imagery: "But the one who *looks* into the perfect law

---

[22]Both Dibelius (*James*, 114) and Davids (*James*, 96) emphasize that γίνεσθε (literally, "become!") is regularly substituted for ἔστε ("Be!," not found in the New Testament). Davids goes on to note that this wording "has continuous force with a charitable assumption ('continue being') rather than the ingressive 'become' which γίνεσθε might be thought to imply." However, given the polysemism and differing semantic investments by enunciator and enunciatee which are so prominent in the Epistle and the clear charges of inconsistency on the part of the implied readers in the remainder of this unit, such an ingressive 'implication' cannot be ruled out.

of freedom and remains, who is not a forgetful *hearer* but a doer of the work, this one will be blessed in/for his [or her] doing." Dibelius commented on these shifting images by noting that such "is the oriental method of exploiting a simile, which is so very contrary to Western logic."[23] Yet if the development is not 'logical,' how are we to understand the rhetorical function of the figures which introduce the sub-unit Jas 1:22 - 2:13?

François Vouga has offered three possible interpretations of the mirror simile.[24] If Jas 1:22-25 were taken as a whole, Vouga argued that the emphasis would be on the contrast between 'not doing' and 'doing' as illustrated by the difference between the actions of those who look into the "mirror" and those who look into the "law." The simile functions to carry forward the stress on perseverance introduced in Jas 1:2-4—"existence is forged by patience and resistance."[25] Alternatively, one can take 1:22-24 as a self-contained saying and 1:25 as a summarizing comment ("comme le commentaire ou la leçon à en tirer"). In this interpretation, the simile functions like the Gospel parables about people who become disciples but fail to maintain their commitment when they return to the routine of life: they "have found a treasure but did not know how or were unable to live it."[26]

Most commentators utilize some form of Vouga's third possible interpretation by treating Jas 1:22-25 as an allegory. The mirror represents the "word" or "perfect law of liberty," and the contrast is between the different responses[27] of those who look into it.[28] What

---

[23]Dibelius, *James*, 116. He goes on to comment that "[o]ne ought to take warning from this insight and should not press the allegory pedantically."

[24]See Vouga, *Jacques*, 64-65.

[25]Ibid., 64: "l'existence se forge dans la patience et la résistance." Similar is the suggestion by Martin (*James*, 50) that "[w]hat is seen in a mirror is meant to lead to action, usually regarded as remedial." Whereas the "thoughtless person" forgets what has been seen in the mirror, the one who looks into the law and continues in it receives the accompanying blessing.

[26]Vouga, *Jacques*, 64: "Il a trouvé un trésor mais n'a pas su ou n'a pas pu en vivre."

[27]Luke T. Johnson ("The Mirror of Remembrance (James 1:22-25)," *CBQ* 50 [1988]: 634) has suggested that the allegorization also includes a contrast between what is "looked at" within the simile: "there is a contrast not simply between two ways of looking but also between *what is looked at*, between the measure of nature and the measure of God's word, 'the perfect law of freedom.'"

[28]Mußner (*Jakobusbrief*, 106) and Cantinat (*Jacques et Jude*, 110) both argued that παρακύπτω has the nuance of a more careful looking into the 'law' than is suggested by the use of κατανοέω with reference to the 'mirror;' cf. the translations

is seen in the mirror (τὸ πρόσωπον τῆς γενέσεως, literally "the face of existence") is variously identified as one's true nature,[29] the *imago Dei* as what God intends the person to be,[30] one's social roles and functions,[31] or simply (without allegorization) one's natural appearance.[32] The focus of the allegory is on how one responds to what is seen: one either simply goes away and forgets because one does not act on what was seen, or one "remains" by "doing the work" and is "blessed."

The difficulty with these allegorical interpretations is that they struggle to allegorize the simile of Jas 1:23-24 in a manner consistent with a transferral of the visual imagery to the law in 1:25 ("looking into the law").[33] Yet, recalling Dibelius's warning about the differences between the 'oriental exploitation of similes' and 'Western logic,' we would do well to avoid even too quickly employing an 'allegorical logic' to the relationship between 1:23-24 and 1:25.[34] But how then is the simile of Jas 1:23-24 to be related to the macarism of 1:25?

---

by Martin (*James*, 49-50) and Adamson (*James*, 82 and 84). Such a distinction is rejected by Davids (*James*, 99) and Dibelius (*James*, 115); indeed, according to LSJ ("παρακύπτω II," 1315) it is the term applied to the "law" which can have the nuance of "to cast a careless glance." As Laws (*James*, 86) observed, the renderings suggested by Mußner *et al.* seem "both inaccurate and to weaken the force of the contrast."

[29]So Ropes, *St. James*, 176.

[30]Martin, *James*, 50; and Sidebottom, *James, Jude, 2 Peter*, 35; cf. Johnson's comment ("Mirror of Remembrance," 640) that the 'perfect law of freedom' provides "the better image of what one should become." Reicke (*James, Peter and Jude*, 22-23) modifies this position somewhat by identifying what is seen with one's new nature as a result of being "birthed by the word of truth" (cf. Jas 1:19); the mirror's "function is to enable the new man in Christ to appear."

[31]Suggested by Vouga, *Jacques*, 65.

[32]Davids, *James*, 98; Dibelius, *James*, 116; Mußner, *Jakobusbrief*, 105; and Cantinat, *Jacques et Jude*, 109. Laws (*James*, 86) assessed this interpretation as "adequate," but suggested that the qualified '*natural* face' may imply "that there is more to be seen of a man than that, and that another, or fuller, image of him may be found in the law." She likens this "image ... found in the law" to "man as he was created to be" (cf. the interpretations along the lines of the *imago Dei* cited above) and to the "reborn self ... [through] the interaction of the 'word' of i. 18, 21" (cf. again Reicke, *James, Peter and Jude*, 22-23).

[33]This effort is clearly seen in the attempts by Martin (*James*, 50-51) and Mußner (*Jakobusbrief*, 106) to present the *imagery* of both Jas 1:23-24 and 1:25 in parallel columns headed "Pictorially/Bildhälfte" (of the mirror simile) and "Actually/Sachhälfte" (of the law).

[34]Dibelius (*James*, 115) himself rejected such allegorizations.

Rather than functioning as some sort of elaborate allegory, or parable, or even developing a marked contrast between "doing" and "not doing," the simile about the mirror merely draws on an all too common experience of life: what we see in the mirror has little impact on how we live our lives, and so we quickly forget what we have seen. A modern parallel might be the experience of glancing at one's watch but having to look again when asked by another as to the time. As Dibelius has stated it,

> The salient point is made clear in v 24: If a person does not conduct himself in accordance with the "word," then what he has heard sticks with him about as much as the mirror image sticks with a person who has observed himself in a mirror: he forgets it.[35]

That is to say, the relationship between the two figures of the "perfect law of freedom" and the "mirror" derives not from the ability of the one to reflect more important aspects of one's nature as compared to the other, but from the relative impact each has, or should have, on the conduct of life.[36]

One final aspect of the figurativization in this introductory section requires attention, namely the identification of the "perfect law of freedom." Historical critics have identified several possible antecedents for the figure "law of freedom" including the Stoic ideal of life in accordance with the rule of reason (the Λόγος),[37] Jewish descriptions of the Torah as providing joy and freedom,[38] and Christian conceptions of

---

[35]Ibid. Cf. Davids's comment (*James*, 98) that "[t]he momentariness and lack of real effect is the point of the parable, not a comparison with a different type of mirror or a different way of seeing;" and Sidebottom's remark (*James, Jude, 2 Peter*, 36), "Out of sight, of mind."

[36]Thus, it is very unlikely that this mirror simile provides a dominant figure for the whole of the Epistle, despite the attempt by Johnson to make it a controlling simile relating the examples of Abraham and Rahab in chapter 2 and Job and Elijah in chapter 5. He tied the Abraham and Rahab examples to the simile by noting the phrasing of the rhetorical question in Jas 2:22 as "do you *see*...": "Where do the readers 'see'? In the mirror of torah. Likewise in 2:24, '*You see* that a person is justified...'" ("Mirror of Remembrance," 643). His argument is too speculative to be convincing.

[37]Cf. Dibelius, *James*, 116-120; and Heinrich Schlier, "ἐλεύθερος, ἐλευθερόω, ἐλευθερία, ἀπελεύθερος," *TDNT* 2:493-496. Davids (*James*, 99) describes this interpretation as "linguistically possible in the Stoic world, although this expression has not yet been found."

[38]Ethelbert Stauffer, "Das 'Gesetz der Freiheit' in der Ordensregel von Jericho,"

the ethical teachings of Jesus as a *nova lex*.[39] After reviewing each of these possibilities, Laws concluded that "James is then reiterating a familiar idea, probably in a familiar phrase; the existence of Jewish parallels does not decide the question of the identity or content of his *law*, of which he gives here no further indication."[40]

While there may be "no further indication" of which of these possible antecedents best predicts the semantic investment in the figure by the implied reader, the inverted parallelisms within this unit and the oppositions of actions in this section suggest that James himself identifies the "perfect law of freedom" with the "implanted word" of 1:21. As Ralph Martin expressed it:

> In this context "law" is for James a norm of conduct, and he can write of the equivalence of the obedient and faithful ποιητὴς ἔργου and the ποιητὴς λόγου. So νόμος and λόγος seem to be equal terms, and this leads to the conclusion that for our writer "the perfect law" is none other than the "word implanted" in the hearts of responsive believers.[41]

Thus, James's "perfect law of freedom" again reminds us of Jeremiah's 'law written upon human hearts' (31:31-34):

> The Law brought freedom because it was the imperative side of the word that was implanted in man and that transformed him from within (Jas. 1:18, 21). ... For James, the Law was not an objectively prescribed norm, ... but the will of God that was written in the heart of the other person.[42]

TLZ 77 (1952): 527-532; and Simon Légasse, "Les pauvres en esprit et les 'volontaires' de Qumran," *NTS* 8 (1961/62): 338-339. Their claims to have found the phrase "law of freedom" within Jewish sectarian writings was rejected by F. Nötscher ("'Gesetz der Freiheit' im NT und in der Mönchsgemeinde am Toten Meer," *Bib* 34 [1953]: 193-194) and Wolfgang Nauck, "Lex insculpta (חוק חרות) in der Sektenschrift," *ZNW* 46 [1955]: 138-140). For the possible combination of Stoic and Jewish ideas in the thought of Philo, see Dibelius, *James*, 117-118.

[39]So Davids, *James*, 96, 97 and 99; and Vouga, *Jacques*, 64, n. 8, and 65. Cf. Cain Felder's view ("Partiality and God's Law: An Exegesis of James 2:1-13," *JRT* 39 [1982/83]: 65) that James's use of "νόμος means Old Testament moral law and the association of that law with the moral teachings of the Jesus tradition."

[40]Laws, *James*, 87.

[41]Martin, *James*, 51. Cf. the comments by Dibelius, *James*, 116; Ropes, *St. James*, 177; Via, "Right Strawy Epistle Reconsidered," 265; and Sidebottom, *James, Jude, 2 Peter*, 36, who is admittedly somewhat hesitant about the identification ("apparently the 'word' of verse 21"). Such an identification is rejected by Laws (*James*, 85).

[42]Goppelt, *Theology*, 2:206. Cf. Martin, *James*, 51.

To be a "doer of the word/work," to "keep the whole law" (2:8) and so be a "doer of the law" (4:11), is to act in accordance with the "will of God written in the heart."

We see then how James utilizes the figurativization in the introductory section 1:22-25 to construct a smooth transition between the conclusion of the first unit ("receive ... the implanted word which is able to save your souls") and his development of the theme "works" of the "word" in terms of a 'living faith' (which is both lived by the believer and "saves"/'makes alive' the believer) in the second unit. Moreover, we learn that "law" for James is not a codification of either ethical absolutes or ritual requirements, but the word of God "implanted" in the believer. Thus, inconsistency arises when believers' actions do not coincide with what they claim to have received; they have "only heard the word" and are not "doing the word."

Jas 1:26 - 2:9 — An Example of Inconsistency

Convictions Emphasized in Jas 1:26 - 2:9

Within this section of the Epistle there are three oppositions of actions. The first and third oppositions parallel one another in the conviction they express and serve to bracket OPP 2:5-6 which gives a conviction about God (expressed in a manner to which the readers would readily assent) that serves as a warrant for why the negative actions of the other oppositions are improper. Whereas the oppositions of actions encountered so far within the Epistle have emphasized convictions regarding "blessedness" and "evil" (i.e., how a person becomes, or fails to become, a believer), OPP 2:1, 4 and OPP 2:8,9 express convictions regarding the "vocation" of believers (i.e., what believers ought to do, or not do, relative to others).

OPP 2:1, 4 — Partiality among Believers. The positive portion of this opposition is stated somewhat elliptically in Jas 2:1 as "not holding the faith with partiality" (μὴ ἐν προσωπολημψίαις[43] ἔχετε τὴν πίστιν) which may be restated as 'not showing partiality among believers.' It is opposed to the negative action in Jas 2:4 of "discriminating among yourselves" (διεκρίθητε ἐν ἑαυτοῖς).[44] As the negative action makes

---

[43]Maynard-Reid suggested (*Poverty and Wealth*, 50) that the plural form of partiality here in Jas 2:1 "giv[es] the impression that there had been several manifestations or varied forms of partiality practiced in the community;" cf. also Ropes, *St. James*, 186.

[44]It could be argued that this is not an "explicit" opposition of actions since the

clear, the receivers of both actions are believers since the distinctions have been made among the readers ("among yourselves").[45]

Neither the positive nor the negative actions express the effects upon the receivers; in this way James places the emphasis on the subjects. Thus, the pertinent aspects of this conviction are related to the contrasting actions of the positive and negative subjects themselves and not their effects upon other believers. Once again, as the negative action makes clear, the pertinent qualification of the subjects is knowledge: the negative subjects have "evil reasonings/thoughts." Their improper knowledge establishes their will to respond in certain ways (saying "Sit here" or "Stand there"). It is not that they are unable to prevent partiality and distinctions within their community, but rather that their "evil thoughts" lead them to respond in a certain way (cf. Jas 1:14-15).

The positive subjects are also qualified by a (proper) knowledge that establishes their will; they have "the faith of our glorious Lord Jesus Christ." The analysis of OPP 1:6 and OPP 1:13-14 in the previous chapter suggested that "faith" within James's system of convictions is a qualification of a person's will which arises from a proper knowledge about God: one is willing to trust God completely because God is "good," "generous," and neither able "to be tempted to do evil" nor "tempts anyone." If the readers "have faith," and thus must already know certain things about God, then their will should be established to act in such a way as not to show "partiality" nor to make "distinctions" within the community. That their knowledge about God should direct their behavior is made explicit by the next opposition of actions.

---

positive action is derived by reconstructing the action 'not showing partiality' from an adverbial prepositional phrase (*"not holding* the faith *with partiality"*). However, the pointed contrast between avoiding partiality and discrimination is certainly clear in Jas 2:1-4. Isolating an opposition of actions in these verses gains further support from the parallel opposition in 2:8-9; see below.

[45]Against this use of ἑαυτούς to support identifying the receivers as believers it should be noted that Mußner (*Jakobusbrief*, 119) translated the prepositional phrase as "in your attitudes" ("'in eurem Innern'—das Urteil wird ja nicht offen ausgesprochen"). Yet Felder ("Partiality and God's Law," 53) rejected this translation as "misleading insofar as it tends to draw attention away from actual 'acts of partiality' that James sets forth in his example." The identification of the receivers as believers also suggests that the persons in the illustration of Jas 2:2-3 are also believers, against those who would identify them as visitors to the Christian assembly (as do Dibelius, *James*, 135 and n. 63; Laws, *James*, 99f; Adamson, *James*, 105; and Easton, *IB* 12:36); see the discussion of this illustration below under figurativization.

OPP 2:5-6 — Honor and Dishonor for the Poor. The second opposition of actions in this section contrasts the actions of God with those of false believers (here identified with the readers). Whereas God "chose the poor with respect to the world" (ἐξελέξατο τοὺς πτωχοὺς τῷ κόσμῳ, 2:5) and honored them by making them "rich with respect to faith and heirs of the kingdom," the readers have "dishonored the poor" (ὑμεῖς δὲ ἠτιμάσατε τὸν πτωχόν, 2:6). This opposition emphasizes two points. First, it serves as a warrant for James's contention that "partiality" is negative; if God has "chosen" and honored the poor (as the readers, with their "piety of the poor," will readily acknowledge), then to "dishonor" the poor is to act contrary to the way God acts (and therefore to act negatively). By showing favoritism to and thus aligning themselves with the rich, the readers have alienated the very people whom God has "chosen" and so have also alienated and separated themselves from God.

Secondly, and more subtly expressed by the effects upon the positive receiver, the opposition again affirms that being "rich in faith and heirs of the kingdom" is something which results from divine rather than human initiative (cf. Jas 1:5 and 17-18). It is because they are "chosen" by God that the "poor" have these benefits, and not because they have earned them by patient endurance of trials (cf. the readers' semantic investment in Jas 1:2-4).

Additionally, the "poor" are said to be "rich in faith" (πλουσίους ἐν πίστει). The simplest explanation of this description is that it parallels the preceding dative qualifier (τῷ κόσμῳ): those who are considered poor from the vantage point of the world are rich from the vantage point of faith.[46] However, the shift in syntactical form creates an ambiguity in that ἐν πίστει might also suggest a parallel as "the poor in the things of the world are rich in (the things of) faith."[47] It may be possible to combine these two nuances as suggested by Cantinat:

Thus, the formula "rich in the faith" would simply say that the poor are rich on account of the received faith, that is to say that they are filled by God

---

[46]So Vouga, *Jacques*, 73-74; Dibelius, *James*, 138; and Davids, *James*, 111.

[47]Cf. Laws (*James*, 103): "Materially poor, they are spiritually rich by virtue of their faith." Cantinat (*Jacques et Jude*, 126) raises this possibility, but then dismisses it: "Cela ne cadre guère avec le reste de la lettre où nous voyons que les destinataires ont bien besoin d'être stimulés dans leur foi (1,2 ss; 4,1 ss)." But it may be that Cantinat has too easily identified the recipients of the letter with those who are "chosen" by God, at least in terms of the semantic investments of the author if not for the readers.

with supernatural goods which are faith and the heritage of the Kingdom. The divine election enriches them with these supernatural goods ..., it gives birth to them by a Word of truth (Jas 1,18), it implants in them the Word which is able to save (1,21), which exalts them (1,9).[48]

The "poor in the sphere of the world" are chosen by God to be "rich in the sphere of faith" by receiving the benefits of the inheritance of the Kingdom and "faith" itself.[49]

Our earlier analysis of James's system of convictions[50] suggested that "faith" was a result of having a proper knowledge about God (God is "good" and "gives generously" [i.e. without "partiality"] "only good gifts"). The conviction about the divine expressed here in OPP 2:5-6 gives further support to the contention that the knowledge which leads to faith is a consequence of divine activity ("God chose the poor"). Yet once the "poor" have become "rich in faith," that faith should establish their will to act in certain ways toward God (to ask for the "wisdom" which they lack) and toward others (to act as God acts, and thereby to "do the word" that has been implanted in them).[51]

OPP 2:8-9 — Love vs. Partiality. As already mentioned, this opposition of actions parallels OPP 2:1, 4 and relies on that parallelism to fill out certain ellipses in its formulation. The positive action is expressed most directly in the citation "Love your neighbor as yourself" (Jas 2:8; see Lev 19:18) and is opposed to the negative action of "showing partiality" (Jas 2:9). The receivers of these actions are identified as people more generally ("your neighbor"), thereby broadening the application of this conviction as compared to the receivers of OPP 2:1, 4 ("yourselves," i.e. other believers).

As with OPP 2:1, 4, the emphasis in OPP 2:8-9 again falls upon the subjects since the receivers are somewhat vague[52] and no effects

---

[48]Cantinat, *Jacques et Jude*, 126; translation mine.

[49]Siding with Cantinat (ibid.) that "faith" and "heirs of the kingdom" are related but not identical terms against Davids's view (*James*, 111-112) that James utilized a form of hendiadys so that "rich in faith" means "heirs of the kingdom."

[50]Cf. the discussions of OPP 1:6, OPP 1:13-14, and OPP 2:1, 4.

[51]Or, as Felder ("Partiality and God's Law," 69) expressed it, James "indicates that anterior to law is 'doing,' motivated by an *imitatio Dei* (e.g., righteousness and mercy), and so offers paradigms for Christian action and social justice."

[52]In addition to the vagueness of "your neighbor" as the receiver of the positive action, note that no receiver is explicitly stated for the negative action (simply προσωπολημπτεῖτε).

on these receivers are explicitly stated. What is most striking about this opposition is how starkly the contrast between actions of the positive and negative subjects respectively is drawn: "you do well" (ποιεῖτε καλῶς) vs. "you commit sin" (ἁμαρτίαν ἐργάζεσθε). The stress, as in the opening section of this sub-unit (Jas 1:22-25), remains on "doing" (here "doing well by completing/fulfilling the royal law" as opposed to "working sin").

If we then summarize the convictions expressed within these three oppositions of actions relative to their contribution to James's system of convictions, it becomes clear that fulfilling one's vocation as a believer (here "loving your neighbor as yourself" rather than "showing partiality") is one way in which one becomes a "doer of the word" and not "only a hearer." Additionally, as OPP 2:5-6 emphasizes, the content of this "royal law" and "implanted word" can be encapsulated in the maxim 'act as God acts;' but one may only have this "wisdom" if it has been received as a "good and perfect gift" from God.

Figurativization in Jas 1:26 - 2:9

James begins this second section with a somewhat ambiguous phrase: "if anyone δοκεῖ to be religious." The ambiguity arises from the fact that the verb may mean either "seems" or "considers oneself." The former translation ("if anyone seems to be religious") would appear to be ruled out by the context; since the one who δοκεῖ to be religious may only be "deceiving his [or her] heart" (ἀπατῶν καρδίαν αὐτοῦ), the issue is not how others perceive one's 'religiosity' but how one perceives one's own.[53] Nevertheless, the ambiguity is instructive in that it reminds us that the readers are indeed concerned not only with how they "consider" themselves, but also with how their religious piety is perceived by others. They want to "seem" religious not only in their own eyes, but perhaps even more so in the eyes of others.

James suggests that an initial clue that one might be deceived regarding one's own piety is a failure to "bridle one's tongue." The most 'natural' understanding of this metaphor is that it refers to improper or morally unacceptable speech; it is "a warning of the need for restraint in speech (including no doubt angry, v. 19, or vulgar and malicious, v. 21, speech)."[54] However, in that the theme of this sub-

---

[53]Cf. Laws, *James*, 88.

[54]Laws, *James*, 88. Cf. Dibelius (*James*, 121, n. 66) who, in rejecting Hofmann's interpretation of "deceiving himself" as "mak[ing] piety into empty talk," asserted that "one should avoid all such specialized conceptions of the

unit is related to "consistency of word and deed," another interpretation of the metaphor is readily apparent: the pertinent restriction on speech is that it be consistent with one's actions.

> James is holding up to condemnation the picture of the use of the tongue when it utters merely formal religious platitudes that have no substance evidenced by practical deeds. The present verse looks back to v 19 with the caution to be "slow to speak" and more especially it looks on to 2:15, 18 where the objector says that he can demonstrate his type of faith by deeds when all he means is that he bids the needy look after themselves.[55]

Thus, the first possibility for understanding the figure as it relates to the theme of this sub-unit is that "bridling one's tongue" would mean to speak only those things that one is willing to put into action. Just what type of "practical deeds" provide the standard by which to judge both speech and action is clearly stated in Jas 1:27: "Pure and undefiled religion before God the Father is this: to care for orphans and widows in their distress and to keep oneself untainted by the world." It may be that the concern for "purity" expressed here reflects investments from the convictions of the implied reader, since at the least concerns for religious purity and remaining "untainted by the world" are not the emphases of James himself in this passage. This difference of emphasis was already sensed by the scribe of P[74] who substituted ὑπερασπίζειν αὐτοὺς for the reading ἄσπιλον ἑαυτὸν τηρεῖν, resulting in "to visit orphans and widows and *to protect them* in their affliction from the world."[56] As Matthew Black commented concerning this textual variant, "No doubt it is a corruption of the usual text, but it is a parti-

---

'bridling of the tongue.'"

[55]Martin, *James*, 52. Martin later adds, "The speaker either promotes true 'piety of action' on behalf of the needy or his profession leads to self-deception when he says but does not do" (53).

[56]Taking ἐν τῇ θλίψει αὐτῶν with the final clause. See D. J. Roberts, "The Definition of 'Pure Religion' in James 1:27," *ExpTim* 83 (1971/72): 215-216. He argued that this variant is supported by the fact that instrumental ἀπό occurs only with passive verbs, not with active ones as in Jas 1:27. B. C. Johanson ("The Definition of 'Pure Religion' in James 1:27 Reconsidered," *ExpTim* 84 [1973]: 119) rejected this argument by noting that ἀπό should be taken not with τηρεῖν as Roberts had done, but with "ἄσπιλον (unspotted) which supplies the passive sense needed to justify the instrumental use with an emphasis on source as in Ja. I[13] (Ἀπὸ Θεοῦ πειράζομαι)." BDF (§182[3], 98) notes that the idea "'[t]o be free from' always takes ἀπό."

cularly happy one."[57] James may be using the readers' concern for religious purity to set up this section's concluding contrast between adultery and murder (Jas 2:11; see the discussion of 2:10-13 below).

But a second nuance of "bridling one's tongue" is also possible; not only must they put into actions what they speak, they must also take care that their actions are consistent with what they profess. This nuance is illustrated by James's admonition not to show partiality and the example of partiality provided by the different treatments afforded to the "man in splendid clothing and wearing a gold ring" and to the "poor person in filthy clothing." As already noted in discussing OPP 2:5-6, what the readers profess to believe is that "God chose the poor with respect to the world to be rich with respect to faith and heirs of the kingdom." Yet this belief is inconsistent with their "deeds" which have "dishonored the poor" and bestowed favoritism upon the rich.

There has been considerable debate among historical critical scholars as to whether the example provided in Jas 2:2-4 reflects an actual event within the life of the community[58] or is simply a stereotypical example,[59] and whether it is set against a special judicial assembly[60] or the gathering of the community in worship.[61] This debate is itself illustrative of the attempt to read the Epistle "from the outside in" discussed in the first chapter of this study. If we are to read the Epistle "from the inside out," we would do well to follow the advice of Cain Felder:

---

[57]Matthew Black, "Critical and Exegetical Notes on Three New Testament Texts: Hebrews 6:11, Jude 5, James 1:27," *ZNW* 30 (1964): 45.

[58]As Martin (*James*, 60-61) believed; he goes as far as to say that it is "depicting [a] familiar scene, which is implied by the use of the indicative mood in what follows (especially vv 4, 6, 7). ... Vv 2, 3 are an example of the 'iterative case in present time' (BDF §371.4)." Reicke (*James, Peter and Jude*, 27) and Easton (*IB* 12:34-36) seem to treat it as an actual event, though they do not explicitly describe it as such. Adamson (*James*, 105) said the "picture is drawn from life," and Cantinat (*Jacques et Jude*, 121) wrote that James "le présente d'une façon si frappante qu'on a tout lieu de croire qu'il s'inspire d'une observation personnellement vécue."

[59]So Dibelius, *James*, 128-130; Davids, *James*, 107; Laws, *James*, 102; Mußner, *Jakobusbrief*, 117; and Roy Bowen Ward, "Partiality in the Assembly: James 2:2-4," *HTR* 62 (1969): 97.

[60]As argued by Ward, "Partiality in the Assembly," 89-97, and followed by Davids, *James*, 105-110; and Martin, *James*, 57-58.

[61]So Laws (*James*, 101), Moo (*James*, 89-90), and Vouga (*Jacques*, 73 n. 8), all specifically rejecting Ward's thesis; cf. also Reicke, *James, Peter and Jude*, 27.

Rather than straining James's example for historical data or precise quotations of or allusions to early Jewish literature, we think that it is more appropriate to examine the possible implications of James's stylized exaggerations in the contrast of the apparel and treatment accorded to the two characters depicted in vv. 2-3, since through this device the author may be attempting to dramatize the fraudulent actions of the assembly, actions which James may see as violations of biblical injunctions in Old Testament law.[62]

Given what we have learned regarding James's system of convictions, it is perhaps better to speak of 'violations of the implanted word received by believers' rather than "injunctions in Old Testament law." To put the question more directly, how does James utilize the specific discursive features of this illustration as an example of how the readers have been inconsistent in what they profess to believe and what they do?

The emphasis in this example clearly falls on the differing instructions given to the two individuals because of the contrasts in their apparel. The "man in splendid clothing and wearing a gold ring"[63] is directed to "Sit here, please."[64] Conversely, the "poor person" is told to "Stand there," or "Sit on the floor."[65] The blatant partiality in the treatment afforded to these persons is obvious; what is more subtle is the way in which James exposes the true allegiance of the readers. Although they characterize themselves as the poor and the oppressed who have been chosen by God (the readers' understanding of themselves as the "Diaspora"), they do not simply try to curry the favor of the rich

---

[62]Felder, "Partiality and God's Law," 55.

[63]Note that the adjective πλούσιος is conspicuous by its absence. Felder (ibid., 56) has suggested this striking absence may indicate that the example "does not present ... a means to argue a 'rich versus poor' theme." Rather, there are "two 'acts of partiality' in his example" with the emphasis on "the shabby treatment which is accorded to the ill-clad man." Cf. Laws, *James*, 103.

[64]As Dibelius (*James*, 131, n. 44), Ropes (*St. James*, 190) and Sidebottom (*James, Jude, 2 Peter*, 38) note, the adverb καλῶς is commonly used to mean "please;" see also Louw and Nida, *Greek-English Lexicon*, §33.177 (1:409). Its more general meaning of "well" is taken here in the sense of "in a good place" by Davids (*James*, 109) and Laws (*James*, 99); so BAGD, "καλῶς," 401; and as an alternative in Louw and Nida, *Greek-English Lexicon*, §87.25 (1:736). Both Maynard-Reid (*Poverty and Wealth*, 55) and Martin (*James*, 62) argued that the instruction is to take a seat of honor, though neither specifically ties it to καλῶς. Reicke (*James, Peter and Jude*, 26) seems to combine both meanings in his translation: "Please sit here in the best place."

[65]On the idiomatic usage of the phrase ὑπὸ τὸ ὑποπόδιον μου (literally, "under my footstool") to mean "on the floor," see Dibelius, *James*, 132 and n. 47; and Laws, *James*, 99.

by preferential treatment[66] but actually identify themselves with the rich. The well-dressed man should "sit *here*," i.e. among the readers, whereas the ill-clad person should "stand *there*," i.e. be both separated and segregated from the readers.[67] As we saw in the discussion of the figurativization of Jas 1:9-12, the readers may claim to identify with the poor, but their actions betray their aspirations to be the rich. "The readers of the epistle have a weakness for the rich and powerful."[68]

James employs a series of arguments in an attempt to persuade his readers that their identification with the rich is improper. First, building on their beliefs regarding the "piety of the poor," he contrasts God's actions toward the poor with their actions toward the poor (OPP 2:5-6). He then shifts the focus to how they are treated by the rich. The rich not only "oppress" the readers in very practical ways ("dragging you into court"),[69] but indeed they are guilty of blasphemy against God in that "the name and the one who bears it [via baptism] belong together; whoever abuses the bearer also abuses the 'honorable name.'"[70] The thrust of James's argument is well summarized by Cain Felder:

> Accordingly, these verses expose the underlying paradox that Christians show deference to the rich, while the oppressions by the rich strongly imply that the rich are not worthy of such honor. Thus, James 2:5-7 involves an antithesis between the poor who are shown to be worthy of honor, but are

---

[66]Reicke (*James, Peter and Jude*, 27) provides an excellent description of the Hellenistic social system of patronage which sheds important light on why the readers might have deferred to the rich persons within their assemblies.

[67]Cf. Davids, *James*, 112; and Vouga, *Jacques*, 73. This spatial distinction is maintained even if one follows the text of P^{74vid}, ℵ, *et al.*, which adds the adverb "here" to the second directive given to the poor person (thus, "Σὺ στῆθι ἐκεῖ ἢ κάθου ὧδε ὑπὸ τὸ ὑποπόδιον μου"). While the variant minimizes the spatial separation somewhat, the social stratification is undiminished. As Laws (*James*, 99) comments, "the *poor man* should most properly *stand over there*, well away, but if he must sit it should be in an equally appropriate, inferior position, *here, under my footstool;*" cf. also Martin, *James*, 62. On the various textual variants, see Dibelius, *James*, 131; and *TCGNT*, 680-681.

[68]Reicke, *James, Peter and Jude*, 27.

[69]For several possible historical reconstructions for the basis of this charge against the rich in Jas 2:7, see Laws, *James*, 106 and Dibelius, *James*, 139-140.

[70]Dibelius, *James*, 141. On the phrase "the good name which was invoked upon you" as a reference to baptism, see also Mußner, *Jakobusbrief*, 122-123 and Reicke, *James, Peter and Jude*, 29. Martin (*James*, 67) and Cantinat (*Jacques et Jude*, 130) are less confident: "Rien n'indique que l'auteur pense plus particulièrement au rite baptismal (cf. Ac 2:38), mais ce n'est pas impossible (cf. Jc 1:18, 21)."

victims of partiality and the rich whose own actions disqualify them for honor, but who nevertheless are beneficiaries of deferential treatment by Christians.[71]

Whereas "pure and undefiled religion before God" would be to identify with the poor and oppressed by "caring for orphans and widows in their distress," the readers have "discriminated" among themselves and "become judges with evil thoughts" because of their "desire" for status and wealth.

James provides the definition for what it means to be impartial by citing Lev 19:18—"Love your neighbor as yourself." This "scripture" provides a means for "performing the royal law" (νόμον τελεῖτε βασιλικὸν κατὰ τὴν γραφήν).[72] Martin described this relationship by arguing that "James is implying ... that obedience to the 'love command-ment' fulfills the royal law, which refers to the entire will of God, especially as revealed in the teaching of Jesus."[73] His stress upon the "teaching of Jesus" as the revelation "the entire will of God" derives from his emphasis upon the presumed sources from the Jesus tradition behind the Epistle (again, reading 'from the outside in'). Yet the relationship between "doing the word" and "remaining in the perfect law of freedom" in the introductory section to this sub-unit (Jas 1:22-25) would suggest that a better identification for the revelation of the will of God within the figurativization of the Epistle would be "the implanted word" which changes the desire/will of the believer. And so the example comes to its climax; showing "partiality" for the rich rather than "caring for orphans and widows" are deeds clearly inconsistent with the "word" which true believers have "received."

Jas 2:10-13 — The Need for Consistency

Figurativization in Jas 2:10-13

Having shown that inconsistency arises from "only hearing" and not "doing the word" and having provided an illustration of an inconsis-tency between the professed beliefs of the readers and their actions, James concludes this sub-unit by underscoring the urgency for 'consis-

---

[71]Felder, "Partiality and God's Law," 59.

[72]With Dibelius (*James*, 142) that 'royal law' "refers to *the* law, of which the commandment in question is only a part." Contra Mußner (*Jakobusbrief*, 124) that the phrase is used directly of the command cited in Jas 2:8 to indicate its superior rank among others within the law as a whole.

[73]Martin, *James*, 67. Cf. Dibelius, *James*, 144.

tency of word and deed.' "For whoever should keep the whole law, but should trip in one thing, he or she has become guilty of the whole thing" (Jas 2:10). Such an indictment strikes most modern readers as overly harsh, and indeed greatly at odds with our conceptions of law and justice. Laws attempted to mitigate the sternness of this statement by noting three uses of the legal term ἔνοχος: "liable for punishment; guilty of crime; or liable in respect of a person or thing against which an offence has been committed (as in 1 Cor. xi. 27)." Concluding that the first two options are too extreme, she opts for the third. "The man who commits one offence must accept that he is responsible and answerable not only in respect of the single precept he has broken, but in respect of the whole corpus of law of which that precept is a part."[74]

Such an interpretation leads Laws, and invariably other commentators who follow a similar track, to associate James with "Jewish legalism."[75] The problem is that such interpretations impose Western concepts of jurisprudence (there is a "corpus of law" consisting of "single precepts") upon a fundamentally different Jewish concept which conceives of the "law" (תּוֹרָה) as a unified whole. Within such a conception, "law cannot be broken up into individual prescriptions" because it is "an ethic involving a general disposition,"[76] a disposition typified by "the will of God."[77] Indeed, the "law" cannot even be broken into broadly defined moral absolutes such as the "love commandment," but is rather the "implanting" of the divine will within the believer so as to transform the very nature, disposition, and desire of the believer (cf. Jas 1:13-21).[78] Inconsistency between any of one's deeds and the word implanted within believers suggests that one has not truly received the word and been transformed by it.

---

[74]Laws, *James*, 112.

[75]"In asserting this principle James would seem to stand squarely within the context of Jewish legalism" (ibid.). Cf. Adamson, *James*, 116-117.

[76]Dibelius, *James*, 146.

[77]Cf. the comments by Mayor, *St. James*, 214-215; Davids, *James*, 117; Easton, *IB* 12:39; Moo, *James*, 95; and Vouga, *Jacques*, 80. Vouga compares this Jewish concept of the unity of law with Hellenistic philosophical ideas of law as "un ordre du monde ... qui doit être obéi dans sa totalité" as part "d'une quête de perfection et de liberté."

[78]This identification between "law" and the "will of God" here within the Epistle is furthered in the ambiguous introduction to the citations from the Decalogue; grammatically, ὁ εἰπών could imply either "the law (ὁ νόμος) has said" or "the one (i.e. God, ὁ θεός) who has said." Ultimately no distinction exists for the "law" is the expression of the "will of God."

James uses the prohibitions against adultery and murder to show again that certain actions by the readers make them "transgressors" of this law. These particular commandments are not chosen simply because of a traditional association between Lev 19:18 and the second table of the Decalogue,[79] nor does their relative sequence indicate simply that James is citing them from a tradition different from the Masoretic Text of Exod 20:13-14.[80]   Rather, as Martin has also noted, the phrasing of Jas 2:11 "suggests that 'murder,' if not adultery, is actually taking place in the congregation."[81]   He concedes that the reference is probably not "to the literal taking of another's life," but more probably to a "spiritualized murder" as suggested by Reicke:

> Of course the readers do not commit murder in the common meaning of the word, but the author understands the commandment against murder in the broadened and deepened sense which Jesus gave it in the Sermon on the Mount (Matt v 21f.). He interprets their wrath and hard words against the people in the community as a violation of this commandment.[82]

Reicke's easy reliance upon the Jesus tradition to interpret the Epistle may however diminish the force of James's charge. James does in fact directly accuse the readers of "murder" in Jas 4:2 and 5:6, and this stunning accusation may arise from failure "to care for orphans and widows" (Jas 1:27) and other needy "brothers and sisters" (2:15-16) within the community.[83]   While they may not have "committed adultery" and so maintained their religious purity ("untainted by the world," 1:27), they have still "become transgressors."[84]

---

[79]As Laws (*James*, 113-114) suggested.

[80]As a number of historical critics theorize; see Dibelius, *James*, 146-147; Davids, *James*, 117; Laws, *James*, 115-116; and Felder, "Partiality and God's Law," 63-64.

[81]Martin, *James*, 70. Note, however, that James does later address the readers as "Adulterers;" see the discussion of Jas 4:4 below.

[82]Reicke, *James, Peter and Jude*, 29.

[83]Death of indigent members of the community as a result of failure of the believers to care for them seems a more likely 'literal' interpretation of the charges of "murder" than Martin's suggestion (*James*, 70) that "verses such as 4:2; 5:6 ... do raise the possibility that the actual killing of other people in internecine strife may be in view."

[84]James's use of the Decalogue citations is thus anything but "curiously inept" as Laws characterized it, faulting James for using two major commandments from the law rather than employing the traditional rabbinic argument of 'light' and 'weighty' commandments (*James*, 113).

In the light of their past failure, James concludes this sub-unit by exhorting the readers to consistency in word and deed. "So speak and so act as ones who are about to be judged by the law of freedom" (Jas 2:12). Both their speech and their deeds will be assessed by their consistency with the "implanted word/law of freedom" in the approaching eschatological judgment.[85] Thus, his emphasis on "keeping the whole law" is not a rigid legalism; "the stress is not on the observance of a sum total of minutiae, but on the maintenance of a complete integrity of word and deed."[86]

Summary of Jas 1:22 - 2:13

This exegesis of Jas 1:22 - 2:13 has shown that both the implied readers and the implied author are concerned with a "consistency of word and deed." However, their emphases in this regard clearly differ. The readers would seem to be quite interested in external appearances. They wish to "seem religious" to others, to have a "pure and undefiled religion" which will keep them "untainted by the world," to speak properly at all times by "bridling their tongues" from socially unacceptable speech and by using their speech to maintain social decorum (those of "splendid" appearance in positions of honor, those who are "filthy" separated and segregated). Even the opening simile of the mirror reflects this concern for externals. By maintaining their religious purity in this way, they strive to "keep the whole law" and so be prepared for the coming "judgment."

James characterizes such religion focused on external matters as "useless." Indeed, those who practice it have been "deceived" because they have "only heard the word" which expresses the will of God but are not "doing [that] word." "Pure and undefiled religion before God the Father," as contrasted with one which merely "seems religious" to other people, is "to care for orphans and widows in their distress" and not to

---

[85]Interestingly, the scribe of P[74] has once again emphasized the implication of James's argument by substituting ἀποστάτης for παραβάτης at the end of Jas 2:11. "Transgression of the law" ultimately becomes "apostasy" in the eschatological judgment. Cf. G. D. Kilpatrick, "Übertreter des Gesetzes, Jak. 2,11," *TZ* 23 (1967): 433.

[86]Laws, *James*, 116. She later continues, "the *law of freedom*, cf. i. 25, is the framework or context within which they speak and act, and the future judgment will take account of that fact." These statements would seem to move her away from her earlier characterization of James as "stand[ing] squarely within the context of Jewish legalism."

shower favoritism upon "the rich who are oppressing" the believers. Those who have been transformed by the "implanted word" will desire to "perform mercy" just as God does by identifying with and "choosing the poor with respect to the world." Only in this way can they "keep the whole law ... of freedom," and share in the divine "mercy [which] triumphs over judgment." The word with which one's deeds must be consistent is "the implanted word," "the law of freedom" which expresses the will of God.

A "Living" Faith (Jas 2:14-26)

Jas 2:14-19 — Faith leads to Action

Convictions Emphasized in Jas 2:14-19

Once again in this section we find an opposition of actions which expresses, in terms of its explicit formulation, a conviction about the vocation of believers. To understand how James utilizes this opposition to clarify his convictions regarding the relationship between faith and works within the process of becoming a believer, we must first remind ourselves that the purpose of religious discourse from a semiotic perspective is the communication of an overall faith-pattern, and not the specific content of the individual oppositions which express that system of convictions. Thus, each opposition of actions is a discursivization of the iterative application of a basic conviction to a particular aspect of the realm of human experience. A single conviction may find expression in a vast number of oppositions of actions discursivized by different aspects of human experience. Why specific actions are chosen to express a particular conviction is part of the overall discursivization process.[87] In studying the oppositions of actions themselves, we are more concerned with elucidating the underlying conviction.[88]

---

[87]That is to say, the realization of the discourse through the development of the discursive syntax (actorialization, temporalization, and spatialization) and the discursive semantics (thematization and figurativization). See Greimas and Courtés, *Semiotics and Language*, "Discoursivization," 85-86; and Patte, *Religious Dimensions*, 259-261.

[88]I.e., we are here focusing on the narrative semantic component of the discourse rather than its discursive structures; see Patte, *Religious Dimensions*, 270-271. These theoretical observations reduce the importance of Dibelius's (*James*, 152) and Mußner's (*Jakobusbrief*, 131) insistence that the illustration in Jas 2:15-16 is not an example of 'faith without works' but rather a comparison of 'faith without works' to an example of 'charity without works.' Even as part of a "comparison,"

OPP 2:16 — Words and Deeds. The only explicit opposition of actions in this section of the Epistle[89] opposes the positive action of believers who give "the things needed by the body" to a destitute "brother or sister" to the negative action of only providing them with a word of blessing ("Go in peace, be warm and well fed").[90] The emphasis within the opposition is squarely upon the effects of these actions upon the receivers:[91] there is no "benefit" for the destitute members of the community if all they receive are pious words. Thus, the opposition focuses on the relative benefits of words and deeds.

We begin by noting, then, that the offering of the blessing itself is not perceived negatively. It is only the offering of words in isolation from "giving" what is "needed by the body" that is of no "benefit" since such words alone cannot provide physical life for the destitute members of the community. In the same way, merely claiming to have faith (πίστιν λέγῃ ... ἔχειν, 2:14) when it is not accompanied by actions (ἔργα δὲ μὴ ἔχῃ, 2:14 / πίστις ... καθ᾽ ἑαυτήν, 2:17[92]) is of no "benefit" in that such "faith" in isolation from "works" is "not able to save"

---

the opposition of actions (and thus to a degree the illustration more generally) presents an iterative application of a conviction to the realm of human experience. Cf. Davids's comment (*James*, 121) on the "parabolic nature" of the example.

[89]Another possible opposition of actions, a polemical dialogue, might be found in the exchange between James and his rhetorical interlocutor in Jas 2:18-19—or does the exchange extend through 2:21, and so include also the invective against the "vain person"? This uncertainty points out the difficulty of reconstructing the limits of this rhetorical diatribe (but, as we shall see, even the roles of the dialogue partners are also problematic) and thus also any polemical dialogue which might be contained within it. See the discussion of the figurativization of Jas 2:18-19 below.

[90]Notice that here again we encounter a very subtle expression of the separation/segregation between the readers and the poor and needy who are told to "*Go* in peace." However, given the highly traditional use of this expression (see Dibelius, *James*, 153, and Martin, *James*, 84-85), this inference of separation should not be over emphasized.

[91]Notice that there is not even a hint that the positive and negative subjects have differing qualifications. Both actions are predicated of believers ("*you* give" of the positive subject, and "someone among *you*" of the negative subject).

[92]With Davids (*James*, 122) that καθ᾽ ἑαυτήν "probably means 'by itself' (i.e. per se, without works)." Contra Ropes (*St. James*, 207-208) who understood the prepositional phrase to mean "in itself," and so as "strengthen[ing] νεκρά, 'inwardly dead'; not merely hindered from activity, but defective in its own power to act." The difficulty with Ropes's interpretation is that James is not contrasting two kinds of faith (a "live faith" and a "dead faith"), but rather arguing that faith unaccompanied by works is "dead" because it does not provide the "benefit" of "saving one's soul/life;" see the discussion which follows.

(μὴ δύναται ἡ πίστις σῶσαι, 2:14) one's "soul/life" (σῶσαι τὰς ψυχάς, Jas 1:21), and so is itself ultimately "dead" (νεκρά, 2:17).

If we relate these parallels to what we have already learned about James's system of convictions, it is possible to explicate the 'convictional logic' which leads James to assert that 'faith in isolation from works is unable to save the soul/life.' "Faith" causes believers to be willing to ask God for "wisdom," a knowledge which establishes their will to act as God would act (to be "doers of the word/work") and so to be "blessed for/in their doing" by having their "souls saved from death." Within OPP 2:16, the negative subject is a believer who knows the will of God in such a situation of need, for the passive verbs within the blessing (θερμαίνεσθε καὶ χορτάζεσθε) are best understood as "divine passives:"[93] "the hope is not simply that somehow or other these wants will be supplied, but that *God* will supply them."[94] Thus, this believer has "wisdom" and so must also have the prerequisite "faith." It is in this light then that the failure to provide "what is needed by the body" is all the more alarming. As Laws has pointed out, the believer as negative subject

> believes that God would wish such need to be relieved (since his prayer is that God will respond to it), yet he does not himself act in accordance with that belief. ... The works of charity are not for James a matter of 'mere humanity', but of live faith in God.[95]

Rather than being a "doer of the word/work" (as the positive subject is), the negative subject is "deceived" (Jas 1:22) by his or her "claim to have faith" and will ultimately discover that such "faith in isolation from works is dead."

Figurativization in Jas 2:14-19

James opens this sub-unit with a tandem of rhetorical questions which clearly set forward the two aspects of the theme "a living faith" that is to be developed. "What is the benefit ... if someone claims to

---

[93]On the use of passive verbs as a circumlocution for avoiding the use of the divine name, cf. BDF § 130(1), 72.

[94]Laws, *James*, 121.

[95]Ibid., 122. Laws was specifically rejecting Sanders's contention (*Ethics in the New Testament*, 125-128) that James was appealing to a "humanistic principle" to support care for the indigent. She characterized Sanders's argument as "anachronistic and inadequate."

have faith but does not have works?" (Jas 2:14a). By this question, James raises the issue of the necessary relation between faith and works which will provide the focus of this first section of the sub-unit. As Dibelius has observed, "the author considers it to be *only natural* that a man who professes (Christian) faith also 'has works.'"[96] Yet we should notice that this is "only natural" for James because of his system of convictions by which he orders and makes sense of the realm of human experience. James's second rhetorical question, "Is the (claimed)[97] faith able to save him [or her]?" (Jas 2:14b), both provides the answer to the first question (there is no "benefit" if such faith is unable to "save") and introduces what will be the focus of the second section (Jas 2:20-26), namely the ability of faith which leads to works to "save" or "justify."

Our earlier analysis of OPP 2:16 provides us with an important check for interpreting the figurativization within the initial rhetorical question of Jas 2:14. Many commentators have heard in the phrase "if someone *claims* to have faith" an implicit charge by James that this "claimed" or "alleged" faith is not *genuine* faith.[98] But within OPP 2:16, James concedes that the negative subject indeed has true faith which has led to receiving "wisdom" regarding the will of God. Thus, it seems more probable that James understands the "claim to have faith" as indicating that it is limited to verbal expressions.[99] The issue for

---

[96]Dibelius, *James*, 152; emphasis mine.

[97]The use of the definite article here (ἡ πίστις) serves to identify this usage of "faith" with the occurrence of "faith" in the previous sentence. For this demonstrative use of the article, see H. E. Dana and Julius R. Mantey, *A Manual Grammar of the Greek New Testament* (New York: Macmillan, 1957), §147(a), 141; and BDF §252, 131-132. Yet, as Dibelius noted (*James*, 152), "[t]he only attributive which is expressed in ἡ πίστις is this: faith, which 'has' no works."

[98]Thus, Laws (*James*, 119) refers to it as "unreal faith," and Moo (*James*, 100) and Martin (*James*, 80) call it a "bogus faith."

[99]This distinction was also recognized by Dibelius (*James*, 152):

For it is not without significance that Jas writes, "if someone should *claim* to have faith," and not "if someone *has* faith" (ἐάν πίστιν τις ἔχῃ). A person whose faith is not expressed in deeds can show it only through words. ... On the other hand, one cannot read into the words "should claim" what was inferred by earlier commentators from the lack of the article before "faith" (πίστιν)—viz., that what is meant here is a false faith, one which is only alleged. Jas certainly never sets the correct faith over against such an alleged faith.

Cf. also Davids's comment (*James*, 120) that the claimed faith "appears only in the person's verbalizations (and ritual actions) but not in ... deeds." Reicke (*James*,

James is not whether "faith separated from works" can be "proper faith," but rather that "having faith and (yet) not having works" or merely "saying" one has faith is not sufficient since it is of no "benefit" in making one alive.

Historical critics have been divided as to whether the illustration James introduces in 2:15-16 is merely a stylized rhetorical device[100] or refers to an actual event in the life of the community.[101] However, since we are here stressing intertextual rather than extratextual relationships, we need go no further than Laws's comments that "[i]t is possible for the readers to conceive of such need existing within the community, ... [and] it is also assumed that there will be members able to supply their need."[102] James may have formulated this example so that the readers were expected to readily identify not with the one who offers the blessing, but with the needy "brother or sister" (recall the prominence of the "piety of the poor" within their beliefs) and thus would have immediately perceived how outlandish such behavior would be. But James has indentified the readers with the speaker ("someone *among you* should say to them"). He then provides rhetorical space for their anticipated objection through the dialogue with an imaginary interlocutor.

The particular objection raised by this interlocutor, however, has been very problematic for critical exegetes because the interlocutor seems to concede James's argument that both faith and works are necessary: "But someone will say, 'You (James) have faith and I (the interlocutor) have works.'" The problem for interpreters of a text without modern punctuation conventions is to determine the extent of the interlocutor's objection and the 'identity' of this interlocutor in terms of her or his relationship to James's own beliefs. Let us take the latter question first, since it may provide some assistance with the issue of the extent of the objection.

Peter and Jude, 32) seems to take it both ways; after stating "[t]his person has no real faith," he continued, "The author does not take issue with faith itself, but with a superficial conception of it which permits faith to be only a formal confession."

[100]So Adamson, *James*, 122; Davids, *James*, 121; Dibelius, *James*, 152-153; Moo, *James*, 103; Mußner, *Jakobusbrief*, 131; and Ropes, *St. James*, 206.

[101]So Martin, *James*, 84; Reicke, *James, Peter and Jude*,32, who relates the blessing to the benediction pronounced by deacons at the close of holy communion; and Christoph Burchard, "Zu Jakobus 2,14-26," *ZNW* 71 (1980): 28-30, who links this example with the one in 2:2-4 and finds here a further example of deference to the rich who are not called upon to assist needy members of the community.

[102]Laws, *James*, 120.

There have been three different theories set forward regarding the identity of James's dialogue partner. The first two take as their starting point the perception of a high degree of correspondence between the opinions of the interlocutor and James himself. Thus, the dialogue partner may be either nothing more than a rhetorical mask from behind which James expresses his own opinion,[103] or may be an ally who comes to assist James in the criticism of the mere speaker of pious words in Jas 2:16.[104] The problem is that the phrase "but someone will say" (ἀλλ' ἐρεῖ τις) was a firmly established conventional form for introducing the objection of one's opponent; as Davids commented, "no one has yet been able to find a case where this common stylistic introduction did not introduce an opposing or disagreeing voice. The evidence just is not strong enough to make this the one exception."[105] But if the interlocutor is an opponent, what is the nature and extent of his or her objection?

Most commentators who interpret the interlocutor as an opponent of James reconstruct the extent of the objection as, "You have faith and I have works." This retort is seen as elliptical and should be filled out as, "You have faith (in isolation from works) and I (also) have works," to which James then responds, "Show me your 'faith in isolation from works'." According to Dibelius, "the main point of the opponent in v 18a is not the *distribution* of faith and works to 'you' and 'me,' but rather the *total separation* of faith and works in general."[106] The pronouns "you" and "me" within the objection are understood "not [to] refer to James and the objector, but are equivalent to εἷς, ἕτερος, 'one,' 'another,' and are merely a more picturesque mode of indicating two imaginary persons."[107] The problem with this reconstruction, as

---

[103]So Vouga, *Jacques*, 87: "Je crois pour ma part que Jc reprend la parole dès le V. 18 (au travers du τις qu'il invoque rhétoriquement pour défendre son propre point de vue) et que c'est aux personnes visées dans les V. 15-17 qu'il s'adresse à nouveau: Vous dites que vous avez la foi, mais quelqu'un vous montrera des actes qui témoignent de sa foi. Il ne suffit pas en effet de confesser qu'il n'y a qu'un seul Dieu: c'est très bien, mais les démons aussi le reconnaissent. ... Dans ce sens, les V. 18-19 seraient une nouvelle illustration des V. 14 et 17, et les V. 20-24.25 enchaîneraient très bien: «Veux-tu savoir que la foi sans les oeuvres est stérile...»."

[104]So Adamson, *James*, 124-125 and 135-137; Mayor, *St. James*, 99-100; Mußner, *Jakobusbrief*, 136-138; and hesitantly Cantinat, *Jacques et Jude*, 146.

[105]Davids, *James*, 124. Cf. the discussion by Dibelius, *James*, 150-151.

[106]Dibelius, *James*, 155; for his full discussion of the problems here, see 154-158. Similar positions are also taken by Ropes, *St. James*, 208-214; Laws, *James*, 122-124; and Davids, *James*, 123-124, though reluctantly.

[107]Ropes, *St. James*, 209. The positions of Dibelius and Ropes have been

proponents of the "ally hypothesis" have been quick to point out, is that the formulation of the objection is a most awkward means to express the idea that "some have faith, and others have works." C. F. D. Moule went so far as to say, "To tell the truth, I cannot think of a *less* likely way to express what J. H. Ropes wants the James passage to mean than what there stands written."[108]

Other exegetes have dealt with the problem of the interlocutor's objection by extending it to include all of vv 18 and 19, with James's response beginning with the invective of Jas 2:20 (ὦ ἄνθρωπε κενέ). Donker supported this extension by arguing for a chiastic arrangement within 2:18-19.[109] Following this reconstruction of the dialogue, the objection is that there are two possible origins for religion—faith and deeds—that are "not only mutually exclusive; they have no logical interplay as well." Thus, a person may choose *either* faith *or* deeds.[110] The *interlocutor's* challenge in 2:18b to "show me your faith without works, and I will show you my faith by works" is an attempt to force James to concede that indeed faith and works are separate entities, thereby undercutting James's own position that they are inseparable. Moreover, the interlocutor levels the same charge at James in 2:19 that exegetes have made for centuries, namely that "faith" for James is nothing more than intellectual acceptance of monotheism.[111]

Although this reconstruction of the dialogue has much to commend it, nevertheless it remains problematic.[112] One of its chief difficulties

---

combined by Scot McKnight ("James 2:18a: The Unidentifiable Interlocutor," *WTJ* 52 [1990]: 362-364) as having "the distinct advantage of understanding the interlocutor's assertion according to the response of James" although he remains troubled by the fact "that this proposal requires that the personal pronouns be undervalued" (364).

[108]Personal note to James Adamson, cited in Adamson, *James*, 137.

[109]See Christiaan E. Donker, "Der Verfasser des Jak und sein Gegner: Zum Problem des Einwandes in Jak 2,18-19," *ZNW* 72 (1981): 236. Martin accepted Donker's chiastic arrangement and argued that it was paralleled by a chiastic arrangement in James's response in 2:20-24 (following a proposal by Lodge, "James and Paul," 201-204); see Martin, *James*, 76-77 and 86-90 for his discussion of the problem. Reicke (*James, Peter and Jude*, 31 and 33) likewise extends the objection through the end of 2:19, though he does not raise the issue of chiasmus.

[110]So R. W. Wall, "Interlocutor and James, James 2:18-20 Reconsidered," unpublished paper summarized by Martin, *James*, 77.

[111]"Darum kann [der Gegner] dem Verfasser vorwerfen, dessen Glaube sei nicht mehr als der Glaube ὅτι εἷς ἐστιν ὁ θεός: das jüdische Gottesbekenntnis" (Donker, "Verfasser und sein Gegner," 239).

[112]Martin himself confessed that it was "[w]ith less than final conviction [that]

is that it makes the example of the 'shuddering demons' a part of the argument of the opponent; thus, the example attempted to demonstrate the separateness of faith and works in that while the demons "believe," they certainly do not have works to support this faith. But as our earlier discussion of the thematization in this section suggested, and as will be established in the discussion of the figurativization in Jas 2:19 below, the example of the demons is best seen as supporting James's contention that indeed faith and works are inseparable.

It seems that the least problematic reconstruction of the dialogue between James and his rhetorical interlocutor in terms of both its form and content is the proposal of Heinz Neitzel. He reconstructed the objection as simply a question: "Do you, James, have faith?" James responds to this question by saying, "I have works. Show me your faith separated from works, and I will show you faith by my works." Thus, Neitzel punctuated the Greek text as follows: ἀλλ' ἐρεῖ τις· σὺ πίστιν ἔχεις;—κἀγὼ· ἔργα ἔχω. δεῖξόν μοι τὴν πίστιν σου χωρὶς τῶν ἔργων, κἀγώ σοι δείξω ἐκ τῶν ἔργων μου τὴν πίστιν.[113] In response to James's perceived over-emphasis on the need for works/action, the interlocutor asks whether James in fact has any "faith" at all, or whether (by inference) he only has "works." James responds that his actions are themselves proof that he has faith, since faith is the prerequisite to receiving wisdom regarding the will of God which establishes how he acts, and challenges them to show their faith in isolation from works.

This reading of the dialogue with the interlocutor shares in common with the other reconstructions the conclusion that at the heart of the disagreement between James and his rhetorical opponent is the issue of whether "faith" can 'exist' in isolation from "works." Whereas his opponent wishes to separate faith from actions, such that even faith in isolation from works might be of some "benefit," James counters in this section (Jas 2:14-19) that "faith" must lead to action/"works;"[114] faith is inseparable from works because "[w]orks are not an 'added

---

we have championed [this] reading" (*James*, 90).

[113]See Heinz Neitzel, "Eine alte crux interpretum im Jakobusbrief 2:18," *ZNW* 73 (1982): 293. This reconstruction differs from the interrogative proposal offered by Dibelius (and rejected because of its complexity; see *James*, 156-157), in that the interlocutor poses but a single question. Neitzel supports his rendering of the grammar (κἀγώ meaning in effect, "and I [would respond]") with examples from Classical and Koiné Greek authors (see "Crux Interpretum," 291-292).

[114]James will return to the "benefit" of this relationship between faith and works in the second section of this sub-unit, Jas 2:20-26.

extra' to faith, but are an essential expression of it."[115]　This much seems clear even if a cloud still seems to obscure attempts to reconstruct the elements of the dialogue in any precise fashion.[116]　The example of the demons brings the development of the sub-theme that faith must be lived to its rhetorical climax.

As we have noted several times already, James's statement, "You believe (πιστεύεις) that God is one, [and] so you should"[117] (Jas 2:19) has been widely used by interpreters to assert that "faith" for James is merely intellectual assent to doctrinal formulas, particularly monotheism. Even demons accede to the existence of only one God, yet there is no doubt that they will be destroyed in the eschatological judgment nor is there any delusion that their "belief" leads to "works of love" which must accompany faith if it is "to save."[118]　Yet, before we can properly relate the demons response to it, we must first examine what beliefs James is expressing by the confession "God is one."

Within a semiotic system which prioritizes issues of ontology, to confess that "God is one" is to believe in "the existence and unity of God."[119]　However, our exegesis of Jas 1:2-21 provided clear evidence that James's pattern of beliefs is constructed within a semiotic

---

[115]Davids, *James*, 121. This expression of the necessary relationship that "faith" must lead to "works" to obtain the "benefit" of salvation would be the point of the conviction expressed by the polemical dialogue between James and his interlocutor. However, since we have seen that this polemical dialogue requires extensive reconstruction and that the convictions expressed by it have already found expression in other oppositions of actions, we need not include this polemical dialogue as an explicit opposition of actions.

[116]Cf. Cantinat's comments (*Jacques et Jude*, 145), "L'exacte interprétation de ce verset est très difficile, la plus difficile qui soit dans le N.T., au dire de Dibelius. ... Mais il est rassurant de constater que les difficultés techniques du texte n'affectent pas beaucoup notre compréhension du passage."

[117]The Greek is καλῶς ποιεῖς, literally "you do well." I will return to other possible nuances of this phrase below.

[118]Cf. as exemplary the comments of Davids, *James*, 126; Dibelius, *James*, 160; Sidebottom, *James, Jude, 2 Peter*, 43; and Thorwald Lorenzen, "Faith without Works Does Not Count before God! James 2:14-26," *ExpTim* 89 (1978): 232. Ropes (*St. James*, 215-216) dissents only slightly. He sees monotheism as "the chief element in faith" but not "the whole of James's conception of faith," though this would still seem to allow construing faith as intellectual assent.

[119]To quote Ropes, *St. James*, 215. This ontological emphasis is seen already in the variant reading of B 614 630 1835 *et al.* (εἷς θεός ἐστιν ["there is one God"]) as compared to the reading of P⁷⁴ ℵ A *et al.* (εἷς ἐστιν ὁ θεός ["God is one"]) which "is in conformity with the prevailing formula of Jewish orthodoxy" (*TCGNT*, 681).

system which prioritizes issues of value. The differences between such systems and their implications for understanding assertions about the divine were examined in some detail in discussing the figurativization in 1:17-18 describing God as "the Father of Lights, with whom there is neither variation nor shadow cast by turning." In our exegesis of those verses, we saw how that God is valued as "pure good" within James's system of convictions and how that experience of God as "pure good" is encountered in the consistency of the divine will. Moreover, we should recall from our elaboration of James's system of convictions that "faith" for James is the result of knowing about God as "pure good."

Thus, within James's system of convictions "faith" necessarily evokes a response from those who know God as "pure good." This conviction is no less true of demons; "in believing that God is one [the demons] believe something about him that evokes a response: that as *one* he is wholly and consistently their enemy, *and they shudder.*"[120] James's point is not that the demons' faith does not lead to works, but precisely the opposite: even the demons act on what they know about God when they tremble in the face of the coming judgment. Laws has well summarized the rhetorical function of James's example:

> He is not concerned to contrast faith, as intellectual assent, with works, but to indicate the necessary outcome of faith, if it is a live faith, and the impossibility of its existing alone. For the demons, belief in the God who is one produces a response of fear. ... The challenge to James's man of faith is to show what response his profession evokes from him.[121]

Thus, James is confident that his actions (and even those of the demons) can demonstrate the existence of his faith, and equally confident that no one will be able to show her or his faith to him "separated from works."

The confrontational nature of this example suggests a second way of reading Jas 2:19. Rather than conceding that the readers do indeed have faith ("You believe that God is one") as he conceded of the negative subject in OPP 2:16, James may be challenging them with a question: "Do you [truly] *believe* that God is one [in that you insist that faith can be separated from one's actions in response]?" Adopting this harsher tone, his words "you do well" (καλῶς ποιεῖς) become ironic. We might paraphrase this second reading of 2:19 as follows: 'If you truly believe that God is one, you do well (and should continue to "do

---

[120]Laws, *James*, 126.
[121]Ibid., 128.

well" in all your actions arising from that faith). But if you insist that faith does not necessarily lead to a response in how one lives, then you have even less understanding of the true nature of faith than the demons who tremble.'

Jas 2:20-26 — Benefit of Faith and Works

Figurativization in Jas 2:20-26

James begins the second section of his discussion of a 'living faith' by asking, "Do you desire proof[122] that faith separated from works is useless?" He proceeds to offer this "proof" by developing a thematic section (no explicit oppositions of actions) which utilizes two examples drawn from the beliefs of the readers. In this way, having already presented his pattern of convictions regarding the relationship between "faith" and "works" of "the word" by the oppositions of actions in the previous sections of this discursive unit, James now attempts to persuade his readers that in fact they should have already "seen" (Jas 2:22, 24) this sequence of relationships within their own belief system. Using a kind of rhetorical jujitsu, James employs his readers' own beliefs to persuade them to accept his belief that "faith" in isolation from "works" is "useless" in that it cannot provide the "benefit" of "saving one's life," and so is itself "dead."

The invective James uses for addressing his audience (whether the readers more generally or the interlocutor more specifically) is unquestionably harsh: "O Vain Person!" (ὦ ἄνθρωπε κενέ). However, the adjective κενός (literally, "empty") as applied figuratively to persons carried several possible nuances. Most scholars point to its usage in

---

[122]Literally, "do you wish to know" (θέλεις δὲ γνῶναι). It will be noted that both the verb (θέλεις) and the vocative construction (ὦ ἄνθρωπε κενέ) are singular (as is the main verb of 2:22, βλέπεις), which has suggested to several commentators that the question and invective are directed only at the interlocutor introduced in 2:18; thus, the readers are only again addressed at 2:24, where the plural verb form is resumed (ὁρᾶτε). See for example Dibelius, *James*, 151 and 160-161; Davids, *James*, 126; Martin, *James*, 90; and Laws, *James*, 128. Adamson (*James*, 132) differs only by his attempt to find the interlocutor already in Jas 2:14, which it will be noted contains plural vocative forms. This shifting between singular and plural forms as well as the semantic parallel between the βλέπεις of 2:22 and the ὁρᾶτε of 2:24 clearly demonstrate that all of Jas 2:14-26 is an attempt by James to convince his imagined audience (the implied reader) that faith isolated from works is of no benefit. Thus, any attempts to draw a sharp distinction between the views of the interlocutor and the implied reader seem unwarranted.

referring "to a complete lack of understanding and insight" in an intellectual sense, and relate it to the Aramaic רֵיקָא ("fool").[123] Although this nuance of intellectual deficiency is supported by the immediate context ("do you desire *to know*"), the broader context of claims unsubstantiated by actions suggests the nuance evidenced elsewhere in Greek literature of "foolish boasting."[124] Finally, it may be that James utilizes the adjective κενός to suggest once again that claims to a faith isolated from works can only be "empty words;"[125] the addressee is "empty" in the sense of lacking any "works" whereby to "show their faith." This final possible nuance would be supported by the pun within James's question: "faith separated from works (ἔργων) is useless (ἀργή, i.e. ἀ+ἐργή, 'workless')."[126]

Two questions naturally arise from James's use of the Abraham and Rahab illustrations: (1) what are the "works" by which each of these notable figures were "justified," and (2) what does it mean for James when he states that they were "justified"? In response to the first of these questions, several exegetes have sought to restrict "works" to acts of mercy or Christian charity. This line of interpretation has been argued most thoroughly by Roy Ward.[127] He related Jas 2:14-26 to what precedes in 2:1-13 (especially vv 12-13) by arguing that the "works" spoken of are "acts of mercy" which "triumph over judgment."

---

[123]See Louw and Nida, *Greek-English Lexicon*, §32.60, 1:33; and Albrecht Oepke, "κενός," *TDNT* 3:659 and 660. Thus, Laws (*James*, 128) renders the phrase as "stupid man," and Martin (*James*, 90) as "you empty-headed person."

[124]Cf. the statement by Epictetus in *Diss.* 2.19.8: "but if I am κενός at a banquet, I astonish the visitors by enumerating the writers (on a particular subject)." Thus, the adjective might be translated here as "pretensious" (MM 340), or the invective as a whole rendered as "you braggart" (Dibelius, *James*, 161 and n. 62).

[125]A similar use of the adjective and its related adverb may be attested in *Herm. Mand.* 11.13: "But [the false prophet] cleaves to the double-minded and empty (τοῖς διψύχοις καὶ κενοῖς), and prophesies to them in a corner, and deceives them by empty speech (λαλῶν ... κενῶς) about everything according to their lusts." See Kirsopp Lake, *The Apostolic Fathers*, LCL (London and New York: William Heinemann and G. Putnam's Sons, 1913) 2:122 and 123.

[126]Regarding this pun, cf. the comments of Laws (*James*, 128) and Vouga (*Jacques*, 88) as representative. It should be noted that there are textual variants which replace ἀργή with either νεκρά (so א A K *et al.*) or κενή (so P⁷⁴), but these readings are most probably assimilations to the vocabulary elsewhere in this section; see *TCGNT* 681.

[127]Roy Bowen Ward, "The Works of Abraham: James 2:14-26," *HTR* 61 (1968): 283-290. See also Adamson, *James*, 122; Davids, *James*, 120 and 127-128; and Reicke, *James, Peter and Jude*, 32.

Ward demonstrated from Jewish and Christian traditions about Abraham that he was widely known for his acts of hospitality. Thus, Ward argued, just as Abraham's faith was understood without explicit reference,[128] so were his "works" of "hospitality." He concluded from this that James is not in fact concerned with "faith" and "works," but only with expounding "mercy triumphs over judgment."[129]

While Ward is correct in emphasizing that 'acts of mercy' are a major concern within this unit of the Epistle (reaching back to the definition of "pure religion" in Jas 1:27), it is indeed strange that if James wished to limit "works" to acts of Christian charity he would have chosen to emphasize Abraham's "work"[130] of "offering his son Isaac upon the altar."[131]   Why not parallel Rahab's "hospitality" to "the messengers" (τοὺς ἀγγέλους; Jas 2:25, cf. Joshua 2) with Abraham's hospitality to "the angels" (הַמַּלְאָכִים; Gen 19:1) en route to Sodom (cf. Genesis 18)?

If we re-examine the story of the "Binding of Isaac" in Gen 22:1-19 and its traditional embellishments, several of its features suggest reasons why James may have chosen this specific incident to expand the definition of "works" beyond acts of mercy. As both the Genesis account and the Jewish traditions regarding the "ten trials of Abraham"[132] make clear, the call to "offer" Isaac was a "test" (cf. Gen

---

[128]Ward, "Works of Abraham," 286; cf. Dibelius, *James*, 161. This contention that Abraham's faith is not explicitly mentioned is puzzling given the citation of Gen 15:6, "Abraham *believed* (ἐπίστευσεν) God." It is certainly true, however, that there are no explicit references to faith on the part of Rahab in Jas 2:24.

[129]Ward ("Works of Abraham," 285) goes so far as to suggest that "faith" and "works" are terms of convenience: "But may it not be possible that James used πίστις and ἔργα for 'linguistic and dialectical convenience'? In the diatribe [of 2:14-26] it would be confusing to contrast 'doing' and 'saying,' since the style demands the use of the verb 'to say' for the imaginary dialogue (as in 2:18)."

[130]The use of the plural "works" (ἔργων in v 21 and τοῖς ἔργοις in v 22) clearly indicates that James is not saying that Abraham "was justified by the [single] work [of] offering his son Isaac on the altar." "Justification" is "by the works" performed throughout his life and not this single act. But the question is, why single out this particular act within the example?

[131]This difficulty has been variously resolved by pointing to the supreme importance of the "Binding of Isaac" in the Abraham tradition (cf. Dibelius, *James*, 162) or by arguing that the ultimate deliverance of Isaac is itself an act of mercy (suggested by Ward, "Works of Abraham," 285) or arose from Abraham's previous acts of mercy (ibid., 288-289; Davids, *James*, 127).

[132]On the specific notion of "ten trials" of Abraham, see *'Abot* 5.3; these trials were later enumerated in *'Abot R. Nat.* 36. Cf. *Pirqe R. El.* 26 and *Jub.* 17:17-

22:1); this would seem to confirm the implied readers' belief that God can be the source of testing (cf. Jas 1:13). James may, however, be wanting to emphasize another part of the tradition by juxtaposing this incident with the quotation from Gen 15:6 that "Abraham believed God." We have seen that within the author's system of convictions faith and belief are related to knowledge about God as "pure good" and the trust that God will only give "good things" to those who ask in faith. It may be then James has in mind that portion of the Abraham tradition spoken of in Heb 11:17-19 where he is said to have believed that God would raise Isaac from the dead if he were sacrificed.[133]   Thus, Abraham's belief in God as "pure good" would have established his will to "offer his son Isaac on the altar."

Another feature of this story that warrants attention is the final pronouncement by "the angel of the Lord" in Gen 22:16-18: "Because you have done this, and have not withheld your son, your only son, I will indeed bless you ... because you have obeyed my voice" (NRSV). Abraham was "blessed" because he had "done" what he heard from the "voice" of the Lord, just as James had earlier asserted that those who are "doers of the work" of the "implanted word" rather than "forgetful hearers" will be "blessed in/for their doing" (Jas 1:25). "Works" are not restricted to acts of mercy, but include all acts of obedience to the implanted word which is received by asking in faith.[134]   It is in this sense that "faith was working with [Abraham's] works and faith was completed by the works;" had Abraham not believed God to be good, his will could not have been established to do what he had heard from the voice of the Lord.

If we then turn to the question of what James means when he states that Abraham "was *justified* (ἐδικαιώθη) by works," the logical place to begin is with the use of the cognate noun "righteousness" (δικαιοσύνη) in Jas 2:23. On the basis of this verbal parallel, it has

---

19:9. For a discussion of Jewish traditions about Abraham more generally and their bearing on Jas 2:21-23, see Dibelius, *James*, 168-174.

[133]For a fine discussion of Jewish and early Christian traditions which interpreted the "Binding of Isaac" as the actual sacrifice of Isaac and subsequent resurrection, see Alan F. Segal, "'He who did not spare his own son ...': Jesus, Paul, and the Akedah," in *From Jesus to Paul: Studies in Honor of Francis Wright Beare*, ed. Peter Richardson and John C. Hurd (Waterloo, Ontario: Wilfrid Laurier University Press, 1984), 169-184.

[134]On the relationship between "works" and "doing" the "implanted word," see Davids, *James*, 127-128. Cf. also Vouga, *Jacques*, 90, n. 16: "[l]es ἔργα (oeuvres) sont ici à nouveau l'obéissance de la foi et non les oeuvres de la Loi."

been argued that "ἐδικαιώθη refers not to a forensic act in which a sinner is declared acquitted ..., but to a declaration by God that a person is righteous, *ṣaddîq*."[135] This characterization, however, is both correct and incorrect. While it is true that there is no indication that James understands the statement "it was accounted to him as righteousness" as a 'forensic act of justification' (à la Paul), nevertheless the introductory questions of this sub-unit (Jas 2:14) make it clear that to "be justified by works" is to be "saved." James is not merely arguing that a 'faith working with works' is more "righteous" before God; he is arguing that only a 'faith working with works' is "able to save" the person's "soul from death." What is at stake is salvation and justification in an eschatological sense.[136]

James draws the example of Abraham to a close in v 24 by sharply contrasting the proper belief that 'works justify a person' (ἐξ ἔργων δικαιοῦται ἄνθρωπος)[137] with the improper belief that 'faith alone justifies a person' (οὐκ ἐκ πίστεως μόνον).[138] The presence of the modifier μόνον clearly indicates that the emphasis is again upon 'faith in isolation from works,' and probably also (given the overall pattern of James's system of convictions) in isolation from even "wisdom."[139] But it must be emphasized that James pointedly does

---

[135]Davids, *James*, 127; cf. also his later comment (132) that "no question of the forensic justification of *sinners* arises, but rather what pleases God." Similar is Mußner's contention (*Jakobusbrief*, 144) that Abraham's combination of faith and works is considered "righteous" by God. Cf. also Martin, *James*, 93-94.

[136]Cf. the comments on the use of σῴζειν in Jas 2:14 by Vouga (*Jacques*, 86) and Martin (*James*, 81-82).

[137]Since an agent is clearly stated within the text ("by works"), it is best to follow the normal syntactical rules and understand that agent to be the subject of the passive verb. Contra the attempt by Davids (*James*, 132) to soften James's contrast between "justified by works" and "justified by faith alone" by taking δικαιοῦται as a 'divine passive' which "has God as the implied active agent."

[138]In that James indicates that a "person being justified by faith alone" would not only be perceived negatively but is in fact impossible within his system of convictions, it may be possible to conceive of this contrast as a kind of elliptical polemical dialogue (an opposition of cognitive actions) opposing the correct belief that 'works justify a person' to the improper belief that 'faith alone justifies a person.' However, since this opposition would require extensive reconstruction of these ellipses and would contribute nothing new to the enunciator's system of convictions, it is better not to include this contrast as an *explicit* opposition of actions.

[139]Thus, the contrast between faith and works here in Jas 2:24 is even more stark than in OPP 2:16 where the negative subject was at least conceded to have wisdom along with faith. See the discussion of this opposition above.

not say that "works alone" can justify a person. Thus, in the light of the pattern of beliefs already established by the oppositions of actions within the Epistle, it is clear that the presence of "works" implies the prior reception of both "wisdom" which establishes the will to act and "faith" which is the prerequisite to receiving "wisdom" as a "gift" from God. The point being stressed by this contrast is not that "works alone" do justify a person (which would be a kind of legalism), but that "faith alone" (i.e., in the absence of a response in one's life) cannot "justify." Again, we see that for James "faith" and "works" cannot exist in isolation from one another.[140]

The inseparability of faith and works and the importance of their working together is driven home by the simile which concludes the unit: "For just as the body separated from spirit is dead, even so also faith separated from works is dead" (Jas 2:26). Reicke has noted that a "modern reader" would tend to allegorize the simile and so "would rather be inclined to reverse the image and picture works as the corporeal element made alive by the working of faith, the spiritual factor."[141] James is not, however, developing an analogy along the lines of a:b::c:d. Rather, his statement that "faith separated from works is dead" is a kind of shorthand expression of his system of convictions. "Faith," although necessary to receive "wisdom" as a gift from God, is not sufficient apart from "works" (i.e., not only "receiving"/"hearing" but also "doing" the "implanted word") to cause one to be "birthed by God" and so can only result in "death" as one's "desire gives birth to sin, and sin [ultimately] gives birth to death." The choice of the "body

---

[140]Cf. Mußner's comment (*Jakobusbrief*, 142) regarding the use of the verb συνεργεῖν in Jas 2:22:

> Er zeigt nämlich, daß es in 2, 18-26 nicht etwa um eine Ausspielung der Werke *gegen* den Glauben geht, sondern um ihre unlösbare Zusammengehörigkeit, um eine lebendige und überzeugende Synthese aus Glauben und Werken. Jak sagt auch nicht—auch dies ist besonders zu beachten—: Die Werke wirken mit dem Glauben zusammen, sondern umgekehrt: Der Glaube wirkt mit den Werken zusammen, d.h., das Primäre ist auch für ihn der Glaube. Eine Alternative Glaube *oder* Werke ist für Jak undenkbar.

Cf. also the comments by Lodge, "James and Paul," 199-200; Davids, *James*, 123; Lohse, "Glaube und Werke," 292; and Ropes, *St. James*, 219.

[141]Reicke, *James, Peter and Jude*, 35. I cannot however concur with his alternate allegorization: "But the author views faith as the formal confession of Christianity, so he is correct in describing it as a body which needs to be animated by the spirit of Christian living and doing." For my critique of the view that "faith" for James is merely "the formal confession of Christianity," cf. the discussion of 2:19 above.

separated from spirit" for the comparison arises from the certainty of resulting "death," not from any presumed similarities between 'body and spirit' and 'faith and works.'

Summary of Jas 2:14-26

Our structural semiotic exegesis has supported our assignment of the theme "a 'living' faith" to this section of the Epistle. The implied readers believed that it was possible for their "faith" about God to be separated from their own actions within life. Though they certainly believed that God desired for the indigent members of the community to "be warm and well fed," they felt the expression of this belief in pious words was sufficient. It may be that it was in fact James's readers who understood "faith" as intellectual assent to Judeo-Christian doctrinal formulas: "God is one," God has "chosen the poor of this world" and cares for them, and so forth. To "believe God" by confessing such beliefs would be "accounted to [them] as righteousness," that is would "justify" and "save" them.

James counters these beliefs by insisting on the need for a 'living' faith. In the first instance, this means that "faith" cannot be isolated from the "works" which necessarily arise from it. If one believes certain things about God, one must live in accordance with those beliefs, just as the "demons tremble" because of their certainty of the coming wrath of God. Secondly, it must be a 'living' faith because it is only a "faith [that] works with [their] works and [is] completed by the works" that is of "benefit" in the sense of "justifying" a person and being "able to save the soul from death." 'Separating faith from works' has the same effect as 'separating the body from spirit'—"death." Faith should not be conceived of as merely intellectual assent, because faith can only be "completed" and lead to "saving one's life/soul" by being 'lived,' that is by "works."

Discursive Structure and Purpose
in Jas 1:22 - 2:26

We concluded the discussion of the first discursive unit of the Epistle (Jas 1:2-21) by raising the question whether there was a conviction not expressed within that unit that would stand between 'receiving wisdom' and 'salvation' within the system of convictions of the author. Our exegesis of Jas 1:22 - 2:26 has confirmed that such a conviction does exist, and indeed that virtually the entire second discursive unit of the Epistle is devoted to expressing that conviction and to persuading the readers to adopt it.   Through a series of parallel oppositions in the first sub-unit (Jas 1:22 - 2:13), James clearly showed that believers must not only "hear"/"receive the implanted word" but must also be "doers of the word" if they are to be "blessed."   The second sub-unit is almost exclusively thematic (containing but a single opposition of actions), and consequently draws heavily upon the beliefs of the implied readers in order to persuade them to adopt this new pattern of belief.[142]

It may be useful to again present schematically the author's system of convictions as developed within the first two units of the Epistle:

Positive	Negative
1. Knowing "God tempts no one." God is the source of "every good and perfect gift" and nothing bad or evil.	1. Knowing "I am tempted by God." Believing God gives both "good and perfect gifts" as well as bad or evil.
2. Having "faith;" being willing to ask because God is "good."	2. Having "doubt." Trusting and mistrusting God who is both good and bad.
3. Asking for "wisdom" from God as a gift.	3. Not asking for "wisdom" from God, or asking with "doubt." Believing one must learn "wisdom" by "enduring trials."

---

[142]Thus, while Jas 2:14-26 is central to the persuasive rhetoric of the Epistle, we should be careful in isolating it as the primary statement of James's own theology or convictions. The figurativization of these verses was chosen because it would be convincing to the readers, not necessarily because it best expresses James's own convictions. Indeed, our discussion of the figurativization in Jas 2:21 pointed to an inconsistency between the figurativization there and James's convictions: Abraham was being "tested" by God when directed to offer Isaac, yet James's own conviction is that "God is unable to be tested by evil, and God tests no one" (Jas 1:13).

4. Receiving "wisdom" from God. Being changed internally by the "implanted word."

4. Receiving nothing from God. Having an internal "(evil) desire."

5. Being a "doer of the word/work." Acting as God acts.

5. Being "a forgetful hearer;" being "deceived [by] oneself;" having one's "desire" give birth to "sin."

6. Being birthed by God; having one's "soul saved from death." Being "blessed for/in one's doing."

6. Having one's "sin" give birth to "death."

What is most striking by its absence in reviewing James's system of convictions is that there are still no convictions which would explain how it is a person initially comes to know God as "pure good."

Now, it may be that such convictions will be found in the second half of the Epistle. But this lacuna is most interesting given a comment by Sophie Laws in speculating upon the Apostle Paul's reaction to reading Jas 2:14-26:

> Yet Paul could surely never have tolerated James's explicit assertion that justification is *not by faith alone* nor his lack of attention to an initial saving act of God that makes faith and consequent good works possible.[143]

Laws is certainly correct that there has been to this point in the Epistle a "lack of attention to an initial saving act of God that makes faith and consequent good works possible;" moreover, the author's pattern of belief would seem to require just such an act by God, a mediator, or someone so that a person can know God as "pure good." But should this blank space in James's system of convictions remain unfilled by the conclusion of the Epistle, it will be more important for us to reflect on its implications for understanding James's purposes in writing than to speculate on Paul's reaction to his "lack of attention" to this important aspect of all expressions of Christian faith.

---

[143]Laws, *James*, 133.

CHAPTER FIVE

"HUMBLING ONESELF" IN THE LIGHT OF "JUDGMENT": JAMES 3:1 - 4:12

When reviewing the descriptions of the organization of the Epistle of James by form critics in chapter one of this study, we saw that Jas 3:1 marked a kind of turning point in their treatment of the letter. Although Dibelius had considered 3:1-12 the last of three "treatises" within the book, he commented that it lacked the "neat arrangement" of the others in that its "ideas bump against or even clash with one another."[1] Following 3:12, the remainder of the Epistle reverted to merely 'grouping' sayings together according to very general themes.

An unintended consequence of this fragmented conception of the organization in this portion of the Epistle by exegetes has been pointed out by Johnson. After reviewing how scholars have addressed several lexical, grammatical, structural and thematic difficulties in the last part of chapter 3 and opening verses of chapter 4 by making broad use of parallels with other literature but seldom looking for parallels within the immediate context of the Epistle of James itself,[2] he commented:

> The habitual perception of James as structurally fragmented ... means that each of these problems is treated in isolation, which only reinforces the initial

---

[1]Dibelius, *James*, 182. For the perception by scholars of an increasing lack of organization following Jas 3:1, see the discussions of the "Structure of the Epistle" in chapter 1 of this study.

[2]Luke Timothy Johnson, "James 3:13-4:10 and the *Topos* περὶ φθόνου," *NovT* 25 (1983): 327-331.

of picking over old exegetical bones will not come about unless the reader be willing to step back once more and see those bones as part of a living organism.[3]

Let us try to follow Johnson's advice by reinvigorating these verses for ourselves as twentieth century readers by considering how the themes of the discursive semantics of this unit might aid in our resolution of the exegetical difficulties presented by its figures.[4]

Discursive Semantic Structure
and Thematization

The central theme of this third discursive unit in the Epistle of James is expressed by a pair of inverted parallelisms. By means of his injunction that "not many of you should become teachers" (3:1), James contrasts the readers' desire to obtain power and high social standing with what is for him the proper attitude of believers in "humbling themselves in the presence of the Lord [so that] the Lord will exalt them" (4:10). He then emphasizes the importance of having this proper attitude by introducing the theme of judgment of individual believers through the inverted parallelism between teachers who "will receive a stricter judgment" (3:1) and the "one Lawgiver and Judge who is able to save and to destroy" (4:12).

This second inverted parallelism underscores a fundamental difference in the perception of the function of teachers between James and his readers. In response to his reminder that there is "one Lawgiver and Judge," James immediately challenges his readers' aggrandized self-perception, asking "so who are you who judges the neighbor?" (4:12). They perceive the role of teachers as being to "judge" others, to exercise

---

[3]Ibid., 331. Johnson identified the literary unit as Jas 3:13 - 4:10 and divided it into two major components: 3:13 - 4:6 which sets forward an indictment against the readers relative to the problem of envy, and 4:7-10 which responds to the indictment with a series of imperatives calling the readers to repentance (332-333). He then relates the terms of the indictment to common discussions of envy (the *topos* περὶ φθόνου) in Hellenistic moral philosophy and Hellenistic-Jewish writings to show how such relationships might assist in dealing with the exegetical difficulties within the passage (334-346).

[4]A similar way of defining our task is by considering exegesis to be the "revitalizing" of the discourse of the text (a necessary step since a "text is *not* living language: it is '*dead language.*' It is no longer a speech.") in terms of Ricoeur's notion of hermeneutics "as the prolongation of the discourse of the text into a new discourse." See the discussion in Patte, *What is Structural Exegesis?*, 5-6.

(punitive?) authority over errant members of the community ("neighbors"). James, on the other hand, views "teachers" not as the dispensers of "(punitive) judgment" but as the recipients of "stricter judgment." Based on the overall theme of the letter established by the inverted parallelism between Jas 1:1 and 5:19-20 (the readers are a "Diaspora" which has "wandered from the truth" and so need someone to "restore" them), we might anticipate that James considers teachers "servants of God and of the Lord Jesus Christ" who "save [sinners'] souls from death and cover a multitude of sins" thereby sparing errant members of the community from harsh judgment rather than inflicting such judgment upon them. But by continuing to withhold this view of teachers from his readers, James places the emphasis here squarely upon the need for humility by all members of the community—especially those, like teachers, of higher status—in the face of impending judgment.[5] We can thus summarize the theme of the discursive unit of Jas 3:1 - 4:12 as "humbling oneself" in the light of impending "judgment."[6]

A third inverted parallelism further supports the identification of the limits of this discursive unit as 3:1 - 4:12 and introduces a major sub-theme developed within the unit. In 3:2, James describes the "mature (τέλειος) person" as one who "does not sin in speech;" such a person stands in stark contrast to "one who speaks against a brother [or sister]" and so "speaks against the law" (4:11). The question of proper and improper speech plays an important role in the development of this unit, but improper speech is only a symptom and not a cause of "sin." This is already apparent in Jas 3:2: "Indeed, we all sin in many things. If anyone does not sin in speech, this one is a mature person who is able to bridle even the whole body." While improper speech may be a kind of 'first among equals,' it is still only one of "many ways" in which

---

[5]Note that what is at stake is the quality of "judgment" (teachers will receive "stricter judgment" and at least by implication all members of the community will be judged). See the discussion of the role of Jas 4:11-12 in the figurativization of this unit below.

[6]These verses have also been treated as a single unit by Moo (*James*, 118) who summarizes their content under the heading "Dissensions within the Community." He places the emphasis upon the problems of speech and their negative impacts upon community life. A similar approach is clearly evident in Davids's heading of the unit 3:1 - 4:12 as "the Demand for Pure Speech" (*James*, 135). In my opinion, this is a major sub-theme within this unit (see the discussion which follows), but not the theme which makes the primary contribution to the discourse as a whole. Cf. also the comments on the closure between Jas 3:1 and 4:11-12 provided by the theme of judgment in Johnson, "*Topos* περὶ φθόνου," 334, n. 32.

people sin. If we inquire as to "from where" evil behavior and speech arise, James responds that it is from "passions which are at war within your members" (4:1). The true problem, in James's view, is the desire for social status (3:1), the "bitter rivalry and ambition" (3:16), and the "arrogance" (4:6) typical of the "(evil) desire [that] gives birth to sin" and ultimately results in "death" (Jas 1:15). The major theme of this unit, as we have seen, is that the solution to this problem of the ultimate cause of sin is to "humble oneself in the presence of the Lord" (4:10; cf. "by meekness receive the implanted word," Jas 1:21).

James develops this theme in two discursive sub-units. The first of these sub-units is marked by two pairs of inverted parallelisms. First, James unmasks the desire of "many of [the readers] to become teachers" (3:1) as nothing more than "rivalry and ambition" (3:14 and 16). The second parallel contrasts the fact that "we all sin in many things" (3:2) with the 'many things' which should typify one "who is wise and intelligent" (3:13) in terms of "the wisdom from above [that is] pure, then peaceful, gentle, obedient, full of mercy and good fruits, impartial" (3:17). This sub-unit extends, then, from 3:1-18 and seeks to show that true "wisdom" is demonstrated not by what one says but by "conduct" which itself evidences "humility characteristic of wisdom" (3:13).

James develops this argument in three sections. He begins (possibly in response to the opening figure of teachers) by describing the proper and positive uses of speech ("the tongue") in guiding human behavior (3:1-5a). But he quickly moves to show how human speech is anything but an unmitigated positive influence. It is capable of expressing both the highest ("we bless the Lord and Father") and the lowest ("we curse human beings who have been made according to the likeness of God") sentiments of the human will (3:5b-12). For this reason, wisdom can be demonstrated not by what one says, but only by the way in which one conducts one's life (3:13-18).[7] It is perhaps not going too far to say that James's advice to those who desire "to become

---

[7]The same division into sections may be found in Moo (*James*, 118-137), although he posits a sharper break between 3:12 and 13 than between 3:5a and 5b (so also Davids [*James*, 135 and 149] although he vacillates on whether to also mark a break between 3:2a and 2b [see his differing assessments on 135 and 136 of Dibelius's argument for such a break; for Dibelius's arguments, see *James*, 184]). Dibelius had argued that there was no connection between the "treatise" of 3:1-12 and 3:13-18 (*James*, 207-208); Mußner (*Jakobusbrief*, 168-169) countered that the related topics of "teacher" and "wisdom" provided some connection (cf. Davids, *James*, 149; and Johnson, "*Topos* περὶ φθόνου," 334, n. 32) but followed Dibelius in seeing a major break between sections at Jas 3:13.

teachers" would be to teach by actions (which will withstand "stricter judgment") rather than simply by words.

The second sub-unit, Jas 4:1-12, is also marked by two inverted parallelisms. James opens the sub-unit by raising a rhetorical question which seems to acknowledge the presence of divisions within the community ("From where do quarrels and disputes among you arise?" 4:1), and closes the sub-unit with an imperative to "not speak against one another, brothers [and sisters]" (4:11). This inverted parallelism is related to the sub-theme of the discursive unit as a whole focused on the issue of proper and improper speech. The second inverted parallelism furthers the central theme of the full discursive unit and provides the dominate theme for this sub-unit: the readers have attempted to fulfill their "evil motives" ("desire," "envy," "passions;" 4:2-3) rather than "humbling themselves in the presence of the Lord" (4:10).[8] These two different actions will provide the grounds for judgment by the "one Lawgiver and Judge."

The division of this sub-unit into sections is complicated by the function of Jas 4:11-12 as "hinge" or transitional verses between the third and fourth discursive units of the Epistle.[9] As we have just seen, these verses contribute not only to the inverted parallelisms marking the discursive unit of Jas 3:1 - 4:12, but also to those marking the sub-unit of 4:1-12. Yet, as the discussion in the next chapter will show, these verses also contribute to the inverted parallelisms marking the final discursive unit of 4:11 - 5:20 and its first sub-unit as well. Because of their 'dual' and transitional functions, it makes sense that they should be treated as a separate section.[10]

---

[8]Although several commentators agree that Jas 4:1-12 should be considered a unit or sub-unit within the Epistle (so Davids, *James*, 155-156; Mußner, *Jakobusbrief*, 175-176; Reicke, *James, Peter and Jude*, 44-47; and Ropes, *St. James*, 252), there is no consensus as to how the unit/sub-unit should be divided into its component sections.

[9]See the discussion of "Inverted Parallelisms and Thematization" in chapter 2 above. It is perhaps uncertainty regarding whether these verses contribute more to what precedes or to what follows which has led some commentators to treat them as an independent unit (so Cantinat, *Jacques et Jude*, 212; Easton, *IB* 12:58; Laws, *James*, 186; and Vouga, *Jacques*, 120). Interestingly, Dibelius dissents ("in spite of certain hesitations") at this point and includes vv. 11-12 as part of a "series of admonitions" in 4:7-12 (*James*, 208; see also 228-229).

[10]At least within the sub-unit 4:1-12; these verses are more integrally involved in the discussion which develops in the final discursive unit of the Epistle, and so there will be treated as the opening verses of a section 4:11-17 in the sub-unit 4:11 -

The delineation of other sections within this sub-unit, however, is more problematic. A major complicating factor is the introduction of a scriptural quotation beginning at Jas 4:5a ("do you think that the scripture speaks for no reason?"). I say "beginning at 4:5a" because there has been considerable scholarly discussion of (if not indeed consternation at) the fact that what follows in 4:5b is neither a quotation nor even a clear allusion to any identifiable passage from scripture. I will return to these questions below; let it suffice here to note that the conjunction οὖν ("therefore") in Jas 4:7 would seem to mark the rationale for the inclusion of the citation or allusion. The conjunction οὖν also appears in 4:4b, there clearly marking the conclusion to be drawn from the rhetorical question of 4:4a. Thus, I propose dividing this sub-unit into three sections: Jas 4:1-4 describing the actions of evil desire as "friendship with the world [and] enmity with God" (4:4), 4:5-10 issuing a call to humble oneself in the presence of God, and 4:11-12 reminding the readers of their impending judgment.

Before proceeding into the exegesis, we need to note an important characteristic of the discursive unit Jas 3:1 - 4:12. There are no convictions of the author emphasized by opposition of actions anywhere within this unit.[11] We have already seen how certain of James's convictions are expressed through the themes of this unit (e.g., convictions regarding the proper functions of "teachers" and that "judgment" awaits all believers), but none of these convictions are emphasized by oppositions of actions. Thus, this discursive unit is fully thematic and will develop its argument by drawing heavily upon the beliefs of the implied readers. In the exegesis that follows, then, we will only be looking at the process of figurativization.

5:9 (see the discussion of thematization in the next chapter). Their role here in 3:1 - 4:12 has been aptly described by Moo "as a brief 'reprise' of the larger discussion of sins of speech that opened the section (3:1-12)" (*James*, 151), although again I believe "sins of speech" to be the sub-theme rather than the primary theme of this unit and so would emphasize the "reprise" of the theme of judgment in Jas 3:1.

[11]There are two possibilities for such emphases of convictions within this unit. The first is found in Jas 3:9 where we have the opposed actions of "blessing" and "cursing;" however, since the receivers are only similar and not truly identical (the receiver of the positive action "blessing" is "God," whereas the receiver of the negative action "cursing" is "human beings who have been made according to the likeness of God"), this is not an *explicit* opposition of actions. There is an explicit opposition of actions in 4:11 ("not speaking against another" *vs.* "speaking against a brother or sister or judging his [or her] brother [or sister]"), but it is related to the themes of the final unit and its first sub-unit.

Exegesis and Commentary

Human Wisdom and Action (Jas 3:1-18)

Jas 3:1-5a — Proper Use of Human Speech

Figurativization in Jas 3:1-5a

James opens this discursive unit by admonishing his readers "not
... to become teachers."[12] The choice of this figure to open a thematic
unit (and its formulation within a prohibition) provides clear evidence
that the teaching office within the church was both highly important and
greatly esteemed within his community. Seizing on his lead in this
regard, many commentators have discussed the roles of and attitudes
about teachers within early Christian communities.[13] However, most
of this discussion about the roles and functions of teachers probably
directs attention away from James's concerns in utilizing the figure.
Since the theme of this unit is focused on the attitudes of individuals
rather than the particulars of their functions within the community,[14]
the details about the teaching office do not seem overly important to
James's development of that theme. What is of importance in this
regard for James's use of this figure to represent the readers' desire to
be teachers is the esteem for and high social status ascribed to teachers
within the community. Thus, their striving for such an office is another
indication of their preoccupation with achieving signs of status[15] (cf.
the στέφανος of Jas 1:12 and their identification with the rich in Jas 2:2-
4). Such longing for the trappings of social rank stand in stark contrast

---

[12]Dibelius (*James*, 182) noted that the imperative of γίνεσθαι is often substituted
for the imperative of εἶναι "precisely in paraenetic imperatives. Therefore the
meaning here is: 'Not many of you are to be teachers.'" I question whether there
is any real distinction between "become" or "be" in this case; the point is to restrict
the aspirations of the readers to assume the (either present or future) role of teachers
(or other positions of high status) within the community.

[13]See especially Laws, *James*, 140-144; cf. Davids, *James*, 136; Moo, *James*,
119; and Joachim Wanke, "Die urchristlichen Lehrer nach dem Zeugnis des
Jakobusbriefes," in *Die Kirche des Anfangs*, Festschrift for Heinz Schürmann, ed.
Rudolf Schnackenburg, Josef Ernst and Joachim Wanke, ETS 38 (Leipzig: St.
Benno-Verlag, 1977), 506-508.

[14]See the discussion above of the inverted parallelisms marking not only the
discursive unit of Jas 3:1 - 4:12 as a whole, but also of those marking the sub-unit
3:1-18 more particularly.

[15]Cf. Dibelius's comment (*James*, 183) that James "does not have in mind the
occasional functioning of Christians as teachers, but rather a certain *thronging*
toward the vocation of teacher" (emphasis mine).

to the attitude of "humbling oneself in the presence of the Lord" (4:10) which provides the goal toward which this unit is progressing.

Recognizing the thematic emphasis on the attitude of individual believers also helps us to distinguish the implied author's investment in the figures of the following verses from those investments by the implied readers. Martin utilized the opening figure of "teachers" specifically as the controlling factor for understanding the subsequent images. Thus, all of Jas 3:1-12 belongs to "a discussion where (i) 'the body' [see 3:2b] in question is the ecclesial one, not the anatomical one, and (ii) the tongue is used in a setting of the congregation at worship." He finds additional support in the "liturgical setting in which 'praising God' is the chief component" (see 3:9-10) and develops corporate interpretations of the metaphors about horses and ships (3:3-4) where the tongue of the teacher is represented by the bit and rudder.[16]   By making such investments of meaning in these figures, Martin is fulfilling the role of the implied reader by emphasizing a concern for status within the corporate life of the community in his understanding of these figures.

But our analysis of the theme of this sub-unit showed that James's purposes here are directed at the attitudes of the individual believer, not the functioning of the corporate body of the community.[17]   James begins to focus on this particular concern for the individual's actions with the confession, "Indeed, we all sin in many things" (Jas 3:2a). The use of πολλά in this sentence is somewhat ambiguous in that it may refer to either the number ("many sins") or the variety ("sin in many things") of sins that are committed.[18]   Either interpretation is possible, but slight preference should be given to the variety of sins since he immediately moves to narrow the focus on speech as a sign that one who does not sin in that area "is able to control even the whole body" (3:2b) and by implication the other sins which it might commit. James also moves to include his readers among those who sin ("we all sin")—since they had been excluded from the first person of the discourse by the

---

[16]Martin, *James*, 103-107. Similar interpretations with an emphasis upon the speech of teachers and their influence over the community may be found in Mußner, *Jakobusbrief*, 157-168 (note especially 158); Wanke, "Urchristlichen Lehrer," 492; and Reicke, *James, Peter and Jude*, 37-38 (although his interpretation of Jas 3:6 seems to shift away from this corporate interpretation of "body" and "tongue").

[17]Thus, corporate interpretations of the figures in Jas 3:3-4 were replaced with individualist readings by Dibelius (*James*, 184-185, especially n. 21), Davids (*James*, 139), and Laws (*James*, 146), although her characterization of the corporate interpretations as "a flight of fancy" is unduly harsh.

[18]Cf. Martin, *James*, 109, who leaves the question open.

statement that "we [teachers] will receive stricter judgment" (3:1b)—and so also to include them among those who will be judged.[19]

James builds on the positive function of speech in controlling actions by means of metaphors involving bits or bridles used to control horses and the rudders used to steer boats.[20] Some have objected that these metaphors do not truly fit, since one cannot say that the tongue actually "controls" the body.[21] If it is considered necessary that there be some kind of direct correspondence, the explanation offered by Moo may provide it:

> just as the bit determines the direction of the horse and the rudder the ship, so the tongue can determine the destiny of the individual. When the believer exercises careful control of the tongue, it can be presumed that he also is able to direct his whole life in its proper, divinely charted course: he is a 'perfect man' (v. 2).[22]

More probably, however, the connection is more general. Given the theme of this unit, it may be that we have here another way of expressing the idea found in Matt 12:34 // Luke 6:45 that "out of the abundance of the heart the mouth speaks." Though the tongue may be small, it is a clear indicator of the internal desires that control all the actions of the person (note that James explicitly mentions that "boats ... are guided by a very small rudder *wherever the will of the pilot desires*" [3:4]).[23]

---

[19]Thus, I perceive the rhetorical move as in the opposite direction from those who see James modestly including himself among his sinful readers (so Martin, *James*, 109; and Reicke, *James, Peter and Jude*, 37 [who continues to exclude the readers by his comment that "no preacher is faultless"]); cf. Davids, *James*, 137.

[20]There is a rather notorious textual problem at the beginning of Jas 3:3 regarding whether to read εἰ δέ ("if") or ἴδε ("see;" cf. *TCGNT*, 681-682). Davids (*James*, 138) provides a fine summary of the problems and scholarly positions. My preference is to follow Davids in reading a conditional clause here. However, both readings make clear that already in 3:3 there is a contrast between the small bit and the large horse controlled by it such as is found in the following metaphors of the rudder and the flame.

[21]Martin makes much of this apparent incongruity in arguing for his view that the "tongue" symbolizes "teachers" who exercise "control" over the "body" of the church; see *James*, 110-111.

[22]Moo, *James*, 122; cf. Adamson, *James*, 143 (despite the attempt by Martin [*James*, 111-112] to enlist him in support of his communal interpretation).

[23]Cf. the comment by Davids (*James*, 140): "It is not that the tongue steers the ship, but that the proper helmsman is often not in control."

Dibelius argued that James had taken a sequence of optimistic metaphors from the classical tradition and shifted them to a pessimistic assessment of the great negative effects of small things.[24] However, nothing yet in this section (Jas 3:1-5a) would have indicated to the reader that James intends these figures to be understood in a negative light; it is only the clearly negative image of the "tongue [as] a fire ... set ablaze by Hell" (3:6) in the next section which brings in the potentially negative effects of the power of the tongue.[25] To this point in the opening section of the sub-unit, James has only offered support of his contention that the one who "does not sin in speech ... is a mature person able to control/bridle even the whole body."

James does, however, prepare the reader for the negative appraisal of human speech that will come in the next section by the ambiguity of his summation in 3:5a—"Likewise the tongue is also a small part, yet it boasts (αὐχεῖ) great things." The idea of "boasting" has already occurred in Jas 1:9 where, we have seen, the readers identified themselves with the "poor/humble brothers and sisters [who] boast (καυχάομαι) in the exaltation" of their eschatological salvation; thus, we may anticipate that the initial inclination of the readers will be to view "boasting" here in 3:5a in positive terms. But James had a more negative view of the "boasting" in 1:9, since it was for him an indication of their striving for the trappings of power and status (see the discussion of this verse in chapter 3 above). The subsequent uses of "boasting" within the Epistle (3:14 and 4:16) will become increasingly negative, culminating in James's denunciation in 4:16—"But now you boast in your pretensions; all such boasting is evil." In the light of the thematic

---

[24]Dibelius, *James*, 185-191, especially 186. As examples of the specific linkage of equestrian and nautical images, see his citations (ibid., 187-188 n. 41) from Stobaeus ("The one in control of pleasure is not he who abstains, but he who partakes and yet is not carried away by it. Just as with both a ship and a horse, it is not the person who does not use them who is in control, but rather the person who guides them wherever he wishes," *Ecl.* 3.17.17) and Theophylactus Simocatta ("We guide horses with reins and whips, and we sail the ship by unfurling the sails and we bring it into harbor by 'bridling' it with anchors. In the same way, Axiochus, it is necessary also to steer the tongue," *Ep.* 70) as well as Lucretius, Dio Chrysostum, and Philo. Dibelius provided a wealth of examples in the notes to these pages.

[25]Cf. Davids (*James*, 140: there was "not so much a pessimistic change in usage, but a slow shift in thought from the power of the tongue to the evil of the tongue to the need for proper control"), and Laws (*James*, 148), who resisted trying to assign any particular images as positive or negative but rather saw them "as building up an argument through a chain of associated ideas."

development in this discursive unit, it does not seem merely coincidental that along with "boasting" in Jas 1:9 we also found mention of "humility" and "exaltation" (cf. Jas 4:10).

Thus, James allows the corporate and individualist, the positive and the negative investments in the figures to play off one another freely in this introductory section. His readers emphasize the positive effects that their speech as teachers will have in controlling the actions of the corporate body of the community. Yet even in the very process of acknowledging the possible positive influence of the tongue, James implies that an individual's speech (specifically its "boasting great things") is more often one of "many things" in which "we all sin" and thereby demonstrate our lack of "control [over] the whole body."[26] Within the section that follows (3:5b-12), James will attempt to persuade his readers to accept his individualist and negative understanding of the figures by making it increasingly difficult for them to sustain their own positive, corporate investments.

Jas 3:5b-12 — Improper Use of Human Speech

Figurativization in Jas 3:5b-12

Although the tongue may exercise a positive influence over a believer's life, James is at pains within this section to show that all too frequently its influence is anything but positive. Despite the heated rhetoric in 3:5b-8, the final verses of this section (Jas 3:9-12) will show that the negative influence of the tongue is not a consequence of it being an unmitigated evil. It is precisely because the tongue is both positive and negative (capable of both "blessing" and "cursing") that it is an "unstable evil" (ἀκατάστατον κακόν; 3:8b) and therefore so pernicious.

James opens this section with another figure along the lines of 'how small an object—how great its effects:' "How small a flame ignites so large a brushwood!"[27] (Jas 3:5b). What distinguishes this figure

---

[26]Martin, despite his persistent emphasis upon corporate interpretations of the figures throughout Jas 3:3-12 (see n. 16 above), later seemed to recognize the polysemism of these figures: "The use of 'body' in several places has a meaning that oscillates between the anatomical human body, of which the tongue forms a small yet powerful member, and the body of the congregation, in which the tongues of teachers exercise a baneful influence" (*James*, 123).

[27]The translation of the Greek term ὕλη by "brushwood" probably better preserves the image of the figure for Euro-Americans than the traditional translation "forest" given our general association of that term with large areas of old-growth hardwood forestation. The dominate forestation patterns and climate of Palestine

from the previous (positive) ones regarding the bit and the rudder is its
unmistakably negative connotations. James explicitly identifies the
tongue ("The tongue is a fire," Jas 3:6) with a flame or spark which
ignites and quickly spreads into a destructive brushfire. Dibelius noted
an interesting relationship in the traditional uses of these figures: "as the
helmsman and the charioteer are typical illustrations of the dominance
of reason, so fire is a favorite metaphor in diatribe to represent the rule
of the passions and desire."[28] Thus, James may have chosen this
particular figure not only to move the readers to consider the (potentially) negative effects of the tongue, but also to prepare the ground for the
emphasis on internal "desires" and "passions" in the next sub-unit.

The emphasis within 3:6 is clearly upon just how evil the consequences of improper human speech may be: "The tongue has been
established among our members as the unrighteous world,[29] staining
the whole body and setting ablaze the course of life,[30] having (itself)
been set ablaze by Hell." Nevertheless, these strong negative images do
not nullify James's earlier positive descriptions of the tongue. The
problem is one of control; but this is no minor problem since, despite
successes in other areas of human endeavor, "no one among humanity
is able to control the tongue" (3:8). Such a declaration would seem to

---

(and much of the eastern Mediterranean basin generally) suggests the term means
something akin to "brushwood" or "undergrowth." See Leonard E. Elliott-Binns,
"The Meaning of ὕλη in Jas. iii. 5," *NTS* 2 (1955/56): 48-50.

[28]Dibelius, *James*, 192. For examples of classical illustrations involving the
helmsman and charioteer, see n. 24 above; Dibelius cited examples of "flame" as
a metaphor for passions from Plutarch (*Praec. coniug.* 4; *De cohib. ira* 4), Philo
(*Spec. leg.* 4.83; *Decal.* 49 and 173), and others on ibid., 192-193 nn. 58 and 59.

[29]This clause is both syntactically and textually problematic; nevertheless, it is
possible to make sense of the traditional text (without making appeals either to the
Syriac [so Adamson, *James*, 185] or theorizing that a marginal gloss has worked its
way into the text [a possibility suggested by Dibelius, *James*, 194-195]). In support
of a translation akin to the one given here, see Laws, *James*, 149-150; Martin,
James, 113-115; Moo, *James*, 125; and Ropes, *St. James*, 234.

[30]As with the astronomical terminology in Jas 1:17, we have here a technical
phrase (apparently an Orphic formulation) that is being employed in a very general
sense. Thus, although arguing from its history that the term should be accented
τροχός ("cycle [of becoming]") rather than τρόχος ("course"), Dibelius (*James*, 198)
concedes that it here "is signifying little more than 'life,' perhaps with a pessimistic
overtone such as others of the period heard in the words 'Necessity' (Ἀνάγκη see
Philo) and 'Fate' (Εἰμαρμένη see Simplicus)." For detailed treatments of the phrase
ὁ τροχὸς τῆς γενέσεως, see ibid., 196-198; and Ropes, *St. James*, 235-239. For its
translation here as "the whole course of life," see Davids, *James*, 143.

indicate that there can be no "mature person" in the terms set down in 3:2b. But we must remember that the discourse of the Epistle is not structured as a logical syllogism. In both 3:2b and 8 we are confronted with more 'poetic' forms of language; as Laws has observed, here we have "the language ... of hyperbole, with an understood exhortation to strive to do precisely what is said to be impossible."[31]

Because it is so difficult to "control/bridle" the tongue, "it is an unstable (ἀκατάστατον) evil, full of lethal poison" (3:8b). This idea of instability was earlier used to describe the "double-minded person [who is] unstable in all of his [or her] ways" (1:8). Thus, the problem with the tongue is not that it is totally evil, but that it is inconsistent by being both good and bad. Again citing Laws:

> At this point, James at last provides a specific example of the evil working of the tongue; and typically for this author the sin described is one of inconsistency, doubleness: *with it we bless the Lord and Father, and with it also we curse men.* James does not pause to commend blessing or to condemn cursing *per se* ..., for it is their incongruity with which he is concerned (and which would presumably for him render the blessing valueless). ...
> James sharpens the incongruity by reminding his readers that men *are made 'in the likeness' of God*, and so both the blessing and the curse are in a way addressed to God.[32]

Is it any wonder that "double-minded persons" (Jas 1:8), who according to James's pattern of beliefs both trust and distrust God whom they believe gives both good ("wisdom") and bad ("trials"), exemplify a similar inconsistency in their own speech?

I suggested in discussing the previous section that James may have invested the figures of the bridle and the rudder with a meaning along the lines of "out of the abundance of the heart, the mouth speaks." This interpretation gains support from his statement in this section that "from out of the same mouth comes blessing and curse" (3:10a). As Martin has stated it, what is "at issue is the observation that what comes out (ἐξέρχεσθαι; cf. Matt 15:19) of a person is what defiles that person (Matt 15:11, 20)."[33] This association would explain how the "tongue ... stains the whole body and sets ablaze the course of life" (Jas 3:6b).

---

[31]Laws, *James*, 154.
[32]Ibid., 154-155. Cf. Davids, *James*, 145.
[33]Martin, *James*, 120.

It is as though one's speech (whether thought of as communicated through the tongue or mouth) cannot hide but must express what is in one's heart. If an individual is τέλειος ἀνήρ then he both praises God and speaks well of persons. But if he is disposed toward deceit and hypocrisy, this will inevitably come out in speech.[34]

The inevitability of one's true inner nature being manifested by one's speech (as a prime example of all one's actions) is then driven home by the flurry of rhetorical questions which concludes this section. "Can a spring pour sweet and bitter [water] from the same opening? Can a fig tree, my brothers [and sisters], bear olives or a grapevine figs? No more so than salty water can be made sweet!" (Jas 3:11-12). Thus, the point ultimately is not merely that speaking both "blessing" and "cursing" is incongruous, but that such should be impossible for one whose nature has been changed "by the implanted word" (see Jas 1:21).

We see then that James has used the progression of figures to virtually foreclose any possibility of the readers maintaining their corporate interpretations. Despite his suggestion that the saying regarding "blessing the Lord and Father, and ... cursing human beings" (3:9) reflects a "liturgical setting" of corporate worship and teaching, even Martin ultimately conceded that those words communicate James's contention that "one's speech ... cannot hide but must express what is in one's heart."[35] James thus utilized this progression of figures to compel his readers to consider their own inner attitudes rather than their social status before other members of the community.[36]

---

[34]Ibid. Note, however, that this interpretation undercuts the corporate understanding of the earlier metaphors that Martin had argued for, or at least provides the basis for the individualist readings.

[35]See again Martin, *James*, 104 and 120 respectively.

[36]This progressive development of figures to incrementally restrict the possible semantic investments by the readers and so lead them to accept the implied author's own investments would seem to be a characteristic of James's argumentative style. Cf. his development of the πειρασμός/πειράζω figures in Jas 1:2-13 whereby he challenges his readers to see their hardships as the result of being "tempted" by their "desires" rather than being "tested" by God (see especially the exegesis of the figurativization in Jas 1:13-16 in chapter 3 above).

Jas 3:13-18 — True Wisdom Shown by Actions

Figurativization in Jas 3:13-18

The final section of this sub-unit emphasizes James's foundational concern that one's actions (particularly one's speech) manifest the person's internal attitudes.[37] It repeats in its basic structure the general movement of the sub-unit as a whole, beginning with the ability of positive actions to demonstrate one's wisdom (3:13; cf. 3:1-5a, especially v. 2b), contrasting that with the detrimental effects of negative actions (3:14-16; cf. 3:5b-12, especially v. 6b), and concluding by emphasizing once again the positive actions which arise from wisdom (3:17-18).[38] The proof of what is inside a person is the actions performed by that person.

If the question then is, "Who is wise and intelligent among you?" (Jas 3:13a), the answer to that question will only be found when the "wise and intelligent ... by good conduct show that [their] works are [performed] by humility characteristic of wisdom"[39] (Jas 3:13b). The difficulties of the Greek syntax within this verse (δειξάτω ἐκ τῆς καλῆς ἀναστροφῆς τὰ ἔργα αὐτοῦ ἐν πραΰτητι σοφίας) arise from the fact that, as Dibelius noted, the clause "combines two thoughts. First, the wise person provides factual proof of this wisdom by a good life. Secondly, the wise person shows this wisdom in meekness."[40]

On this first point, it is clear that the relationship between "good conduct" and "wisdom" is a repetition of the pattern exhibited earlier between "faith" and "works." As Hartin described it,

---

[37]Cf. Davids's comments (*James*, 149) on the relationship between 3:12b and the following section 3:13-18: "James has moved from the impossibility of one nature producing two results to the observation that one's works reveal his true inspiration."

[38]On the "consciously constructed unity" within the section Jas 3:13-18 provided by the inclusio between 3:13 and 17-18, cf. Hartin, *James and Q*, 97-98.

[39]Reicke (*James, Peter and Jude*, 41 and n. 24 on 65) noted that σοφίας may be either a qualitative genitive ("wise humility") or a genitive of limitation ("humility as concerns wisdom"). I have preferred the former since the actions which characterize "the wisdom which is from above" are a particular concern of this section (see especially Jas 3:11), and James does not seem to want to restrict "humility" just to the domain of "wisdom" (cf. 4:10).

[40]Dibelius, *James*, 209. Contra Ropes (*St. James*, 244) that the wise person "is here called on to prove not (as many commentators suppose) his wisdom (which would require δειξάτω τὴν σοφίαν), but his meekness." Note, however, that πραΰτης is itself not in the accusative case here, but rather in the dative ("show ... by humility").

Jas 3.13 argues that the way of life should demonstrate that works are influenced by wisdom. These works will show wisdom, just as they illustrated faith. Wisdom, then, must be demonstrated in action. It is not just an intellectual concept, but something that involves the very life of the believer.[41]

This interrelationship is not surprising since both "faith" and "wisdom" are antecedent to "works"/"conduct" within James's system of convictions; it is the presence of "faith" which makes possible the reception of "wisdom" that determines what one's actions ("works"/"conduct") should be.[42]

But it is the second point—that one demonstrate the presence of such wisdom "by humility"—that is of particular concern to James in what follows. More precisely, his concern is that the attempts by the implied readers to "show wisdom" are characterized by "bitter rivalry and ambition" (3:14a) rather than humility.[43] This much is clear, even if ambiguity continues to cloud any precise understanding of the related prohibition (μὴ κατακαυχᾶσθε καὶ ψεύδεσθε κατὰ τῆς ἀληθείας). Some commentators have argued that there must be an implied object for verb "boast," and have suggested translations along the lines of either "do not boast about what is actually sinful (e.g., rivalry and ambition) and thereby lie against the truth"[44] or "do not boast about your wisdom (which your rivalry and ambition prove you lack) and so deny the truth."[45] Dibelius, however, specifically rejected any attempt to supply an object, preferring to translate the clause as "do not boast with lies in defiance of the truth."[46] Yet another possibility is that the prepositional phrase κατὰ τῆς ἀληθείας is the *de facto* object of both verbs, and the clause should be rendered as "do not degrade and lie against the truth."[47] Each of these possibilities in its own way makes

---

[41]Hartin, *James and Q*, 100.

[42]See the schematic presentation of James's system of convictions at the end of chapter 4.

[43]Cf. Reicke, *James, Peter and Jude*, 41-42: "The recipients of the epistle do not behave [with good Christian behavior in humility]. According to vs. 14 they strive after wisdom as a means of success in society only, displaying aggressiveness and ambition."

[44]So Ropes, *St. James*, 246; Laws, *James*, 160; and Mußner, *Jakobusbrief*, 171.

[45]So Mayor, *St. James*, 127-128; Moo, *James*, 133; and Martin, *James*, 131.

[46]Dibelius, *James*, 210; cf. Cantinat, *Jacques et Jude*, 189. Davids (*James*, 151) characterized this rendering as a form of hendiadys.

[47]On the translation of κατακαυχάομαι as "to degrade," see Louw and Nida, *Greek-English Lexicon*, §33.370 (1:431). This reconstruction of the syntax gains

the point that the presence of "bitter rivalry and ambition" proves one has not "by meekness received the implanted word" (Jas 1:21).

James emphasizes that the attitude of "rivalry and ambition ... is not the wisdom which comes down from above" (3:15), i.e. the wisdom which is "a good gift and ... perfect present ... coming down from the Father of Lights" (Jas 1:17). It is important to note that by saying that such "is not the wisdom" given by God, he is not implying that in his view there is some other kind of wisdom which might be characterized as "earthly, unspiritual, demonic."[48] There is no other wisdom for James than that which has been given by God. The attitude that leads to rivalry and ambition is "earthly, unspiritual, [and] demonic," and may not be characterized as "wisdom."[49] Indeed such attitudes are for James a virtual 'anti-wisdom.'

Whereas "rivalry and ambition" result in "rebellion and every bad deed" (Jas 3:16), "the wisdom from above is first of all pure, then peaceful, gentle, obedient, full of mercy and good fruits, impartial" (3:17). But by this string of adjectives, James

> tells us what effects divine wisdom should produce—for almost all of these adjectives describe what wisdom does rather than what it is. It is again clear that James does not view *wisdom* as a series of correct propositional statements, but as a quality that motivates certain kinds of behavior.[50]

Within James's system of convictions, "wisdom" is a knowledge about God and God's purposes which establishes the believer's will to act as God acts.[51] Rather than resulting in "bitter rivalry and ambition," "the fruit of righteousness [and so also wisdom] is sown in peace by those who make peace" (3:18).

---

some support from the variant reading of $\aleph^{(2)}$ syr^p 33 with the word order τῆς ἀληθείας καὶ ψεύδεσθε (with the preposition κατά no longer needed to relate it to the verb with that prefix). This option was rejected by Ropes (*St. James*, 246) because "the idea of 'boasting over (*or* against) the truth' is out of place in the context;" however, the alternative translation of "degrading the truth" would not seem to violate the context.

[48]As has been inferred by Moo, *James*, 134; Davids, *James*, 152; Ropes, *St. James*, 247-248; Dibelius, *James*, 210; and Vouga, *Jacques*, 105-106, among others.

[49]Cf. Hartin, *James and Q*, 104; and Laws, *James*, 162-163.

[50]Moo, *James*, 135. Cf. Laws, *James*, 163; and Martin, *James*, 133.

[51]Cf. Hartin, *James and Q*, 108; and Davids, *James*, 154.

Summary of Jas 3:1-18

Looking back on the unfolding of this discursive sub-unit, we see that the corporate interpretation of the figures in Jas 3:2b-5a suggested by Martin does in fact reflect the initial investments in meaning by the implied readers. They perceive themselves as "mature persons" who do not commit errors in what they say, and so they desire to "become teachers." The use of the 'so small yet so great' images might even indicate for them a kind of (false) humility; although they recognize that they are only a tiny part of the community, they seek to control and direct its conduct. What motivates them, however, is nothing more than "bitter rivalry and ambition," and the result (as will again be emphasized in Jas 4:1-4) can only be "rebellion and every bad deed."

James attempts to redirect the attention of his readers. By investing the figures within this sub-unit with individualist meanings and applications, he endeavors to lead them to be more introspective and less obsessed with their status before others. He once again stresses that their actions will demonstrate their true motivation either as being established by "faith" in God as "pure good" and by "wisdom" regarding God's will (cf. Jas 2:14-26), or as being established by their own "(evil) desires." If their actions emerge from "faith" and "wisdom," there will be the positive benefit of "peace;" but if their actions continue to be driven by "ambition," the only possible consequence can be "rebellion and every bad deed."

The Grounds for Judgment
(Jas 4:1-12)

Jas 4:1-4 — The Actions of Evil Desire

Figurativization in Jas 4:1-4

We saw in the previous sub-unit that there seem to be competing tendencies between James and the implied readers over whether the figures within this unit should be invested with corporate or individualist meanings. Those same tensions are clearly in evidence in the opening verse of this section. James's initial rhetorical question appears clearly to have a corporate reference: "From where do quarrels and disputes[52] among you arise?" (4:1a). However, the rhetorical question

---

[52]The terms for "quarrels" (πόλεμοι) and "disputes" (μάχαι) employed here are extremely harsh, normally having the meanings "wars" and "battles" respectively. However, both were often used in paraenetic texts to refer to strife and quarrels (see

which he offers in answer would seem to rely on the individualist interpretation of the previous sub-unit for its substantiation: "Do they not originate here, from your passions which are at war within your members?" (4:1b).

Not surprisingly, some commentators have tried to monolithically impose either individualist or corporate meanings upon the language. Those who favored corporate interpretations of the figures in Jas 3:3-5 likewise saw the "members" in 4:1b as different persons in the Christian community.[53] Conversely, some have preferred to emphasize the second rhetorical question and "to understand the division as within the individual, himself in his own body torn by differing desires, ... [as] would be consistent with James's recurrent theme of the divided man (cf. 1:6-8, 2:4, 2:14-17, 3:9-10)."[54] Other commentators proposed mediating positions so that the "disputes among you" in 4:1a "refer to inner-community conflicts occasioned by the party spirit of the teachers," while the "war within your members" of 4:1b reflects "a movement from external conflict in the community to its internal basis."[55]

James uses these tensions/ambiguities to great rhetorical effect. His system of convictions strongly supports understanding the figure of "war within your members" as an internal struggle between the competing "passions" of the "double-minded person." But as the preceding sub-unit demonstrated, such internal attitudes will inevitably lead to actions resulting in "quarrels and disputes" between the various members of the community as well. If there is "war" (στρατεύομαι) rather than "peace" (cf. Jas 3:18) within the individual believer, then there will be "wars" (πόλεμοι) rather than "peace" among the members of the community. James continues to juxtapose internal evil desires and external evil acts in the following verses.

The staccato fashion of the phrasing in Jas 4:2-3 presents some difficulty in reconstructing the relationship between the individual

---

Dibelius, *James*, 216 n. 44, for examples). The verbal cognates of both terms are found in Jas 4:2.

[53]Thus, Ropes comments (*St. James*, 253), "The war is between pleasures which have their seat in the bodies of several persons, not between conflicting pleasures throwing an individual into a state of internal strife and confusion. Since the pleasures clash, the persons who take them as their supreme aim are necessarily brought into conflict." Cf. also Martin, *James*, 140 and 144-145; and Reicke, *James, Peter and Jude*, 45-46.

[54]Laws, *James*, 168. Cf. Dibelius, *James*, 216.

[55]Davids, *James*, 156-157. Cf. also Mußner, *Jakobusbrief*, 176-177; and Kugelman, *James and Jude*, 45-46.

phrases. Two such structures have been proposed. The first is a chiastic arrangement suggested by Dibelius:[56]

a₁ You desire—
    and you do not have;

ἐπιθυμεῖτε—
    καὶ οὐκ ἔχετε

b₁ you are jealous and
    envious—
    and you do not obtain
    (what you covet);

φθονεῖτε καὶ ζηλοῦτε—
    καὶ οὐ δύνασθε ἐπιτυχεῖν

b₂ you fight and strive—
    and you do not have
    because you do not
    ask;

μάχεσθε καὶ πολεμεῖτε—
    καὶ οὐκ ἔχετε διὰ τὸ μὴ
    αἰτεῖσθαι ὑμᾶς

a₂ you ask—
    and you do not receive
    because you ask with
    the wrong motive ...

αἰτεῖτε—
    καὶ οὐ λαμβάνετε, διότι
    κακῶς αἰτεῖσθε κτλ.

It should be noted that Dibelius has here adopted a conjectural emendation to the Greek text first suggested by Erasmus in substituting φθονεῖτε ("you are jealous") for φονεύετε "you murder") at the beginning of b₁. He favored this emendation because he felt that "murder" neither fit the immediate context of the juxtaposition with "envy" (ζηλοῦτε) nor the general context of Jas 4:2-3, and further these "two Greek roots for 'jealousy' appear together frequently in related texts."[57] Several commentators adopt this chiastic arrangement while maintaining φονεύετε by "metaphorically" interpreting the "murder" either as the withholding of aid from or oppression of the poor,[58] or as related to deaths variously brought about by involvement in political insurrection movements.[59]

---

[56]See Dibelius, *James*, 218.

[57]For his full argument supporting the conjectural emendation, see ibid., 217-218. Adamson (*James*, 167-169) also adopts the emendation. Ropes (*St. James*, 254) also perceived φονεύετε καὶ ζηλοῦτε as an "impossible anticlimax," but maintained the traditional text and employed the "anticlimax" as an argument for a major break after "you murder" (see discussion of the alternative structure below).

[58]So Davids, *James*, 157-159; and Mußner, *Jakobusbrief*, 178-180.

[59]So Reicke, *James, Peter and Jude*, 45. Similar interpretations of the meaning

There are, however, some significant difficulties with this chiastic ordering of the phrases. The first is that the καί which marks the second stiche of element b₂ is lacking in some manuscripts.[60] The stylistic balance of b₂ is further disrupted by the fact that the stiche "you do not have because you do not ask" is both significantly more complex than the second stiche of the first two elements and not as clearly related to the content of the first stiche of b₂ ("you fight and strive"). Secondly, element a₂ breaks the formal symmetry both in that its first stiche carries forward the thought of the second stiche of b₂ rather than continuing the parallelism between the initial stiche of the first three elements and by its unbalanced length.[61]

Beyond these stylistic issues there is also a contextual problem with this interpretation. Whereas the rhetorical questions of 4:1 stressed James's conviction that external actions ("quarrels and disputes") originate from internal desires ("your passions which are at war within your members"), Dibelius's chiastic arrangement tends to reverse this relationship. It seems as if the external actions of the second stiche in each element of the chiasmus explain the origin of the internal attitude expressed in its opening stiche. Thus, "you desire [because] you do not have; you are jealous and envious [because] you do not obtain; you [must] fight and strive [because] you do not ask." This ordering of the relationships is certainly inconsistent with James's pattern of beliefs, and there is no clear evidence that it might reflect the beliefs of his readers.

The second option for structuring the phrases of Jas 4:2-3 is as couplets, and in the case of the first two as parallel couplets:[62]

---

of "murder" in 4:2 have been offered by Michael J. Townsend, "James 4:1-4: A Warning against Zealotry?" *ExpTim* 87 (1976): 211-213; and Martin, *James*, 140-141 and 146.

[60]The καί is omitted in A B and the Koiné witnesses; it is found in ℵ P Ψ and numerous minuscules, but its authenticity is called into doubt by the insertion of the conjunction δέ in other (albeit late) minuscules. Its importance to the chiastic arrangement is evident from Dibelius's own emphasis of the καὶ οὐ(κ) repetition at the beginning of the second stiche of each element (see above).

[61]Indeed, element a₂ is two-thirds the length of the other three elements combined (31 syllables as compared to 48), a fact suppressed by Dibelius's ellipses. It may be for similar reasons that Adamson (*James*, 167-169), Martin (*James*, 139-141 and 145-147), and Vouga (*Jacques*, 111 and 113-114) each utilize Dibelius's basic punctuation of Jas 4:2, but do not accept a chiastic ordering of the full content of Jas 4:2 and 3.

[62]Cf. Ropes, *St. James*, 254-258; Laws, *James*, 169-172; Cantinat, *Jacques et Jude*, 197-200; Kugelman, *James and Jude*, 46-47; Moo, *James*, 139-142; and Johnson, "Topos περὶ φθόνου," 329-330. Mayor (*St. James*, 136-137) initially

You desire but do not have, (so) you murder.	ἐπιθυμεῖτε, καὶ οὐκ ἔχετε· φονεύετε.
And you are envious but unable to obtain, (so) you battle and wage war.	καὶ ζηλοῦτε, καὶ οὐ δύνα- σθε ἐπιτυχεῖν· μάχεσθε καὶ πολεμεῖτε.

The final clause of 4:2 and 4:3 may also be structured as a couplet, although it lacks the periodic balance of the initial pair:

You do not have because you do not ask; you ask but do not receive because you ask with evil motives in order that you might squander it on your passions.	οὐκ ἔχετε διὰ τὸ μὴ αἰτεῖσθαι· αἰτεῖτε καὶ οὐ λαμβάνετε, διότι κακῶς αἰτεῖσθε, ἵνα ἐν ταῖς ἡδοναῖς ὑμῶν δαπανήσητε.

On stylistic grounds, this structuring of the phrases in Jas 4:2-3 is more satisfactory since it does not require either conjectural emendation or doubtful variant readings.

But the strongest arguments in support of this structuring are contextual in that it provides a better response to the rhetorical questions of 4:1 in terms of the theme of this discursive unit. Both of the paired couplets establish an internal conflict by the thwarting of one's "passions," which then leads to injurious actions within the community culminating in their "battling and waging war" (μάχεσθε καὶ πολεμεῖτε) which parallels the "quarrels and disputes" (πόλεμοι καὶ ... μάχαι) of the opening rhetorical question. This parallel supports a "metaphorical" interpretation of not only those "battles and wars," but also of the "murders." Yet we should be careful not simply to 'spiritualize' this "murder" as no more than hatred (cf. Matt 5:21-22). As we saw in discussing the reference to the commandment against murder in Jas 2:11, there is reason to believe that James may consider the readers' failure "to care for orphans and widows" (1:27) and other indigent believers (2:15-16) as a kind of "murder."[63] This interpretation will be rein-

---

seems to favor this structure, but then leans toward the conjectural emendation and the resulting parallel structure φθονεῖτε καὶ ζηλοῦτε as in Dibelius and Adamson (see n. 57 above).

[63]See again Davids's discussion of the charge of "murder" in 4:2 (*James*, 159).

forced by the charge against the "rich" in Jas 5:6. The final "couplet" indicates that such internal division is unnecessary: "you do not have because you do not ask" for what is needed from "the God who gives to everyone generously" (Jas 1:5). It also warns that requests arising from "evil motives" will not be answered: recall from Jas 1:7-8 that the "double-minded" (δίψυχος) and "unstable" (ἀκατάστατος; cf. the ἀκατάστατον κακόν of 3:8) person will not receive anything from God.

James brings this section to a close by capturing his readers' attention with the striking address "Adulteresses!" (Jas 4:4a). This vocative may have been suggested to him both by the earlier association between "murder" and "adultery" (2:11)[64] and the usual association of "passions" (ἡδονή) with sexual desire.[65] But the address is striking not only for its harshness, but perhaps even more because it is the only feminine vocative form within the Epistle.[66] What significance should be attached to this choice of gender for addressing the readers?

An intriguing possibility has been suggested by John Schmitt. He has argued that the specific choice of the feminine gender is by way of an allusion to Prov 30:20:

> The ὁδὸς γυναικὸς μοιχαλίδος ("the way of an adulterous woman") is that "having washed herself from her deed, she says she has done nothing wrong" (ἄτοπον, "out of place, unnatural"). ... The point for James is not just the idea of infidelity, but also the style of this sinner. She commits her deed and feels no remorse. She is detached from any consequence of her evil ways. This sinner has lost, or is suppressing, the moral sensitivity that should characterize a friend of God.[67]

Such is certainly an attractive explanation since it is in keeping both with the portrayal of the impunity with which the readers are accused of acting and with the call to repentance in the following section. But it does not adequately relate to the immediately following imagery regarding 'friendship with the world vs. friendship with God' (Jas 4:4) to be conclusive. More likely is the commonly held view that the choice of gender reflects the prophetic tradition of Israel as God's unfaithful wife, transferred to the church more specifically by the early Christian

---

[64]Cf. John J. Schmitt, "You Adulteresses! The Image in James 4:4," *NovT* 28 (1986): 334-335.

[65]See Louw and Nida, *Greek-English Lexicon*, §25.27 [1:292].

[66]A fact not lost on the scribes of ℵ² P Ψ and the Koiné witnesses who inserted μοιχοὶ καί into the text. Cf. *TCGNT*, 682-683.

[67]Schmitt, "You Adulteresses!," 336.

imagery of the "bride of Christ."[68] However, since neither image can claim further development either here or elsewhere within the Epistle, it seems best to leave the question open.[69]

James concludes this section by once again emphasizing that evil actions and desires ("friendship with the world," 4:4) are problems of the human will: "Therefore, whoever *desires* [βουληθῇ] to be a friend of the world is made an enemy of God."[70] Those attitudes and actions which would conversely express a "desire" to be "a friend of God" (cf. Jas 2:23b) will provide the focus for the figurativization of the central section in this discursive sub-unit.

Jas 4:5-10 — Humbling Oneself before God

Figurativization in Jas 4:5-10

In discussing the discursive structure of this sub-unit at the beginning of this chapter, we noted the enigmatic presence of an introduction to a quotation from "scripture" (ἡ γραφή) in Jas 4:5a ("Or do you think that the scripture says for no reason ...") where what follows is clearly not a verbal citation of any passage from either the Hebrew Bible or the New Testament. Given the clearly formulaic language, most commentators have concluded that James must be quoting from some either unknown or no-longer extant apocryphal book.[71] But prior to asking

---

[68]Cf. Dibelius, *James*, 220; Davids, *James*, 160-161; Martin, *James*, 141; Cantinat, *Jacques et Jude*, 201; and numerous others. Schmitt challenges this explanation at its very foundation by questioning whether such "marital symbolism between God and Israel" ever existed. For his critique of this imagery, see "You Adulteresses!," 331-334 and idem, "The Gender of Ancient Israel," *JSOT* 26 (1983): 115-125. However, I remain unconvinced, particularly regarding his arguments relative to Hosea (see "You Adulteresses!," 333 and "Gender of Israel," 119-123).

[69]The ambiguity introduced by these two possibilities is also significant in terms of the general pattern of competing corporate and individualist investments in figures throughout this discursive unit. Schmitt's proposal fits well with the implied author's individualist investments in figures elsewhere in the unit, but the investment drawn from the corporate image of Israel as God's unfaithful wife appears to be more consistent with the immediate context. Thus, the corporate investment of the figure "adulteresses" is possible for James as well as for the readers, and so here we cannot make a sharp distinction between the implied author's and the implied reader's investments.

[70]Cf. Adamson, *James*, 170; and Martin, *James*, 148.

[71]Cf. Davids (*James*, 162) and Adamson (*James*, 170-171) who provide summaries of the proposals offered by various scholars. More recently Moo (*James*,

what James may be citing or alluding to, we need to understand what idea is expressed by the ensuing clause.

The clause contained in Jas 4:5b (πρὸς φθόνον ἐπιποθεῖ τὸ πνεῦμα ὃ κατῴκισεν ἐν ἡμῖν) is ambiguous since morphologically τὸ πνεῦμα can be either nominative or accusative case and thus related to the verb ἐπιποθεῖ as either its subject ("the spirit which [God] caused to dwell in us longs enviously") or its object ("[God] longs jealously for the spirit which [God] caused to dwell in us"). The former possibility is preferred by Laws since "it would compare with other of James's descriptions of man: as δίψυχος, uncertain about his requests in prayer (i. 6-8), and as a battlefield of conflicting desires (iv. 1-3, esp. *v.* 2, ἐπιθυμεῖτε)."[72] She proposed that ἐπιποθεῖ marks an allusion to Ps 83:3 (LXX, ET 84:2) which describes the longing of the human soul for God. She summarizes the argument as follows:

'Is scripture meaningless? (*v. 5a*). Is this (according to scripture) the proper manner of the soul's desire? (*v. 5b*).' The answer implied if the allusion is taken must be, Surely not! The object of the soul's desire is God, and the things of God; and in that situation, as scripture also says, He gives grace (*v.* 6).[73]

However, it is doubtful that on the basis of a single word the readers would have recognized Jas 4:5b as an (antithetical) allusion to Ps 83:3 calling for a negative response to the rhetorical question.

Lewis Prockter has also argued for taking "the spirit" as the subject of the clause in 4:5b, but he specifically rejects Laws's suggested allusion. He proposed identifying "the scripture" with the Septuagintal rendering of Gen 8:21: "because the inclination of man presses relentlessly towards evil from his youth" (his translation). Primarily on the basis of this identification, he attempted to interpret Jas 4:4-6 as a midrash on the Noah story.[74] His proposal is even less convincing than Laws's, for he cannot provide even a single verbal parallel between Jas 4:5 and Gen 8:21.

146; cf. Martin, *James*, 149) has suggested that the formula introduces only a broad allusion to the concept of God's jealousy for the chosen people.

[72]Sophie S. Laws, "Does Scripture Speak in Vain? A Reconsideration of James iv. 5," *NTS* 20 (1973/74): 213.

[73]Laws, "Does Scripture Speak in Vain?," 214-215; cf. Johnson, "*Topos* περὶ φθόνου," 346.

[74]Lewis J. Prockter, "James 4.4-6: Midrash on Noah," *NTS* 35 (1989): 625-626.

What if we should follow Laws's proposal in taking Jas 4:5a as itself a rhetorical question, but were to defer the quotation proper to the clear citation of Prov 3:34 in Jas 4:6b? The result would be, "Or do you think that the scripture speaks for no reason? ... Therefore it says, 'God opposes the arrogant, but gives grace to the humble.'" What would then be required in 4:5b would be some grounds for asserting that "[God] gives even more grace" (4:6a) for which 4:6b would serve as a prooftext. Just such a foundation would be laid by taking "the spirit" as the object of "longs" and supplying "God" as its unexpressed subject: "God longs jealously for the spirit which [God] caused to dwell in us, and [so] gives even more grace." This translation finds support in the immediate context if indeed the vocative "Adulterers!" in 4:4 is an allusion to the marital symbolism between God and the chosen people.[75] It would gain further support from James's earlier image of God's "will to give birth to us by the word of truth that we might be a kind of first fruit of God's creations" (Jas 1:18). Even though the spirit which God placed within the human person often prefers "friendship with the world" and so finds itself at "enmity with God" (4:4), God still "longs jealously" for that spirit[76] and gives "even more grace" to those who are "humble."

But who are these "humble ones" (ταπεινοί) to whom God "gives grace"? As Ropes has noted, the immediate context would seem to require that the term is "[h]ere applied primarily to those who are humble toward God (cf. v. 7 ὑποτάγητε, v. 10 ταπεινώθητε ἐνώπιον Κυρίου), but not without thought of the same persons' lowly position in the community" (cf. Jas 1:9).[77] But since this call to "submit to" and "humble oneself before" God comes only *after* the citation of Prov 3:34, it is likely that the readers would have again (as in 1:9) invoked their "piety of the poor" and seen themselves as already the recipients of God's "grace." James makes clear by what follows, however, that in his view it is only those who humble themselves before God who will be "given even more grace" and "exalted" (Jas 4:10).

James summarizes his point with a carefully constructed series of imperatives in 4:7-10. The calls to "submit" and "humble oneself" form

---

[75]Cf. Ropes, *James*, 260 and 264; and Moo, *James*, 144-146.

[76]Cf. Dibelius, *James*, 224 and excursus on 223.

[77]Ropes, *St. James*, 266. Ropes mistakenly gives the reference as Jas 1:10 (which refers to the "rich," not the "humble/poor").

an inclusio surrounding three couplets, each expounding on how one expresses such an attitude:[78]

ὑποτάγητε οὖν τῷ θεῷ.

{ ἀντίστητε δὲ τῷ διαβόλῳ, καὶ φεύξεται ἀφ' ὑμῶν·
{ ἐγγίσατε τῷ θεῷ, καὶ ἐγγιεῖ ὑμῖν.

{ καθαρίσατε χεῖρας, ἁμαρτωλοί,
{ καὶ ἁγνίσατε καρδίας, δίψυχοι.

{ ταλαιπωρήσατε καὶ πενθήσατε καὶ κλαύσατε·
{ ὁ γέλως ὑμῶν εἰς πένθος μετατραπήτω καὶ ἡ χαρὰ εἰς κατήφειαν.

ταπεινώθητε ἐνώπιον κυρίου, καὶ ὑψώσει ὑμᾶς.

Therefore, submit to God.

{ Resist the devil, and he will flee from you;
{ come near to God, and (God) will come near to you.

{ Cleanse (your) hands, sinners,
{ and purify (your) hearts, double-minded ones.

{ Lament, and mourn, and weep;
{ let your laughter turn to sadness and your joy to dejection.

Humble yourselves in the presence of the Lord, and (the Lord) will exalt you.

But how is it that these attitudes and actions express one's "desire" to be "a friend of God" (cf. Jas 2:23b) and not "a friend of the world ... [and] an enemy of God" (4:4)?

To answer that question, we need to consider how these stylized phrases might be invested with specific meanings in terms of James's system of convictions. To "resist the devil" expresses a call to resist the "rivalry and ambition" which results from the desire for status that James describes as "earthly, unspiritual, demonic" (3:14-15). Such resistance is only possible if one "comes near to God" and "asks for wisdom" that will change one's will, having "faith" that "God will come near" and will "give" that wisdom "generously" (cf. 1:5). "Cleansing [one's] hands" would be to cease those actions that are injurious to the

---

[78]Adapted from Davids, *James*, 165; cf. Hill, "Analysis of James 3-5," 12; and Ekstrom, "Discourse Structure of James," 26-27.

community; but this too is only possible if the "double-minded ones" first "purify [their] hearts" by "receiving with meekness the implanted word" (1:21). The "laughter" and "joy" that come from "friendship with the world" must be turned to the "sadness" and "dejection" of knowing one has become "an enemy of God." Once believers in this way "humble [themselves] in the presence of the Lord," they will gain the only worthwhile status, for God "will exalt them."

Jas 4:11-12 — Judgment of Speech and Acts[79]

Figurativization in Jas 4:11-12

The final section of this sub-unit emphasizes why having a proper attitude of 'humility' is so important. In the first instance, having such an attitude will mean that believers will "not speak against one another" (4:11), and so "quarrels and disputes" will not arise within the community (4:1). But in clarifying what he intends by "speaking against a brother [or sister]" by the parallel "speaking against and judging the law" (cf. also the question of 4:12, "so who are you who judges the neighbor?"), James reintroduces the theme of judgment from 3:1. There is "one Lawgiver and Judge" who will judge both what is said ("speaking against another/the law") and what is done ("judging the neighbor/the law," "not doing the law"). And there can be no doubt but that this "one Lawgiver and Judge" is the same "Lord" before whom believers are to "humble" themselves.

For James, this "judgment" is both potentially positive and potentially negative for those who will receive it—and not merely because for some it will be more strict than for others (3:1b). The Lord as "the one Lawgiver and Judge" is able both to "save"/"exalt" (4:10) and to "destroy." Moreover, "judgment" awaits everyone, even those of prominence within the Christian community. How is this view of God as a "judge who is able to save and to destroy" to be related to James's conviction that God is the source of "every good and perfect gift" (1:17) and nothing bad or evil? Might not believing in God as such a "judge" lead to "doubt" and "double-mindedness" since one does not know whether to expect "salvation" (good) or "destruction" (bad) from God?

---

[79]Here we are only concerned with those features of 4:11-12 related to the themes of the discursive unit Jas 3:1 - 4:12 and sub-unit 4:1-12. In the next chapter we will consider other semantic features of 4:11-12 in discussing their role in the final discursive unit of the Epistle.

We need to begin by stressing something which has already been stated, namely, that "judgment" is both potentially positive and potentially negative *for those who will receive it*. While "judgment" will have obviously negative consequences for those who are "destroyed" as a result, that does not mean that God's act of destruction itself is perceived as bad or evil by James (consider the example of the "demons [who] shuddered" in the certainty of their impending judgment [Jas 2:19]). In James's system of convictions, it is a good thing for God to destroy those whose "evil desire ... has conceived [and] given birth to sin" (1:14-15). But "judgment" will also "save" others' "souls from death" (1:21), bringing to them the positive consequences of "exaltation" (1:9, 4:10) and a "crown of life" (1:12).

Additionally, there is no reason for any individual to "doubt" whether God will give salvation or destruction to her or him in particular (even the demons have no doubt about what they will receive!). People will be judged on the speech and actions which arise from their will to act. If one knows that God is good (even in destroying evil and those who do it), then one can have the "faith" to ask God for the "wisdom" needed to change internally so as to be willing to act as God acts and be "blessed for one's doing" (1:25) in the judgment. On the other hand, if one strives to gain "wisdom" on his or her own through the trials and vicissitudes of life because he or she cannot trust a God who is believed to be both good and bad to give it, then one will receive nothing from God to change the internal "evil desire" which "gives birth to sin" and ultimately "death" and destruction in the judgment.[80]

Summary of Jas 4:1-12

Whereas in previous sub-units of the Epistle we have been able to trace considerable movement between the initial investments of meaning which the readers brought to the figures and the investments which James seeks to persuade them to adopt, only one example of such movement is clearly evident within this sub-unit. In discussing the citation of Prov 3:34 in Jas 4:6 ("God gives grace to the humble" [ὁ θεὸς ... ταπεινοῖς δὲ δίδωσιν χάριν]), I suggested that the readers may have once again invoked their "piety of the poor" so as to see themselves as already the recipients of God's "grace." But with the imperatives which follow in 4:7-10, James quickly moves to convince

---

[80]See again the presentation of James's system of convictions at the end of chapter 4.

his readers that the ταπεινοί who will receive "grace" and be "exalted" by God are those who "humble themselves in the presence of the Lord."

If we compare this particular point with the theme of the Epistle as a whole (the readers are a "Diaspora" which has "wandered from the truth" and so need someone to "restore" them), it appears that with this sub-unit we have come to the heart of one the central purposes of the Epistle. James believes that his readers should by now see that their "desires" for "friendship with the world" and even for positions of status within their Christian community have lead them "away from the truth" and indeed made them "enemies of God." In an effort to "restore" them, he urges them to once again "humble themselves in the presence of the Lord," to "come near to God" in the confidence that "God will come near" to them.

Discursive Structure and Purpose
in Jas 3:1 - 4:12

James does not emphasize any new convictions in this discursive unit of the Epistle, but the pattern of beliefs we isolated in the opening units have been an invaluable aid in helping us to distinguish his investments of meanings in the figures used here from the initial semantic investments of his implied readers. He draws on a number of images familiar to inhabitants of the Hellenistic world in an effort to convince them that their actions are not "works" of the "implanted word" and as such expressions of God's will. On the contrary, their actions have been typical of the "rebellion and every bad deed" which arise from "bitter rivalry and ambition" that are "earthly, unspiritual, demonic" (3:14-15). And so James urges them to "humble themselves in the presence of the Lord" who is the "one Lawgiver and Judge able to save and to destroy" (4:10-12).

The primary focus of the theme of this discursive unit has been on how individuals should respond in the light of impending judgment. They must have their inner nature "purified" so that their actions which arise from it will be able to withstand even "stricter judgment." Yet James has also provided indications that believers have more than just a responsibility for preparing themselves for judgment, particularly in the ambiguity over corporate or individualist investments in the figures of the second sub-unit. Although "not many ... brothers [and sisters] should desire to become teachers" (3:1, the readers' improper concern for status within the corporate life of the community), there is still obviously a need for "teachers" like James himself within the community. Moreover, he stresses that individuals' inner attitudes impact directly on corporate life: the "passions ... at war within" them lead to "quarrels/wars" (πόλεμοι) within the community (4:1). Believers are not to "speak against" or "judge the neighbor" (4:11), but what responsibilities might they have toward that "neighbor"? These are the themes that James will develop in the final discursive unit of the Epistle.

CHAPTER SIX

"BRINGING BACK" ONE'S "NEIGHBOR": JAMES 4:11 - 5:20

On the basis of our analysis of Jas 3:1 - 4:12 in the previous chapter, we were able to conclude that one of James's chief concerns in that unit was to call his readers to prepare themselves individually for their coming encounter with the "one Lawgiver and Judge who is able to save and to destroy" (4:12). But we also noted that there are indications, especially in the 'hinge' verses of 4:11-12, that James believes his readers have a responsibility not only for themselves, but also for other members of their religious community. The themes of the discourse shift their focus from the individual to the community as a whole.

In commenting on the final saying of the Epistle (5:19-20), even Dibelius noticed a connection between the communal concerns expressed there and those in 4:11-12:

> The closeness of individuals to one another brings with it the fact that each observes and passes judgment upon what the other does. Disruptions of the community can only be avoided if criticism by one brother of another can be directed into the proper path—i.e., if it does not lead to slander or alienation (4:11; 5:9), but rather to the beneficial influence of one brother upon the other.[1]

But in that James so strongly prohibits "criticizing" and "judging" fellow members of the community ("Who are you who judges the neighbor?"

---

[1]Dibelius, *James*, 259.

[4:12]), it seems somewhat unlikely that he would have conceived of the possibility of such actions having a "beneficial influence" if they are performed by believers. We need to carefully consider the development of the themes within this discursive unit if we are to understand how one may "bring back" one who has "wandered from the truth" without judging/condemning them.

Discursive Semantic Structure and Thematization

The primary theme of this final discursive unit of the Epistle is defined by a pair of closely related inverted parallelisms. The 'inverted content' of "speak[ing] against or judg[ing] a brother [or sister]" (Jas 4:11a) is paralleled by the 'posited content' of "restor[ing]" "anyone among you [who] should wander from the truth" (5:19). The related inverted parallelism helps to specify what James envisions as "wandering from the truth" by paralleling this 'posited content' with the contrasting 'inverted content' of "judging the law" and "not [being] a doer of the law" (4:11b). This second parallelism suggests that the primary way in which believers may "wander/err" (see the play on πλανάω/πλάνη in 5:19-20) is by failing "to do the works" of the "law/word" which has been "implanted" within them by God (cf. Jas 1:21-25). James urges his readers to "restore [such wanderers] to the truth" rather than "judging/condemning" them.

As in the previous discursive unit (3:1 - 4:12), James again introduces the theme of judgment into this final unit by means of an inverted parallelism. In this instance, the "one Lawgiver and Judge who is able to save and to destroy" (4:12) is the 'inverted content' paralleled by the 'posited content' of "saving [a sinner's][2] soul from death" (5:20). The role of the language of the "one Lawgiver and Judge" as both the 'posited' content of one unit and the 'inverted' content of the following unit is both interesting and instructive. In the preceding unit, James utilized his belief that there is "*one* Lawgiver and Judge" to show that believers should not assume the role of "judge" and should in fact prepare themselves for "judgment" (the posited content of Jas 3:1 - 4:12). But within the unit now under consideration, James utilizes the readers' belief in God as "Lawgiver and Judge who is able ... *to destroy*" (the inverted content of 4:11 - 5:20; see especially 5:1-6) to

---

[2]Taking the antecedent of αὐτοῦ as ἁμαρτωλόν rather than ὁ ἐπιστρέψας. On the ambiguities in 5:20, see the discussion in the exegesis and commentary below.

raise the issue of what a believer's responsibility might be toward those
in danger of such "judgment/condemnation." At least toward those who
have been members of the community and are now at risk of divine
condemnation ("if anyone *among you* should wander ...", 5:19), their
responsibility is to try to "restore [such] sinners from the error of their
way ... [and] save their souls from death" (5:20, the posited content of
4:11 - 5:20). Whereas the theme of the preceding unit focused on
'sparing oneself from judgment,' the theme of this unit emphasizes
'sparing others from judgment.'

James develops this theme in two sub-units, the first elaborating
on the nature of the coming judgment (4:11 - 5:9) and the second more
specifically on the believer's responsibility to others (5:10-20). The
limits of the first sub-unit are marked by two inverted parallelisms. The
admonition "do not speak against (μὴ καταλαλεῖτε) one another ... [or]
judge/condemn (κρίνων)³ a brother [or sister]" (4:11) is paralleled by
the admonition "do not grumble (μὴ στενάζετε) against one another ...
so that you may not be condemned⁴ (μὴ κριθῆτε)" (5:9). The emphasis
upon judgment is underscored by the second inverted parallelism
between the "one Lawgiver and Judge" (4:12) and his announcement that
"the Judge stands before the door" (5:9).⁵ The twofold theme of the
sub-unit may be summarized as "the Judge and judgment."

James deals with the criterion which the "one Lawgiver and
Judge" employs for judgment in the section Jas 4:11-17.⁶ His concern

---

³I have included "judge/condemn" as part of the prohibition since James uses
it in the following clause to clarify the nuance of "speak against" within this verse:
ὁ καταλαλῶν ἢ κρινῶν τὸν ἀδελφὸν αὐτοῦ. Cf. Davids's comment (*James*, 169) that
"the use of καταλαλεῖ and κρίνει is to show that the one action does both acts, not
that the person directly slanders the law."

⁴Whereas the uses of the verb κρίνω in Jas 4:11-12 are somewhat ambiguous as
to whether they should carry the general nuance of "judge" of the more specific
nuance of "condemn," the more general usage can be ruled out here in 5:9 because
we have seen in the previous discursive unit that even believers will be "judged" (cf.
the "stricter judgment" of teachers in 3:1). Thus, while believers cannot entirely
avoid "judgment" by not "grumbling against one another," they can in that way
avoid "condemnation."

⁵Cf. the comments by Moo, *James*, 170: "As he has done in 4:11-12, James
connects speaking against others with judgment. There, however, he likened critical
speech to judgment; here he warns that criticism of one another places a person in
danger of judgment. ... To reinforce his warning, James reminds his readers again
that this judgment is imminent: *the Judge is standing at the doors*." Cf. also
Sidebottom, *James, Jude, 2 Peter*, 59.

⁶Jas 4:11-17 is also treated as a single section by Martin, *James*, 159-162; and

within this section is to once again emphasize that one's actions must be determined by the divine will ("if the Lord wills," 4:15), and that failure to do what God desires to be done within the world will lead to "sin" ("for the one who knows to do good but is not doing it, it is sin" [4:17]) and ultimately "condemnation" and "death" (cf. again 1:15 and 5:20). His second section (5:1-9) presents the nature of the judgment/condemnation that the "one Lawgiver and Judge" will bring by taking up one of the stock images from the readers' "piety of the poor," namely the judgment of the rich. James utilizes the apostrophe to the "rich" in 5:1-6 (cf. the apostrophe to the merchant class in 4:13-16) as a rhetorical device to direct the attention of those within his community ("brothers [and sisters]", 5:7) toward those whom they believe to be the quintessential "others" who are *outside* of the community. In the discussion of the figurativization of this section we will consider the competing investments that James and his readers make in this figure in terms of the lesson to be drawn from the 'judgment of the rich.'[7]

The second sub-unit is likewise marked by two inverted parallelisms. The first is formed by James's admonition to "take as an example of perseverance in suffering the prophets who spoke by the authority of the Lord" (5:10) and his own offering of Elijah as an example of "a person with the same nature/sufferings[8] as us" (5:17). The second parallelism links the attitude that "we consider (as) blessed the ones who endured" (5:11) with James's concern that there are those who have not "endured," i.e. who have "wandered from the truth" (5:19). We might describe the theme of this sub-unit as "being a patient prophet," for James introduces the specific example of Elijah within the context of communal support and prayer and links the personal endurance of the prophets and the readers (5:10-11) with the prophetic concern for assisting the 'endurance' of others (5:19-20).

The introductory section of this sub-unit (5:10-11) draws on the readers' beliefs regarding the need to patiently endure human suffering (cf. the readers' semantic investments in Jas 1:2-4). The central section

---

Adamson, *James*, 175-181.

[7]Thus, the vocative ἀδελφοί in 5:7 does not introduce a new section, as suggested by Davids (*James*, 171) and Martin (*James*, 186). Jas 5:7-9 is connected with 5:1-6 by the conjunction οὖν, as Davids himself later conceded: "The response of the suffering Christians (ἀδελφοί) is given in the light of the sure and present judgment of the rich (οὖν); one cannot read 5:7-11 separately from 5:1-6" (*James*, 181). Cf. also Laws, *James*, 208; and Vouga, *Jacques*, 133 n. 2.

[8]"Included in the idea of 'like nature' [ὁμοιοπαθής] is the thought of suffering (πάθος)." Martin, *James*, 212; cf. Reicke, *James, Peter and Jude*, 60 and 66 n. 41.

(5:12-18)[9] describes the importance of communal prayer and praise as a response to both the misfortunes and blessings of life. Rather than the prohibition of oaths in Jas 5:12 being an isolated saying within its present context,[10] James includes oaths here as an example of an improper means of invoking God's name as a response to the difficulties of life.[11] God's name is properly invoked as a sign of submission to God's will, and not as a guarantor of the veracity of or one's commitment to expressions of her or his own will (cf. 4:13-16). As Martin has expressed it,

> Prayer that moves the human exigency to conform to the divine plan is seen to be the appropriate attitude expressing faith and confidence. Hence the import of the phrase in v 14b: ἐν ὀνόματι τοῦ κυρίου, which is not a magical or mechanical talisman and not an exorcistic form of words; rather it is the phrase that marks out the sphere of faith in which God's perfect will is acknowledged and trusted as the best—whatever the outcome.[12]

And by the concluding section of the Epistle (5:19-20), James reminds his readers that the prophetic responsibility for others extends beyond mutual prayer to include "restoring" those who have "wandered from the truth" and not conformed their activities to that divine will.

---

[9]This division differs slightly from the view of a number of commentators that 5:13-18 should be considered a section; see Moo, *James*, 175; Adamson, *James*, 196; Sidebottom, *James, Jude, 2 Peter*, 61; Davids, *James*, 191-192; Cantinat, *Jacques et Jude*, 244-245; and Vouga, *Jacques*, 140. On the inclusion of 5:12 with 13-18, see the discussion which follows.

[10]Cf. Dibelius, *James*, 241-242; Sidebottom, *James, Jude, 2 Peter*, 60; Moo, *James*, 173; Mußner, *Jakobusbrief*, 211; and Davids, *James*, 188-189, who also alludes to Francis's suggestion ("Form and Function," 125) that the phrase πρὸ πάντων followed by oaths and health wishes was a common Hellenistic epistolary device for closing letters. I will return to Francis's argument in the next chapter; yet it should be noted here that even if one accepts this view that the prohibition of oaths and instruction regarding prayer for healing reflect variations on epistolary generic expectations, it would not follow that 5:12 must mark the beginning of a new unit or sub-unit. It is still possible to connect 5:12-20 with 5:10-11 if the organizing principles are not restricted to only formal generic structures.

[11]Laws (*James*, 219-220) similarly suggested that 5:12 should be related to the discussion of worship and prayer in 5:13-18 ("there are wrong, and right, ways of addressing or calling upon God"); cf. Ropes, *St. James*, 300. Although Martin identified Jas 5:12-18 as a section (*James*, 197-200), he commented that "[t]he scene abruptly changes at 5:13" (ibid., 214).

[12]Martin, *James*, 202.

Exegesis and Commentary

The Judge and Judgment (Jas 4:11 - 5:9)

Jas 4:11-17 — Knowing and Doing the Law

Convictions Emphasized in Jas 4:11-17

James constructs three oppositions of actions within this section of the Epistle, but, as the analysis will show, he does not introduce any new convictions here. Rather, he utilizes these oppositions of actions to once again emphasize certain convictions that he has been at pains to communicate to the readers throughout the Epistle. James constructs a closely knit pair of oppositions in 4:11 to underscore that believers must "do the law" (cf. Jas 1:22-25 and 2:14-26, and point 5 in the presentation of James's system of convictions at the end of chapter 4 above). In keeping with the theme of this unit, his concern is specifically with "doing the law" in terms of a believer's dealings with other believers. The third opposition is a polemical dialogue within the apostrophe to the 'merchants' in 4:13-16, and it once again stresses the importance of one's will being established by God's will (i.e., having "wisdom;" cf. Jas 1:5-8 and 1:21, and point 4 in James's system of convictions).

OPP 4:11A and OPP 4:11B — Not Judging Believers. In the first half of Jas 4:11, we find an opposition between the positive action of a believer "not speaking against another" which is opposed to the negative action of a believer "speaking against a brother [or sister] or ... judging his [or her] brother [or sister]." This opposition of actions is crucial to the theme of this discursive unit, and indeed contributes a portion of the content to the inverted parallelisms which mark both the discursive unit of 4:11 - 5:20 and the sub-unit of 4:11 - 5:9. James utilizes this opposition to underscore his conviction regarding how believers ought *not* to act toward one another ("judging/condemning"); his conviction regarding how they should rather act toward one another will be underscored by OPP 5:19.

It is that opposition (and the related inverted parallelisms between 4:11-12 and 5:19-20) which makes explicit what the respective effects of the positive and negative actions of OPP 4:11A are for those believers who either receive or do not receive "judgment/condemnation" from their fellow believers. The end product of "condemnation" would be the "death" of one's "soul" (5:20), whereas "not being judged" but rather "being restored" by another believer "will save [one's] soul from death and will cover a multitude of sins" (5:20).

James makes explicit the respective qualifications of the positive and negative subjects of OPP 4:11A by OPP 4:11B, which opposes the negative action "speaking against the law and judging the law" to the positive action of "doing the law." The negative subject of OPP 4:11A who "speaks against and judges" others is one who also "speaks against and judges the law." In terms of James's system of convictions, this indicates that such a person has not internalized God's will, that is, has not "received the implanted word" (1:21) which would make God's will his or her own. Conversely, the positive subject of OPP 4:11A who "does not speak against another" is one who "does the law" (cf. 1:22-25), that is who knows and performs God's will because her or his desires have been changed by "receiving the implanted word." Thus, as Dibelius observed, "[s]lander is not a transgression against the authority of merely one commandment, but a transgression against the authority of the law in general, and therefore against God."[13]

OPP 4:13, 15-16 — Knowing 'If God Wills'. The body of this section consists of a polemical dialogue comprised of an apostrophe to merchants,[14] whom James characterizes by the statement, "Today or tomorrow we will go to such and such a city, and we will work there for a year and will conduct business and will make a profit" (4:13). James clearly marks such attitudes as negative when he later comments that by such statements they "boast in [their] pretensions; all such boasting is evil" (4:16). The proper attitude, for James, is expressed by the statement, "If the Lord wills, we will both live and will do this or that" (4:15). The positive statement demonstrates that the problem is not with planning future activity ("If the Lord wills, ... we will do this or that"), but with whether the divine will determines those plans.[15]

But what role does the divine will play in determining the future plans of believers? Some have emphasized James's statement regarding the ephemeral quality of human life ("For you are a vapor appearing for a short time, and then disappearing," 4:14b), and concluded that James intends to communicate the idea that God controls the course of events

---

[13]Dibelius, *James*, 228. Cf. Davids, *James*, 169-170.

[14]It should be noted that James does not actually identify the persons addressed beyond the reported content of their speech; he simply employs the participial construction οἱ λέγοντες ("the ones who say"). However, the content of their statement is in keeping with the general interests and business patterns of the merchant class. See the discussion of the figurativization below.

[15]Cf. Davids, *James*, 173; and Martin, *James*, 166.

and thus humans cannot accomplish any plan which God does not will to come about.[16] Therefore, James is encouraging his readers to "preface such remarks by some contingent reminder"[17] and to "*qualify all of their plans ... with reference to the will of the Lord.*"[18]

However, given the importance of the divine will within James's system of convictions in determining what actions one should perform, more would seem to be at stake in his phrase "if God wills" than simply an acknowledgment of 'contingency.' It is what "God wills" (rather than what the person "desires") that should provide the very content of the believer's plans for the future. The problem is not simply that the merchants do not respect divine sovereignty, but that their "attitude reflects a proud complacency that suggests a 'this-worldly planning' and a blatant desire to become rich."[19] This meaning finds further support in that the negative subject (the merchants) is qualified by a lack of knowledge ("actually you do not know about tomorrow," 4:14a), and knowledge within James's system of convictions is related to the goodness and will of God. These two nuances were balanced well by Moo: "What James encourages is not the constant verbalization of the formula *If the Lord wills*, which can easily become a glib and meaningless recitation, but a sincere appreciation for God's control of affairs and for his specific will for us."[20]

Figurativization in Jas 4:11-17

In commenting on the image of God as the "one Lawgiver and Judge who is able to save and to destroy," E. M. Sidebottom remarked that these "[c]onventional words ... ill-accord with the doctrine of 1.17ff." describing God as the source of "every good and perfect gift."[21] But what we must keep in mind is that these "conventional

---

[16]So Reicke, *James, Peter and Jude*, 48-49; and Martin, *James*, 160 and 166. Gerhard Delling ("ἀλαζών, ἀλαζονεία," *TDNT* 1:227) argued that this is the nuance of their "pretensions:" "ἀλαζονεῖαι are expressions of the ἀλαζονεία which acts as if it could dispose of the future whereas this is really under the control of the will of God."

[17]Martin, *James*, 166.

[18]Moo, *James*, 156, emphasis mine.

[19]Martin, *James*, 165.

[20]Moo, *James*, 157; cf. Davids, *James*, 173.

[21]Sidebottom, *James, Jude, 2 Peter*, 55. He went on to suggest that the resolution of the apparent conflict is that "the point stressed [here in 4:12] is that God is the ultimate power as well as the ultimate court of appeal, not that he is

words" are capable of bearing multiple semantic investments. We have
seen how James was able to understand the expression "to save and to
destroy" in terms of his system of convictions regarding God as 'pure
good' when discussing the role of this figure as the posited content of
the sub-unit 4:1-12 (see the discussion of figurativization in Jas 4:11-12
at the end of the previous chapter). But as an introductory figure to the
sub-unit 4:11 - 5:9, it draws primarily on the convictions of the implied
readers—whom it will be recalled are confused (in James's opinion) on
precisely the issue of believing God to be a source of both good and bad
(cf. the discussions of Jas 1:2-4 and 1:13-16 in chapter 3). It is
precisely this belief in God as one who brings destructive judgment that
sets the mood for this sub-unit of the Epistle.

Who are these "ones who say, 'Today or tomorrow...'"? Based
on the description provided of their planned activities ("we will go to
such and such a city, and we will work there for a year and will conduct
business and will make a profit"), it seems that James is envisioning
traveling merchants rather than local shopkeepers.[22]   It has been
suggested that this description is inherently disparaging since the verb
ἐμπορεύομαι can have the meaning "to cheat" as well as the meaning
"to conduct business."[23]   While such an association may have occurred
to the readers as a result of a general disdain for the social and economic
elite, it does not appear to be an essential component of James's
investment in the term.[24]   Nor is there much point in determining

---

destructive."   However, God's role in 'destructive judgment' is clearly in view
within this sub-unit; see especially the judgment of the rich in 5:1-5.

[22]So Laws, *James*, 190:   "*emporeuomai* ['to conduct business'] carries the
nuance of the distinction between the *emporoi*, the wholesale traveling traders, and
the *kapēloi*, the local retailers."   Cf. Maynard-Reid, *Poverty and Wealth*, 71.

[23]See Ross, *Epistles of James and John*, 82 n. 6; and Maynard-Reid, *Poverty
and Wealth*, 71, who mistakenly translates ἐμπορευσόμεθα as "we will go."
Moreover, he introduces an element of anti-Semitism by joining this nuance of
'cheating' with his citation (ibid., 125 n. 19) of A. T. Robertson's comment that the
word "presents a vivid picture of the Jewish merchant of the time" (see Archibald
Thomas Robertson, *Word Pictures in the New Testament*, vol. 6, *The General
Epistles and the Apocalypse* [New York and London: Richard R. Smith, Inc.,
1933], 55).   It should be noted that Robertson makes no reference to any possibility
of 'cheating' as a nuance of this word in the context of Jas 4:13.

[24]Indeed, according to Louw and Nida (*Greek-English Lexicon*, §§ 57.196
[1:580] and 88.148 [1:759]) no negative associations are attached to the use of the
verb in meaning "to conduct business," although its secondary meaning "to cheat"
may derive from its use in some contexts "to refer to the process of selling cheap
merchandise at a high price."   According to LSJ ("ἐμπορεύομαι," 1:548), the

whether James envisions such merchants to be actual members of the community which he is addressing;[25] for him, the example of the 'merchants' is paradigmatic of all those who act without reference to what "God wills."

Commentators have been about equally divided on the question of whether the phrase ποία ἡ ζωὴ ὑμῶν in Jas 4:14 should be considered an extension of the object of the verb ἐπίστασθε (thus, "you do not know what will be tomorrow, *what your life will be like*"),[26] or as an independent question (thus, "What is your life?").[27] While either reading is possible, the interrogative seems better suited as an introduction to the following statement recalling the ephemeral quality of life—particularly given the related images of the passing away of the lifestyle of the rich in Jas 1:10-11 and 5:2-3. In each instance these images are drawn from the convictions of the readers, specifically from the traditional "piety of the poor." Thus, it is unlikely that Dibelius is correct in arguing this question provides the focus of James's own attention within this section.[28] Rather, as the analysis of the polemical dialogue in Jas 4:13-16 revealed, James's emphasis is upon one's will to act properly being predicated upon the divine will.

---

meaning "to cheat" applies only with the accusative of person (as in 2 Pet 2:3).

[25]Somewhat uncharacteristically, Dibelius (*James*, 234-235) argued that this paraenetic example arose from a particular concern of the author within his community. Yet he avoided being overly specific ("[t]he matter is related vividly, but not at all in detail"), seeing it as a general reference to a "bad habit seeping in from the world" with the increasing involvement of community members in trade.

[26]So Martin, *James*, 158; see also Mußner, *Jakobusbrief*, 190; Reicke, *James, Peter and Jude*, 48; Davids, *James*, 172; Vouga, *Jacques*, 121 and 123; and the punctuation of NA-26 and *UBSGNT*.

[27]So Ropes, *St. James*, 278; Dibelius, *James*, 230-231 and 233; Cantinat, *Jacques et Jude*, 216-217; Laws, *James*, 191; Adamson, *James*, 178; and Moo, *James*, 155. The interrogative construction is supported by the inclusion of γάρ in P74vid A K L P which, according to *TCGNT* (684), "appears to have been inserted (perhaps under the influence of the following clause) in order to prevent ambiguity." The reading without the conjunction (ℵ* B 614 and versions) is favored by those who take the "what" with the verb (see the commentators cited in the previous note).

[28]Dibelius, *James*, 231. This assertion appears somewhat strange in the Hermeneia edition of his commentary in that the translator and editor (Michael Williams and Helmut Koester) have subordinated the question within their reconstruction of the anacoluthon and translation of the passage, setting it off between dashes as a kind of parenthetical (see ibid., 230; likewise Adamson, *James*, 178). Dibelius did not provide a translation within the German original of the Meyers Kommentar.

This emphasis is further underscored by the saying which he uses to bring this section to a close: "Therefore, for the one who knows to do good but is not doing it, it is sin for him [or her]." This reference to "do[ing] good" is yet another expression of the idea James has stressed by such phrases and terms as "doing the word/work" (1:22-25), "works" (in 2:14-26), and "good conduct ... [and] works" (3:13);[29] to "do good" is to act in accordance with the divine will made known to the believer by "receiving the implanted word" (1:21). The "sin" described here is therefore more encompassing than simply a failure to use one's resources to charitable or beneficial ends.[30] The 'sins of omission' here in 4:17, like the 'sins of commission' arising from evil "desires" in 1:15, result from a failure "to do" the things which one "knows" God desires to be done in the world.[31] Nevertheless, the specific failure to "do good" by providing for the needs of others (see again Jas 2:14-17) supplies a smooth transition into the next section of this sub-unit.

Jas 5:1-9 — Judgment upon Rich Oppressors

Convictions Emphasized in Jas 5:1-9

James emphasizes only a single conviction by an opposition of actions within this section of the Epistle. Unlike the vast majority of oppositions of actions within the Epistle which have believers for their positive subjects,[32] OPP 5:1, 5 seems to have the divine as its positive subject. It appears that, whereas the rich have afforded themselves every luxury (Jas 5:5, the negative action), God is going to bring "miseries" upon them as an act of judgment (Jas 5:1, the positive action). Yet, the previous oppositions expressing convictions about the divine have underscored God's positive actions toward human beings ("giving" to believers rather than "rebuking" them in OPP 1:5, and "honoring" the poor whom believers themselves have "dishonored" in

---

[29]Cf. Cantinat, *Jacques et Jude*, 219; Davids, *James*, 174; and Martin, *James*, 161.

[30]As Davids (*James*, 174) suggested concerning a "deeper level ... viewing the whole motive of gathering wealth rather than doing good with it (i.e. sharing it with the poor) as a failure to follow known standards of Christian guidance."

[31]Cf. Martin, *James*, 161-162; and Mußner, *Jakobusbrief*, 192.

[32]Eleven of the thirteen other oppositions of actions within the Epistle have believers as their positive subjects (see Appendix B). That the vast majority of oppositions concern the actions of believers should not come as a surprise given the paraenetic interests of the book.

OPP 2:5, 6). What precisely is the conviction that James is trying to emphasize within this section?

OPP 5:1, 5 — "Misery" and "Luxury" of the Rich. James clearly opposes two actions that have the "rich" as their respective receivers. He views positively the action of "miseries coming upon the rich" (ἐπὶ ταῖς ταλαιπωρίαις ὑμῶν ταῖς ἐπερχομέναις, 5:1), and negatively their own actions of providing themselves with 'luxury' by "revelling upon the earth, living indulgently ... [and] fattening [their] hearts" (ἐτρυφήσατε ἐπὶ τῆς γῆς καὶ ἐσπαταλήσατε, ἐθρέψατε τὰς καρδίας ὑμῶν, 5:5). This opposition presents us with two problems: (1) exactly who is the subject of the positive action causing "miseries to come upon the rich," and (2) why does James view these particular acts as positive and negative respectively?

One answer would be that James shares his readers convictions relative to the "piety of the poor;" since the rich have indulged themselves at the expense of others, they deserve to be punished by God ("The wage that was robbed from the laborers who reap your fields cries out against you, and the cries of the harvesters have entered the ears of Lord Sabaoth," Jas 5:4). Thus, God is the positive subject within the opposition of actions who sends "miseries ... upon the rich" as an act of judgment. But we have seen elsewhere in the Epistle that James distances himself somewhat from the readers' "piety of the poor" theology. Rather than facilely accepting this solution, we need to consider what the effects of these actions are for the positive and negative receivers respectively, since the ambiguity regarding the identity of the positive subject clearly places the emphasis within this opposition on these respective effects.

At first glance, we seem to be confronted with the irony that the effects upon the receivers of the positive action seem to be negative: the "miseries" (ταλαιπωρίαι) which are coming upon them should cause them to "wail greatly" (κλαύσατε ὀλολύζοντες,[33] 5:1). But we need to remember that the imperative verb within this construction has already occurred in conjunction with the verbal stem related to the noun "miseries" used here: "Lament, and mourn, and weep" (**ταλαιπωρήσατε καὶ πενθήσατε καὶ κλαύσατε**, Jas 4:9a). James utilized those words to call to his readers "to humble themselves before the Lord" so that they

---

[33]Literally, "cry crying aloud/wailing." The adverbial participle ὀλολύζοντες was probably included for its onomatopoeic quality; cf. Laws, *James*, 197; and Martin, *James*, 175-176.

might be "exalted" (4:10) rather than "condemned." There is also a connection with the saying regarding the rich in Jas 1:9-11. Not only is the imagery in 1:11 about the passing beauty of the flower clearly paralleled by the figures in 5:2-3a of the decay of material possessions, but we also find here in OPP 5:1, 5 a reason why "the rich may boast in his [or her] humiliation" (1:10). If the "humiliation" brought about by the decay of their wealth leads to repentance and "humbling themselves before the Lord," they like the "poor/humble brother [or sister]" will have cause "to boast in their exaltation" (1:9; cf. 4:10).

Therefore, even "miseries" may have a positive effect if they should lead the rich to repentance.[34] Conversely, the 'luxuries' which the rich have afforded themselves will have a decidedly negative effect. Rather than "humbling themselves" and taking God's will as their own, they have fulfilled their own evil "desires"[35] and will as a result receive death on the eschatological day of judgment ("you have fattened your hearts for the day of slaughter," 5:5)[36] rather than life.

But who is the subject who performs this ultimately positive action of bringing "miseries" upon the rich? The answer resides in James's earlier discussion of the "blessings of trials" (Jas 1:2-12). Just as "trials" served as a warning of eschatological judgment and were to lead one to pray in faith, asking God for what is needed (see the exegetical summary of this section in chapter 3), so also are these "miseries" a

---

[34]Cf. Mußner, *Jakobusbrief*, 193; and Cantinat, *Jacques et Jude*, 220-221. Ropes (*St. James*, 282), Dibelius (*James*, 235), Davids (*James*, 174-175), Vouga (*Jacques*, 128), and Martin (*James*, 173) all rejected the suggestion that this apostrophe to the rich is a call to repentance. In a sense they were right. Strictly speaking James is not here calling "the rich" to repentance as he earlier called his readers, for if they repent it will only be because of the "miseries" that come upon them. Additionally, as with any use of the rhetorical device of apostrophe, the words are actually directed at the author's audience and not those persons addressed by the vocative (see the discussion below of the figurativization in this section). Nevertheless, at the narrative semantic level these verses do express James's belief that "miseries" may lead to repentance for those who are not already believers.

[35]As Reicke noted (*James, Peter and Jude*, 51), "The illustration of the heart that is growing fat through sumptuous living is not based on anatomical observations, but on the usual conception of the heart as the seat of the will, and in this case of the lusts and desires." Cf. Ropes, *St. James*, 290; and Moo, *James*, 165-166.

[36]Cf. Davids, *James*, 178-179; Ropes, *St. James*, 290; Laws, *James*, 203-204; Mußner, *Jakobusbrief*, 197-198; Cantinat, *Jacques et Jude*, 228; and Martin, *James*, 180. Contra Dibelius (*James*, 239) who suggested that "'the day of slaughter' could also mean any day of disaster upon which things turned out terribly only for the poor, or upon which the poor had to suffer precisely from the rich."

warning regarding the imminence of judgment and a summons to call upon God. "Miseries" serve the same function for non-believers that "trials," in James's system of convictions, serve for believers. And just as he did not identify the source of "trials" in 1:2-12, James leaves the origin of the "miseries" here in 5:1-6 shrouded in intentional ambiguity. One thing is certain however; God is not, for James, the one who brings these "miseries." He has already emphasized his convictions in this regard by OPP 1:13-14: "God tempts/tests no one,"[37] and is a source of only good (cf. Jas 1:17-18).

Figurativization in Jas 5:1-9

In this section of the Epistle, James is clearly drawing on imagery from the traditional indictments of the rich within the "piety of the poor" so important to his readers. Yet, these images are not simply formulaic; they reflect the economic plight of poor, independent farmers oppressed by wealthy agriculturalists holding large estates who exercised considerable control over the markets.[38] James employs these images both to utilize his readers' beliefs that God will imminently intervene to judge the rich as a reason to "patiently endure" until their eschatological deliverance ("Therefore have patience [μακροθυμήσατε], brothers [and sisters], until the advent of the Lord," 5:7a), and to again warn them not to adopt the desire for wealth and status typical of the "rich."[39]

---

[37]That earlier opposition of actions may also provide a clue as to the identity of the positive subject here in OPP 5:1, 5. James stated in 1:14 that "each one is tempted/tested when he [or she] is dragged away and enticed by his [or her] own evil desire." Thus, it may be that the rich in some sense bring "miseries" upon themselves by their very drive for 'luxury.' Yet this explanation seems almost a non sequitor; if the rich pursue the negative action of fulfilling their evil desires it results in the positive action of bringing misery upon them. It is better to simply respect James's ambiguity and leave open the question of the identity of the positive subject.

[38]For fine summaries of economic factors in first century Mediterranean culture which led to this oppression, see Martin, *James*, 174-175; Maynard-Reid, *Poverty and Wealth*, 87-90; and Heinz Kreissig, "Die landwirtschaftliche Situation im Palästina vor dem judäischen Krieg," *Acta Antiqua Academiae Scientiarum Hungaricae* 17 (1969): 239-253. Martin (despite his citation of Kreissig) is clearly dependent upon Maynard-Reid, who is himself drawing directly from Kreissig. Shimon Applebaum noted these factors were more applicable in areas of Judaea under Greek control than in Jewish population centers; see "Judaca as a Roman Province; the Countryside as a Political and Economic Factor," *ANRW* II.8 (1978): 368-370.

[39]This two-fold semantic investment has been recognized by several commentators. Ropes (*St. James*, 282) commented that "[t]he purpose of the verses [5:1-6]

Given the theme of this sub-unit, James's own primary investments seem related to being prepared for judgment. They must "patiently endure" rather than "wander from the truth" because "the Judge stands before the door" (5:9b). Indeed, as the charge that the rich "have stored up treasure (even) in the Last Days" (5:3b) makes clear, James believes that "the end times, in which they have a last chance to repent and put their goods to righteous uses, are already upon them."[40] He underscores this point by the proverbial images of the corrosion of precious metals[41] and moth-eaten garments. These images were traditionally used to indicate

> not only temporality, but also uselessness .... The garments which are food for moths and the money which is tarnishing are not being used by their owner, and yet they could have been used by the poor. ... Temporality is one side of the coin, but the very temporality of goods points to their being withheld from the service for which God intended them.[42]

The charge here, however, goes beyond the earlier indictment that people have failed to utilize their wealth to benefit the needy (Jas 2:15-16); they have withheld even the wages rightfully owed to the poor (5:4).[43] This leads James to extend these images by stating that "their corrosion ... will eat your flesh as fire" (5:3), thereby introducing the

---

is partly to dissuade the Christians from setting a high value on wealth, partly to give them a certain grim comfort in the hardships of poverty (*cf.* 5[7-11])." Cf. also Reicke, *James, Peter and Jude*, 52; and Davids, *James*, 174.

[40]Davids, *James*, 177; cf. also Laws, *James*, 200, and the discussion of OPP 5:1, 5 above.

[41]Windisch concludes from the statement that "your gold and silver are rusted (κατίωται)" (5:3) that the author is from a lower socio-economic group: "Der den unteren Schichten angehörige Vf. scheint nicht zu wissen, daß Edelmetall im allgemeinen den Rost nicht annimmt" (Hans Windisch, *Die katholischen Briefe*, 3d ed., rev. Herbert Preisker, HNT 15 [Tübingen: J. C. B. Mohr (Paul Siebeck), 1951], 31). But the widespread use of these images (cited even by Windisch himself; cf. also Dibelius, *James*, 236-237; and Davids, *James*, 176) militates against drawing such conclusions about the socio-economic status of the author.

[42]Davids, *James*, 176. Cf. Dibelius, *James*, 236; Mußner, *Jakobusbrief*, 194; and Martin, *James*, 174. Contra Ropes, *St. James*, 285, who characterized such interpretations as "needless and far-fetched."

[43]Cf. Martin, *James*, 179. This charge is heightened by the variant reading ἀφυστερημένος ("defraud") in ℵ and B*. As Moo noted (*James*, 163 n. 1), "The difference in meaning is not great, since [ἀπεστερημένος] certainly connotes an illegitimate, fraudulent action." See also Laws, *James*, 201.

nuance of "a threat: Rust will eat you own flesh—i.e., you yourself will perish just as your riches."[44]

The climactic charge which James raises within this apostrophe to the rich is that they have "condemned" (cf. Jas 2:6b) and "murdered the righteous" (5:6a). Once again, this charge of "murder" is rooted in traditional themes of the "piety of the poor" (see especially Sir 34:22 [NRSV 26-27], "To take away a neighbor's living is to commit murder; to deprive an employee of wages is to shed blood").[45] What is more problematic is the clause by which James concludes the apostrophe: οὐκ ἀντιτάσσεται ὑμῖν. Most interpreters take the clause as a simple indicative ("[the righteous one] does not resist you").[46] But the clause might also be rendered as a question ("Does not [the righteous one] resist you?"), in which case the resistance offered by the righteous would be understood as their remonstrance before God ("the cries of the harvesters have entered the ears of Lord Sabaoth," 5:4).[47]

One other possible interpretation of the clause, however, seems to be more in keeping with the theme of this sub-unit. Schökel argued that the final clause of 5:6 should be rendered as a rhetorical question with "God" as its implied subject. This question, thus, repeats the idea expressed in Jas 4:6 (citing Prov 3:34) that "God resists (ἀντιτάσσεται) the proud."[48] Judgment does indeed await those who act with reckless

---

[44]Dibelius, *James*, 237.

[45]Cf. Maynard-Reid, *Poverty and Wealth*, 93; Davids, *James*, 179; and Ropes, *St. James*, 291. Moo believes that the judicial term καταδικάζω "suggests rather that the rich are using, and perhaps perverting, the legal processes available to accumulate property and gain wealth" (*James*, 166); in this regard, cf. Jas 2:6b.

[46]So Dibelius, *James*, 239; Cantinat, *Jacques et Jude*, 229; Laws, *James*, 206-207; Martin, *James*, 172 and 181-182; and Moo, *James*, 166-167.

[47]So Davids, *James*, 180; and Ropes, *St. James*, 292.

[48]Schökel argued that Jas 4:6 - 5:6 was a commentary on Prov 3:34. He proposed that Jas 4:7-12 comments on the second stiche of the quotation and 4:13 - 5:6 on the first. He summarized the argument of the unit as: "God gives grace to the humble, therefore humble yourselves before God; God opposes the arrogant, you behave arrogantly, should not He oppose you?" He supported his interpretation of the final clause of Jas 5:6 by noting the normal use of οὐ to introduce rhetorical questions, the stylistic use of such questions to close units, and the emphasis on social justice as better fitting this context than a call to Christian patience. See Luis Alonso Schökel, "James 5,2 [sic, '5,6'] and 4,6," *Bib* 54 (1973): 74-76. However, his identification of 4:6 - 5:6 as a formal unit within the Epistle is problematic. First, he begins by stating that "[a]ncient writers made no use of titles and subtitles outside of the text, they introduced them in the text" (ibid., 73). But if the quotation of Prov 3:34 is such a "title/subtitle" announcing the commentary to follow, then it

disregard for others in an attempt to fulfill their own evil "desires." Like those who "doubt ... [and are] double-minded, unstable in all their ways," the rich described here should not "suppose they will receive anything from the Lord" (Jas 1:7-8).

But if we shift James's question slightly so as to ask, "Why does 'God resist the rich' by withholding things from them and threatening judgment?", it seems that his answer might differ from the beliefs of his readers. Recalling our analysis of OPP 5:1, 5, it is possible to conclude that James believes God's "resistance" toward the rich, like the "miseries coming upon them," is for the purpose of bringing them to repentance, and not simply to bring punitive judgment upon them. If we follow this interpretation, then the call to "patience" in Jas 5:7-8 takes on a decidedly different nuance than enduring present affliction as one awaits the divine vindication of the "poor." James could be encouraging his readers to have patience in the hope that some of those who remain outside will yet be brought into the community.[49] But as they patiently wait, they must also "strengthen [their] hearts" (5:8b) by "stand[ing] firmly in the faith, not ... giv[ing] way to doubt."[50]

Summary of Jas 4:11 - 5:9

Our structural exegesis of this sub-unit of the Epistle has shown that James and his readers have markedly different understandings of the purposes of the eschatological "miseries" which are to be visited upon "the rich." His readers hear within the apostrophe to the rich the divine vindication of the poor by the destruction of the rich and their goods. They recognize within James's reminder that there is "one Lawgiver and

---

breaks the connection between 4:6 and what precedes. Additionally, his argument regarding the context relative to the theme of "patience" is undercut by what immediately follows in 5:7, as he himself admits: "The transition to 5,7 is simple and traditional: since God himself opposes the wicked, man should wait patiently" (ibid., 75). While these observations suggest that Jas 4:6 - 5:6 need not be a separate unit, they do not militate against the basic view that Jas 4:6 supports interpreting 5:6b as a rhetorical question with "God" as its implied subject. Cf. Maynard-Reid, *Poverty and Wealth*, 94-95.

[49]Might it be that the concept of a 'spiritual harvest' lies behind his statement, "Consider how the farmer waits for the precious fruit of the ground, having patience concerning it until it receives the early and late rains" (5:7b)?

[50]Davids, *James*, 184; cf. Günther Harder, "στηρίζω," *TDNT* 7:655-657. Note also the stark contrast between the believers who should "strengthen their hearts because the advent of the Lord has come near" and the rich who have "fattened their hearts in the Last Days."

Judge" that it is God who will bring this judgment and not they themselves.   Thus, "the righteous do not resist [the rich]," but rather are
"patient ... because the advent of the Lord has come near."   They will
not have to suffer the oppression of the rich for much longer.

But for James, these eschatological "miseries" need not lead to the
destruction of "the rich" themselves.   Rather, by recognizing the
ephemeral quality not only of their material possessions (5:2-3a) but also
of their very lives (4:14b), they can be brought to repentance (5:1).   The
believers are to patiently await their own "exaltation" (4:10) at the
"advent of the Lord" in the hope that others will cease their singular
pursuit of their own plans and desires for wealth and luxury and so have
their "souls saved from death."[51]   God "resists" the rich not solely as
a means of exacting vengeance upon them, but also as a final opportunity for "restoring" them as well.   God "resists" and allows "miseries to
come upon" non-believers in the hope they too will be "saved from
death."   But this does not necessarily indicate that similar means should
be used by believers to "restore" other believers who may have "wandered from the truth" by—like the rich—following their own "desires."
We have already emphasized that believers are not to "speak/grumble
against" or "judge/condemn" other believers.   The appropriate means for
"restoring" those "errant" members within the community will be
addressed in the final sub-unit of the Epistle.

Being a Patient Prophet (Jas 5:10-20)

Jas 5:10-11 — Patient Endurance

Figurativization in Jas 5:10-11

James introduces this sub-unit by providing a pair of "example[s]"
from the traditions of his readers that he encourages them to imitate.[52]

---

[51]George Peck ("James 5:1-6," *Int* 42 [1988]: 295-296) provided a balanced
appropriation of this text for twentieth century Christians of Euro-American cultures:
We could not responsibly assert that James directly authorizes the church to
undertake the overthrow of the established economic order.   Yet at the same
time we would be avoiding the central issues of the text were we to imply by
a passive stance that our situation is exactly the same as that of the epistle's
first readers.   Given where and who we are, and the plain meaning of
James's portrayal of what God is up to in these matters, how can we in good
conscience remain content to leave intact the crippling inequities with which
so many of our sisters and brothers must daily contend?   (ibid., 296)
Cf. also the comments by Maynard-Reid, *Poverty and Wealth*, 94-95.

[52]As Lee has noted, "Even in the sense of an example ὑπόδειγμα is not merely

The first example is "the prophets who spoke by the authority of the Lord."[53] While the readers' view of themselves as the people of God scattered in and persecuted by a hostile world (cf. their investment in the opening "Diaspora" figure) might have led them to emphasize the "suffering" of the prophets, for James "it is not the suffering which forms the example but the fact that those who suffered did in fact endure patiently."[54] It is this same emphasis on "endurance" that is underscored by the second example of Job.

James's inclusion of Job in this context has been perceived as problematic in two respects. The first is that the canonical portrait of Job is hardly that of a man who patiently and passively endures hardship. Consequently, some interpreters have suggested that the proverbial "patience of Job" developed in the extra-canonical traditions provided the source of the example known to the readers.[55] However, in that the theme of this unit is related to the concern that some within the community might "wander from the truth," it seems better to stress the nuance of "endurance" rather than "patience" for James's use of ὑπομονή with reference to Job; the primary example which the readers are to imitate is of the "perseverance of Job."[56]

The second problem in the Job illustration is that James relates the readers' knowledge about "the perseverance of Job" to their knowledge of τὸ τέλος κυρίου. Martin has proposed that τέλος here means "purpose," and that the whole example of Job in Jas 5:11 is a kind of theodicy. According to Martin, James's readers believed

---

like δεῖγμα a sample, but involves the notion of something suggested as a basis for imitation or instruction" (E. Kenneth Lee, "Words Denoting 'Pattern' in the New Testament," *NTS* 8 [1961/62]: 168).

[53]The Greek grammar in this verse has presented some difficulties for translators. Since τοὺς προφήτας is in the accusative case, it is the secondary object of λάβετε (its primary object being ὑπόδειγμα). The genitives τῆς κακοπαθίας καὶ τῆς μακροθυμίας are best taken as an example of hendiadys (cf. BDF § 442 (16) [228]; Ropes, *St. James*, 298; and Davids, *James*, 186), and despite the separation by the verb and vocative are best understood as modifying ὑπόδειγμα (thus, the prophets are "an example of perseverance in suffering").

[54]Davids, *James*, 186.

[55]See Dibelius, *James*, 246; Cantinat, *Jacques et Jude*, 239; and Davids, *James*, 187 for references. This emphasis upon "the patience of Job" is clearly found within the *Testament of Job*.

[56]Cf. Moo, *James*, 171-172; Martin, *James*, 189; Reicke, *James, Peter and Jude*, 53; and A. Strobel, *Untersuchungen zum eschatologischen Verzögerungsproblem: Auf Grund der spätjüdischen-urchristlichen Geschichte von Habakuk 2,2 ff.*, NovTSup 2 (Leiden and Köln: E. J. Brill, 1961), 257.

that God had forgotten them and was dealing harshly with their situation in a way that was out of character. Hence James' role is to offer a theodicy, that is, to reassert the divine character as good (v 11: he is πολύσπλαγχνος ... καὶ οἰκτίρμων), and the actions of God in allowing suffering to come are appealed to as serving a benign purpose (v 11). ... And that summons to ὑπομονή ... is the main facet of Job's experience on which James fastens in order to drive home the single point that his readers should learn how to see *their* troubles as part of God's design (τέλος).[57]

Martin's emphasis upon "the divine character as good" is quite in keeping with James's system of convictions; however, his emphasis on "suffering ... as serving a benign purpose" is more in keeping with the readers' convictions. It is the readers who believe God has a "purpose" or "design" in human suffering (namely that they learn patience and wisdom from their trials; see their investments in Jas 1:2-4). If we consider the example of Job in the light of James's own beliefs about the "blessings of trial" (Jas 1:2-12), then we would stress that Job "found his closest communion with God in the midst of adversity."[58]

But if τὸ τέλος κυρίου does not, for James, refer to "the purpose of the Lord," to what does it refer? The simplest explanation is that it refers to the "end" of the story of Job when God restores possessions and family to him. The terms τέλος and סוֹף are used in other texts to indicate "the end of the matter,"[59] and such a use here "provides a concrete example of the 'blessing' mentioned earlier ["we consider (as) blessed the ones who endured," 5:11a], and explains the final clause: Job's 'end' shows that the Lord is indeed compassionate and merciful."[60] Yet a reference to the past experience of Job need not exhaust James's investment in the term. He may also be looking to the ultimate 'end that the Lord will accomplish' at the eschaton in bringing an end to suffering.[61] There is thus a clear connection between Jas 5:10-11

---

[57]Martin, *James*, 189; cf. 194-195 and Mußner, *Jakobusbrief*, 207.

[58]Martin, *James*, 195. Thus, we again have an example of a commentator conflating the investments of the implied author and the implied readers and presenting both as the intentions of the writer.

[59]See Dibelius, *James*, 246.

[60]Moo, *James*, 172. Cf. Davids, *James*, 188; Laws, *James*, 216-217; and Sidebottom, *James, Jude, 2 Peter*, 59-60.

[61]Cf. the arguments in Robert P. Gordon, "ΚΑΙ ΤΟ ΤΕΛΟΣ ΚΥΡΙΟΥ ΕΙΔΕΤΕ (Jas v.11)," *JTS* 26 (1975): 91-95. He found the antecedent to the particular phrase "the end of the Lord" in the phrase קֵץ קָרֵם קִיצָא דה' within the Fragment-Targum (paralleled in other rabbinic texts) used to refer to the Passover as the appointed time of divine deliverance (ibid., 93-94). He relates the themes of the targumic material

and the conclusion in 5:19-20. Believers must "endure," that is not "wander from the truth," if they (like the prophets and Job) are to be "blessed" and have their "souls saved from death."

Jas 5:12-18 — Praying in Faith

Figurativization in Jas 5:12-18[62]

Within this central section of the final sub-unit, James directs his readers' attention to their communal responsibilities within the context of their relationships with the divine. His use of the phrase "above all things" (πρὸ πάντων) in introducing the section both signals the approaching close of the Epistle[63] and emphasizes the significance of what follows.[64] Moreover, we should probably understand it as applying not specifically to the prohibition of oaths in 5:12, but as highlighting the importance of this complementarity of the believer's relationship to God and to other believers. The responsibilities believers have to deal honestly, pray, and rejoice with other believers all are bound up in the believer's relationship with God.

It is this context which gives the prohibition of oaths its specific quality within the Epistle.[65] James is not concerned with the specific

---

and the Epistle of James: "the Exodus as the appointed end of the Israelites' sufferings in Egypt corresponds to the Parousia as the *terminus ad quem* of the sufferings of the Christian communities addressed in the letter of James" (ibid., 94). Cf. Strobel's suggestion that the Passover liturgy influenced Jas 5:7-11 ("Exkurs: Die passatheologische Einheit Jak 5, 7-11," *Eschatologischen Verzögerungsproblem*, 254-264).

[62]There is a possible opposition of actions in Jas 5:12. The positive action of "let your 'Yes' be yes, and [your] 'No' be no" could be opposed to the negative action of "swear[ing] either by Heaven or earth or any other oath." The problem is that there are no explicit receivers to these actions; to whom specifically should one avoid giving oaths? Additionally, if we were to analyze these actions as an opposition, they would seem to repeat the conviction already emphasized by OPP 4:13, 15-16 regarding the limits of human knowledge. Since nothing major is added to James's convictions and the receivers are problematic, it is better not to include this as an explicit opposition of actions.

[63]See Francis, "Form and Function," 125, for the customary use of this phrase in closing Hellenistic letters.

[64]Cf. Davids, *James*, 189; Laws, *James*, 219-220; and Martin, *James*, 203. Mußner (*Jakobusbrief*, 211) takes an almost opposite approach when he takes the phrase as marking a virtual afterthought; he paraphrases the opening of 5:12 as, "Vor allem darf ich nicht vergessen, euch noch diese Mahnung zu schreiben ...."

[65]Most historical critics devote considerable attention to the possible literary

formulae which should be employed in oaths or with whether any formula should be used, but with the importance of a believer's dealings with others being characterized by unquestionable truthfulness.[66] The believer's relationship with God factors into this demand in different ways. One should not invoke the divine ("do not swear by Heaven") as a guarantor of one's (apparently) dubious veracity. Moreover, a lack of honesty in dealing with others—particularly if one enlists God as an accomplice—is an obvious form of "wandering from the truth" (5:19) that breaks one's relationship with God and will cause one "to fall under condemnation" (5:12).

Reicke has suggested that this prohibition of oaths may also be related to the call for patient endurance since "[a]mong the recipients of the letter, swearing appears to have been a means of expressing impatience with their lot and bitterness at the oppressive social order."[67] How then should believers respond to their lot? James responds, "Is anyone among you suffering misfortune? Let him or her pray. Is anyone happy? Let him or her sing praise." (Jas 5:13) Believers are to acknowledge their dependence upon God in times of both suffering and joy.[68] And both prayer and praise in terms of James's system of convictions are to be "understood as a disposition of trustful submitting to God's good will (see 1:2-9), ... and the efficacy of prayer is connected with [the] willingness to submit to the divine plan and to await God's intervention."[69]

---

relationships between Jas 5:12 and Matt 5:34-37. See as examples Dibelius, *James*, 250-251; Davids, 188-191; Martin, *James*, 203-204; G. Stählin, "Zum Gebrauch von Beteuerungsformeln im Neuen Testament," *NovT* 5 (1962): 117-118; and Paul S. Minear, "Yes or No. The Demand for Honesty in the Early Church," *NovT* 13 (1971): 6-7. There have even been attempts to use the saying here as a means for assessing Jesus's own hermeneutics; see Gerhard Dautzenberg, "Ist das Schwurverbot Mt 5,33-37; Jak 5,12 ein Beispiel für die Torakritik Jesu?," *BZ*, NF 25 (1981): 47-66. But as throughout this study, we are more concerned with its function within the Epistle than with its pre- and post-history.

[66]Cf. Dibelius, *James*, 249-251 and most commentators.

[67]Reicke, *James, Peter and Jude*, 56.

[68]Contra Moo (*James*, 175-176) and Martin (*James*, 206) who contended that the "happiness" spoken of here is an inner attitude "independent of prevailing conditions." The pointed parallel between "Is anyone suffering misfortune? ... Is anyone happy?" suggests that James is describing proper responses toward the divine in just such extremely different circumstances. Cf. Davids, *James*, 192.

[69]Martin, *James*, 200-201.

James's continuing instructions regarding the specific prayers for those who are sick and prayers of confession (5:14-16) firmly establish the communal context of all prayer and praise. The responsibility of believers to each other is underscored both with regard to the leaders within the community ("let [the one who is sick] call[70] the elders of the church," 5:14) and to all other members of the community ("confess [your] sins to one another and pray on behalf of one another so that you may be healed," 5:16). This may be, in fact, somewhat of a false distinction. As Reicke noted in his discussion of the office of "elder" within early Christian churches,

> Generally the elders seem to have been laymen in the sense that they were engaged in ordinary professions and occupations. It was some time before the individual congregations were able to employ full-time ministers. Yet the elders mentioned in Acts and the later epistles are not exclusively laymen. They are supposed to be appointed and ordained by apostles or disciples of apostles (Acts xiv 23; Titus i 5).[71]

At a minimum it can be said that James does not offer any explicit indication that such responsibilities are incumbent only upon those who may have the charism of healing.[72]

James concludes this section by assuring his readers that "the effective prayer of a righteous person is capable of much" (5:16b). Several proposals have been offered to explain the nuance of the enigmatic participle ἐνεργουμένη within this statement.[73] Since this

---

[70]The widely attested view that προσκαλέω indicates that the person is "too ill to go to the elders" (see for example Davids, *James*, 192; and Martin, *James*, 206) suggests over-interpretation. This common word states only that the one who is sick should "summon" the elders and need not imply that she or he is bedridden.

[71]Reicke, *James, Peter and Jude*, 58-59.

[72]As is suggested by Dibelius's comments (*James*, 252-253) that "their healing power must be connected with [the elders] official character." This emphasis on "miracle workers" arises at least in part from his characterization of the healings as exorcisms. I doubt that such an interpretation is warranted in that James elsewhere uses language about the demonic, but there is no such language within these verses. Cf. Davids, *James*, 194; Laws, *James*, 228; and Martin, *James*, 211. Neither should we go to the opposite extreme and assume that James is explicitly rejecting charismatic healing, as has been suggested by Gary S. Shogren, "Will God Heal Us? A Re-examination of James 5:15-16a," *EvQ* 61 (1989): 100. It may be that the specific role of the elders described in 5:14 is restricted to the anointing with oil which may have already been perceived as a sacerdotal function. On sacramental views of this anointing, see Moo, *James*, 178-179.

[73]Dibelius (*James*, 256), Cantinat (*Jacques et Jude*, 256), and Laws (*James*,

section encourages the readers to acknowledge their dependence upon God regardless of the current circumstances of their lives, Davids is probably correct in his view that "this participle points to God as the active agent"[74] regardless of how one interprets the syntactical technicalities.[75] It is this confidence that James illustrates by his allusion to the Elijah cycle in 1 Kings. As with the earlier reference to the "endurance of Job" (Jas 5:11), commentators have often pointed to inconsistencies between the details of James's illustration and the narratives of the Hebrew Bible.[76] But Vouga has noted that the accounts of the cessation and restoration of rain frame the narratives recounting Elijah's prophetic activity, and so here serve as a symbol of his divine mission.[77] Just as God answered Elijah's prayers and so enabled him to fulfill his prophetic mission, so God will also answer the prayers of believers as they perform their mission in behalf of others.

Before continuing to the final section of this sub-unit, we need to notice one other facet of James's discussion of prayer for fellow believers. By relating healing and forgiveness ("The prayer offered with faith will heal/save [σώσει] the sick, ... and if he [or she] has committed sins, they will be forgiven," 5:15), James "retains something of the

---

234) took the participle as a simple adjective ("energetic prayer"). Ropes (*St. James*, 309), Mayor (*St. James*, 177-179), and Mußner (*Jakobusbrief*, 227-228) construed it as a temporal participle ("when it is exercised/actualized/effective"). Adamson (*James*, 199) took it as an adverbial modifier of the main verb ("is very powerful *in its operation*").

[74]Davids, *James*, 196-197.

[75]Cf. Martin, *James*, 211-212. Both Mußner (*Jakobusbrief*, 228) and Mayor (*St. James*, 178) agreed with this interpretation, although Mußner identified the participle as a dynamic middle (*Jakobusbrief*, 227 n. 4) and Mayor was emphatic that it must be passive (*St. James*, 177-179).

[76]Cf. Dibelius, *James*, 256-257; Davids, *James*, 197; and Martin, *James*, 212-213. Robert Eisenman ("Eschatological 'Rain' Imagery in the War Scroll from Qumran and in the Letter of James," *JNES* 49 [1990]: 173-184) attempted to connect patristic traditions about James the Just as a rainmaker with the illustration of 5:17-18. He suggested that the three and one half years without rain is an allusion to the interval between James's martyrdom (c. 62 CE) and the beginning of the Jewish Revolt (66 CE), "which was no doubt seen in some circles as the beginning of [the] process of eschatological final judgment" (ibid., 179). Eisenman's lack of concern for relative dates and fanciful connections make his article less than convincing.

[77]"Jc fait allusion à des traditions juives ..., développées à partir de 1 R 17,1; 18,1. 41-46, qui encadrent le récit de toute son activité prophétique. La prière d'Elie a pour origine, pour objet et pour visée la mission que Dieu lui a donnée." Vouga, *Jacques*, 144.

long-established connection between sickness and sin."[78]   Rather than straining the evidence in an effort to determine whether James is offering a theodicy to explain why some believers are not healed,[79] it is better to note that the three previous uses of σῴζω within the Epistle (see 1:21; 2:14; and 4:12) all have a soteriological and eschatological nuance.[80] James is thus stressing that believers should be concerned with both the spiritual and physical well-being of other believers as the end approaches, and so provides a smooth transition into the closing section of the Epistle with its climactic use of the verb σῴζω.

Jas 5:19-20 — The Task of a Prophet

Convictions Emphasized in Jas 5:19-20

Having come to the final verses of the Epistle, it is appropriate to remind ourselves that we still have not encountered an opposition of actions that explains how a person initially comes to know God as "pure good" and so is able to begin the process of becoming a believer. We had noted this lacuna in summarizing James's system of convictions at

---

[78]Laws, *James*, 229. Dibelius (*James*, 254-255) argued that no connection exists here between healing and forgiveness.   The verbs σῴζω and ἐγείρω have their technical meanings of "to heal" and "to restore to health," and the κἄν of 5:15b "evidently introduces a second promise" of forgiveness.

[79]Martin argued that by this relationship "James implies that sometimes sin is a cause of illness" (*James*, 210), and that it is only "those who are ill *because of sin* (and have confessed this sin) [that] have access to the channel through which they can receive healing from a divine source" (ibid., 212; emphasis mine).   Better is Laws's interpretation (*James*, 229) that "James thinks of a possible, but not inevitable, association rather than a direct cause and effect relationship."

[80]Cf. Vouga, *Jacques*, 142.   Vouga also offered his own theodicy in terms of these verses.   He maintained that within this context "save" (5:15) and "heal" (5:16) are synonymous, and concluded from this that while it is certain that God will "save" the sick, "c.-à-d. *en la fidélité de Dieu qui accompagne le frère dans sa maladie et sa souffrance*," the question is left open as to whether God will actually grant a physical recovery from the illness itself.   "Maintenant l'ambiguïté de ἐγερεῖ, Jc laisse Dieu *libre* de la manière dont il répondra: sera-ce par la guérison, ou en donnant au malade de vivre sa maladie autrement?   Jc laisse cette question ouverte."   Cf. Ambrosius Verheul, "The Paschal Character of the Sacrament of the Sick: Exegesis of James 5:14-15 and the New Rite for the Sacrament of the Sick," in *Temple of the Holy Spirit: Sickness and Death of the Christian in Liturgy* (New York: Pueblo Publishing Company, 1983), 252-253, who likewise stresses the eschatological aspects of σῴζω and ἐγείρω in terms of final deliverance from suffering in the resurrection of the believer.

the end of our analysis of Jas 1:22 - 2:26 (see the end of chapter 4). There were no convictions emphasized by oppositions of actions within the discursive unit Jas 3:1 - 4:12, and the previous oppositions within this final unit of Jas 4:11 - 5:20 have repeated convictions expressed earlier in the Epistle. Will the final opposition of actions within the Epistle fill in this gap?

OPP 5:19 — Restoring Errant Believers. James concludes the Epistle by opposing the positive action of a believer "bringing back/restoring" a fellow believer (ἐπιστρέψῃ τις αὐτόν) to the negative action of a believer "wandering from the truth" (τις ἐν ὑμῖν πλανηθῇ ἀπὸ τῆς ἀληθείας). That both the subjects and receivers are believers is clearly indicated by the communal vocative address (ἀδελφοί μου) and James's identification of the wanderer as "someone among you." Thus, the negative action is clearly that of apostasy, and the positive action of "restoring" takes place *intramuros* and is not an evangelistic or missionary activity. In the light of James's overall system of convictions, we can also identify this apostasy as the rejection of or failure to perform the will of God (cf. the discussion of Jas 4:17 above).[81]

James does not provide any explicit description of the qualifications that allow a believer to restore an errant believer, nor does he give much insight into the qualifications of the negative subject. Since this errant believer "wanders from the *truth*," we may infer that the negative subject lacks (or perhaps more accurately has lost) some type of knowledge, specifically knowledge regarding the will of God. The paucity of evidence regarding the qualifications of the subjects again indicates that James emphasizes the effects of the actions on their respective receivers.

Although James specifies the effects of the positive action in some detail ("the one who restores a sinner from the error of his [or her] way will save his [αὐτοῦ] soul from death and will cover a multitude of sins," 5:20), it is not entirely clear which, if in fact any, of these effects

----

[81]Similar observations have been made by Mußner (*Jakobusbrief*, 230 n. 4), Davids (*James*, 198), and Martin (*James*, 217-219); however, both Davids and Martin suggest that this wandering may be considered by James to be the consequence of demonic activity. Martin cites Jas 3:15 and 4:7 in support of this interpretation. Yet it should be emphasized that 3:15 and 4:7 *describe* certain actions as demonic, not as actually being caused by demons. Indeed, this explanation of "wandering" is inconsistent with James's conviction that sin arises from human desire and not from external sources; see the discussion of 1:13-16 in chapter 3 above.

apply to the receiver of the positive action. The ambiguity is introduced by the pronoun αὐτοῦ which modifies "soul." Just whose "soul" is saved from death—the "sinner" (ἁμαρτωλόν, the receiver of the positive action) or the "the one who restores" (ὁ ἐπιστρέψας, the subject of the positive action)?[82] And is it the same person who gains the benefits of "covering a multitude of sins"? It is certainly likely that at least the first effect ("save his [or her] soul from death") applies to the errant believer as the receiver of the action 'restoration,' and so we may apply these effects to the receiver here in our analysis of OPP 5:19. Thus, the errant believer who is "restored" gains 'life' and 'forgiveness' ("saved from death," "sins covered"), but those believers who continue to "wander from the truth" will receive 'death' (since they are not "saved," nor are their "sins covered"). Nevertheless, we will need to return to the other possibilities opened by this ambiguity in discussing the semantic investments in these figures.

But where does the conviction expressed by this opposition of actions belong within James's overall pattern of belief? The action of "restoring" an errant believer must be a crucial part of a believer's vocation; it is thus a "work" of the "word," a means of acting as God has acted in redeeming the believer in the first place. Thus, in terms of the schema of James's system of convictions presented at the end of chapter 4, this opposition is another expression of the fifth stage leading to blessedness and provides an example of being a "doer of the word/work."[83] Yet, since it is 'acting as God has acted in redeeming the believer,' it may be possible to draw some inferences by way of

---

[82]This ambiguity was not lost on the scribes who transmitted the text. While some attempted to solve the problem by transposing αὐτοῦ to follow the prepositional phrase (ἐκ θανάτου αὐτοῦ, i.e. "from death itself;" P[74] B 614 1108 1611 it[ff]), other scribes simply omitted the problematic pronoun (K L Ψ and most minuscules). Cf. *TCGNT*, 686; and Martin, *James*, 217. Neither of these variants completely removes the ambiguity; while the absence of the possessive pronoun (it is simply "a soul") may make it slightly more likely that the "soul" will be identified as the sinner's, it does not rule out identifying the soul as that of the restorer.

[83]Notice that our earlier analysis of James's convictions has shown that the effect of being a "doer of the word/work" is being "birthed by God" (1:18) and having one's "soul saved from death" (1:21)—the sixth and final stage in achieving blessedness. This would support the view that restorer's soul is (also) "saved from death" (5:20) by virtue of having brought back an errant believer. Again, we will return to the multiple investments in this closing verse in discussing the figurativization below.

parallel with regard to the actions of God or the mediator in bringing a person to know God as "pure good."[84]

To find such parallels, however, we must consider a broader context than just Jas 5:19-20. Since the theme of this discursive unit as a whole (4:11 - 5:20, "bringing back" one's "neighbor") is obviously related to the conviction expressed by OPP 5:19, it will provide an appropriate context for our consideration. How is it that believers are to conduct themselves relative to one another according to this unit? To begin with, they are not to "speak against" or "judge" one another (4:11), nor are they to "grumble against one another" (5:9). These actions would seem to parallel James's conviction that God does not "reproach/reprimand" (ὀνειδίζοντος) but rather "gives to everyone generously" (διδόντος ... πᾶσιν ἁπλῶς; cf. OPP 1:5). Additionally, believers are to deal honestly with one another, to pray and rejoice together, to share in one another's periods of suffering and sickness, and to confess their sins to one another (5:12-16). By these actions they demonstrate their reliance upon God, that "the Lord is compassionate and merciful" (5:11), and that the "advent of the Lord" which will bring an end to all human suffering "is near ... [for] the Judge stands before the door" (5:7-9).

We may conjecture from this, and from James's designation of himself as a "servant of God and of the Lord Jesus Christ" (1:1), that the mediator performs similar actions which served to convince non-believers that God is "pure good" so that they may have trust/faith that God will meet their needs, etc. But we can only "conjecture," because James provides no oppositions of actions that emphasize convictions about the mediator. As we noted in the conclusion to chapter 4, this silence regarding the initial saving activities of the mediator will have significant importance for our understanding of the Epistle's purpose.

Figurativization in Jas 5:19-20

In beginning to discuss the figurativization in these verses, we first need to choose the appropriate English terms to describe the activity which James encourages from his readers. Several commentators have chosen to describe the activity of "restoring a sinner" who has "wan-

---

[84]On how the pattern of belief in one category (e.g., believers) may be used to aid in understanding and filling out the pattern of belief in another category (e.g., the divine, mediator[s]), see Patte, *Structural Exegesis for New Testament Critics*, 51-53. For a more detailed discussion of the theoretical basis for such comparisons, see idem, *Religious Dimensions*, 115-128.

dered from the truth" by the use of "conversion" language.[85] However, our analysis of OPP 5:19 indicated that what is in view is not the making of new "converts" to the Christian religion, but of "bringing back" Christians who have apostatized. In order to avoid confusion on our part, it is probably best to maintain the less technical language provided by a more literal translation of James's figures of "restoring" errant believers rather than introducing "conversion" language.[86]

We have already noted the ambiguity introduced into these verses by the uncertain antecedent of the possessive pronoun αὐτοῦ that modifies ψυχήν in 5:20. Whose "soul" is it that is "saved from death," and who gains the benefit of "covering a multitude of sins"? Several resolutions to this ambiguity are possible. It could be that both of these promises are offered as a reward to the one who "restores" errant believers; by performing this "work," one not only "saves his [or her own] soul," but "covers the multitude of sins" that have been committed by both these members of the community.[87] Yet, "turning a sinner back from the error of his [or her] way" and so "saving his [or her] soul from death" is such a natural image. Thus, many commentators apply the first promise ('salvation') to the sinner, and the second promise ('forgiveness') to either the restorer or both.[88] Since the two promises are, however, most likely parallel expressions, still other commentators prefer to apply both promises to the errant believer.[89]

In the majority of instances in the Epistle where we have encountered such ambiguities it has been possible, on the basis of the general patterns of their belief systems, to assign certain possible

---

[85]Cf. Laws, *James*, 238 et passim; Reicke, *James, Peter, and Jude*, 62; Moo, *James*, 190; and Martin, *James*, 219, who makes a point of stressing that "radical conversion can describe the initial turning to God at the time of salvation ... [and] can also refer to 'turning back' to God from whom one has strayed." The same is true of both the translation and German original ("bekehren" and "Bekehrung") of Dibelius (see *James*, 257-258).

[86]That it really is our problem rather than one for the author and first readers of the Epistle is supported by the fact that the verb ἐπιστρέφω had not "already acquired the technical religious meaning of the modern verb 'convert,' although such passages as Mt. 13[15] (Is. 6[10]), Lk. 1[16] 22[32], ... [and] 1 Thess. 1[9] show that the process had already begun." Ropes, *St. James*, 314; cf. Adamson, *James*, 202-203.

[87]So Cantinat, *Jacques et Jude*, 261-262; and Adamson, *James*, 202-204.

[88]So Dibelius, *James*, 258-259; Ropes, *St. James*, 315-316; Laws, *James*, 239; and Mußner, *Jakobusbrief*, 253.

[89]So Reicke, *James, Peter and Jude*, 62-63; Davids, *James*, 200-201; Moo, *James*, 190; and Martin, *James*, 220.

semantic investments to the readers and others to the implied author. In this case, however, both possible investments are in keeping with the beliefs and concerns of the author. Given the theme of this final discursive unit, it seems almost certain that James is encouraging the implied reader to follow his own example in "restoring" those who have "wandered from the truth" so that their "multitude of sins" might be "covered" and their "souls saved from death" in the coming eschatological judgment. Yet in the very process of making this point, James underscores "that the Christian who is walking the way of righteousness is responsible for the 'wanderer' ... and that there is some type of blessing for the one who rescues the brother or sister from error."[90] Indeed according to James's system of convictions, it is precisely by performing such "deeds of the word" that one finally receives ultimate blessedness (cf. Jas 1:22-25).

Summary of Jas 5:10-20

James begins this sub-unit by reminding his readers that their community "considers as blessed the ones who endured" (5:11). He encourages them to "take as an example ... the prophets" not only because they demonstrated "perseverance in suffering" (5:10), but also because they accepted the responsibility of calling those who had "wandered from the truth" to turn back "from the error of their way" (5:19-20). By assuming this responsibility for their brothers and sisters, they will not only assist those who might err in their "endurance" but will themselves be "blessed for their doing" (1:25), having their own "souls saved from death" and finding forgiveness for their "many sins."

Discursive Structure and Purpose
in Jas 4:11 - 5:20

In summarizing the sub-unit Jas 4:1-12 in the previous chapter, we noted that James's call of the readers to repentance in those verses was one of the central purposes of the Epistle. Within this final unit, James exhorts his readers to follow his example by "restoring" others within their community who may be "wandering from the truth." He begins in 4:11 - 5:9 by reminding them one final time that the standard of judgment will be whether believers have accepted the divine will as their own, and by stressing the urgency of the situation since "the Judge is standing at the door." He then directs their attention to the means for

---

[90]Martin, *James*, 220.

accomplishing this vocation. They cannot "restore" others by "grumbling against one another" and "condemning" their sisters and brothers in the faith; rather, they must encourage "patient endurance" by directing the attention of "wandering" and "suffering" believers toward God's goodness and provision through communal prayer, praise and confession. This vocation of restoring errant believers with which James challenges the readers in the closing verses of the Epistle encapsulates his own purposes in writing to them.[91]

In reviewing the inverted parallelisms between the opening and closing verses of the Epistle in chapter two of this study, we focused on the connection between James's description of his readers as "the twelve tribes of the Diaspora" and his concern for those who "wander from the truth." Yet, there are other parallelisms between the introduction and conclusion of the Epistle. As Ralph Martin has pointed out,

> James sets out his thoughts on prayer [5:13-18] in the context of suffering. He has come full turn, since he began his letter with a reference to trials (1:2) and now ends his letter on the same note (this *inclusio* pattern frames the theme of suffering that occupies much of the sections in between the opening and closing of the epistle, in particular 1:12; 2:6-7; 5:1-11).[92]

It is thus time for us likewise to come full circle and to once again look at the Epistle as a whole. Has the structural semiotic analysis which we have pursued confirmed our initial hypotheses and provided us with answers to our questions regarding the (apparent lack of) structure and organization in the Epistle and what the author hoped to accomplish by writing it in this way?

---

[91]Cf. Davids, *James*, 26 and 201; Reicke, *James, Peter and Jude*, 62; and Martin, *James*, 221.

[92]Ibid., 205.

CHAPTER SEVEN

"RESTORING" THE "DIASPORA": EVALUATING THE THESIS

In the introduction to this study I likened readings operating within a communication paradigm to the process of reading a text "from the inside out." Such an approach to reading attempts to "reveal the selections, orderings and arrangements made by the author in moving from the deep to surface structure"[1] of a text, to imaginatively recon-struct something like the operation of transforming concepts into (hopefully) persuasive expression. It is just such an approach that we have employed in our exegesis of the Epistle of James by beginning with elucidating James's system of convictions from the inverted parallelisms of his themes and his explicit oppositions of actions and then turning to his selection and use of figures to persuade his readers to adopt this pattern of belief as their own. But having explored in this manner the details and intra-relationships of the Epistle, we come now to its outer textual reaches—the Epistle as a whole.

Our analyses of the discursive semantic structures and themati-zation within the Epistle have supported the division of the Epistle into four discursive units that was proposed in the later sections of chapter two of this study. It remains for us to consider how these four units contribute to the development of the overall theme of the Epistle (isolated by the inverted parallelisms between Jas 1:1 and 5:19-20), namely James's desire to "restore" the readers to the "truth" from which

---

[1]Louw, "Discourse Analysis," 102.

they have "wandered." Our procedure in this final task will be similar
to that which we have used previously. We will begin by reviewing
those religious purposes of the Epistle related to its communication of a
specific pattern of religious beliefs, the system of convictions of the
implied author "James." Next, we will consider an overarching figure
of this writing developed by its use of epistolary features. Finally, we
will consider how the various discursive structures and features inter-
relate to achieve James's purposes for writing this text.

The Religious Purposes of the
Epistle of James

Our theoretical overview of structural semiotics in chapter two of
this study emphasized that one of the major purposes of religious
discourse as viewed from this perspective is the communication of a
system of convictions (technically a "micro-semantic universe")
regarding how to perceive and order the realm of human experience.
With regard to religious paraenetic discourse in particular, this "'causing
to believe' [by adopting the author's system of convictions] becomes the
dominant function, but 'causing to do' remains the ultimate objective of
the discourse."[2] To conclude our analysis of the religious purposes of
the Epistle, we need to summarize this system of convictions and then
inquire as to how it relates to the paraenetic objectives (the "causing to
do") of this text. We will construct our summary of James's pattern of
beliefs by narrativizing the courses of action which alternatively lead
individuals either to having their "souls/lives saved" or to "death."

The Process of Becoming a Believer
According to James's Faith

To assist our conceptualizing of the interrelationships between
James's individual convictions about "believers" with regard to what is
"blessedness" and "evil," we will develop two idealized stories—one in
which a believer progresses through a process culminating in salvation
and the other in which a potential believer follows a different sequence
which ends, for James, in "death."[3] The choice of this particular
category of convictions is a function of the fact that the vast majority of

---

[2]Patte, "Method for Didactic Discourses," 91. See the fuller discussion of these
issues in the section on "A Major Goal of Religious Discourse" in chapter 2 above.

[3]On the use of such narratives to present a system of convictions, see Patte,
Structural Exegesis for New Testament Critics, 47-53.

oppositions of actions in the Epistle concern believers.[4] The 'plot' for our stories will be provided by the sequence of actions in the schematic presentation of the hierarchy of convictions which we have developed through our study of those oppositions of actions.

We must remind ourselves, however, that our study of these oppositions, particularly in the second discursive unit of the Epistle (1:22 - 2:26), has highlighted the fact that James's presentation of convictions begins this process of becoming a believer *in media res*.[5] Of the convictions explicitly stated within the Epistle, the initial stage in obtaining blessedness is 'knowing God is the source of "every good and perfect gift" (1:17) and of nothing bad or evil.' Yet how does one come to have this (positive) knowledge so that one does not fall victim to believing that 'God gives both "good gifts" and bad gifts (e.g., "temptations/trials" [πειρασμοί], 1:13a)'? Our analysis of the oppositions of actions which have the divine as their subject (OPP 1:5 and OPP 2:5, 6) as compared with OPP 5:19-20 regarding the vocation of believers suggested that God or the mediator ("the Lord Jesus Christ," 1:1) must perform good acts for potential believers if they are to have this essential knowledge. But James gives no indication of what those good acts were or might be. We must begin, then, where the implied author begins.[6]

Once a person comes to know that God is "pure good," it is possible for her to have "faith" (1:6) in God, that is to have trust that God will give those things which are needed. What is most needed, in James's pattern of beliefs, is "wisdom," (1:5) a knowledge of and insight into the will of God. God will give this wisdom "generously" to those who ask in "faith" (1:5-6). But when the believer receives this wisdom

---

[4]Eleven of fourteen oppositions of actions in the Epistle have believers as their positive subjects; see Appendix B.

[5]See the conclusion to chapter 4 of this study.

[6]This observation confronts us directly with the fact that any given discourse presents only a "micro-semantic universe" and not a complete "semantic universe" which could "potentially include all the elements of human experience" (Patte, *Religious Dimensions*, 80). The very 'convictional logic' of the implied author's pattern of beliefs would demand that someone or something communicate knowledge about the divine as 'pure good' to people so that they do not succumb to the evil which results from believing the divine to be both 'good' and 'bad.' While the silence of the discourse at precisely this point frustrates our attempts to fully understand the human author's theology (the full system of arguments which might be used to express and support the more foundational convictions), it is an essential key to understanding the purpose of the specific discourse the Epistle of James. We will return to this issue in the next section.

as a gift from God, it does more than simply provide her with knowledge and insight. This gift of wisdom is "receiving the implanted word" (1:21) from God that changes a person internally so that she not only knows what God's will is, but accepts it as her own and "desires" to perform it. It is then possible for her to be a "doer of the word/work," rather than simply one who "hears" (1:22-25). Specifically, she will accept the vocation of performing "works" on behalf of other believers (such as "caring for orphans and widows" [1:27b] and meeting the needs of the indigent [2:15-17] rather than being "tainted by the world's" [1:27c] striving after status and luxury) in demonstration of God's goodness about which she has "heard." Finally, she will be "blessed for/in her doing" (1:25) by being "birthed by God" (1:18) and so having her "soul saved from death" (1:21, 5:20).[7]

Conversely, James's beliefs about evil arise from the possibility that a person will have "doubt" (1:6) about God as "pure good" and so will both trust and distrust God. As a result, he will not ask for "wisdom" as a gift but will rather try to learn God's will through "enduring trials" (1:2-4), which are in fact what he believes to be God's "gifts" to him, and so they confirm his "doubt." Because "he does not ask," he does "not receive anything from God" (4:2-3, cf. 1:7-8) and his internal evil "desires" (1:14-15) are not replaced by a "desire" to perform God's will. Over time he becomes a "forgetful hearer" who has "deceived himself" (1:22) by "thinking himself to be religious" (1:26). Rather than being "birthed by God" (1:18), his "desire gives birth to sin; and when it has matured, sin gives birth to death" (1:15).[8]

---

[7]Luke Timothy Johnson makes a number of similar points in summarizing his reconstruction of James's concept of discipleship. He likewise begins with "[t]he ultimate dependence of all on God" as a source of good gifts, identifies "wisdom" with the "implanted word" which gives "to humans another way of viewing and measuring reality," and summarizes James's call to be "doers of the word" as "living out the demands of the law of the kingdom, 'Love your neighbor as yourself' (2:8)." See Luke T. Johnson, "Friendship with the World/Friendship with God: A Study of Discipleship in James," in *Discipleship in the New Testament*, ed. Fernando F. Segovia (Philadelphia: Fortress Press, 1985), 176.

[8]Cf. Johnson's discussion of the "double-minded" person who is a "friend of the world" in ibid., 174-177. His discussion there is a fine description of James's concept of the evil "desires" that drive the actions of those who have not been changed internally by the "implanted word." However, he missed James's belief that the foundational problem is believing God to be a source of both good and evil when he identified double-mindedness with "the desire to live by both measures [the standard of the evil world and the standard of the divine will] at once, to be friends with everyone" (ibid., 176).

More Specific Religious Purposes
of the Epistle

As we begin to inquire regarding the specific religious purposes of the Epistle as a refinement of its general purpose as religious discourse, we need to summarize what we have learned about the implied reader constructed by the author. James has envisioned his audience as and directed his argument toward people who are already believers. This point has been underscored not only by his figurativization of the implied readers (e.g., the vocative ἀδελφοί [μου] occurs fifteen times in the Epistle), but also by the limits of the system of convictions presented in the Epistle. The foundational conviction within his hierarchy of blessedness presumes that a person has already begun the process of becoming a believer since he or she should already know God is "pure good." Nevertheless, what prompts James to compose this text is his concern that they have "wandered from the truth" (5:19), or are at least in danger of doing so, and would not receive the blessedness promised to the believer.

But is "wandering" a figurativization of a failure to maintain "orthodoxy" or "orthopraxis"?[9] Certainly James is concerned about ethical failures on the part of his readers, as the paraenetic emphases make abundantly clear. They have "dishonored the poor" whom "God has chosen" (2:5-6). They have offered only pious words in place of assistance to those who are in need (2:15-16). Their strivings for status have produced "quarrels and disputes" within the community (4:1), with members "speaking against" and "condemning" one another (4:11). But each of these specific ethical failures is only a 'symptom' of what is for James the underlying 'disease.' Ethical failures are symptomatic of people who have not "received the implanted word" (1:21) that would transform their evil "desires" (1:14-15) into a willingness to perform the will of God revealed in "the wisdom which is from above" (3:17-18).

Thus, the most foundational symptom of the disease which plagues the implied readers is an absence of "wisdom" (1:5). James argues that they lack this wisdom because they have allowed their "piety of the poor" and certain aspects of "wisdom theology" to convince them that God is a source of bad as well as good. True enough, James admits, they believe that God uses bad things such as trials/temptations to accomplish a good end, namely that they will learn the wisdom which

---

[9]Again borrowing Martin's terms for discussing the 'wanderer' in Jas 5:19 (*James*, 219).

they need to achieve blessedness (cf. 1:2-4). But these beliefs have had the decidedly negative effect of making them both trust and distrust God. It is this disease—a "double-mindedness" about a God who is both good and bad rather than complete "faith" in a God who is "pure good"—that caused them to "wander" and placed them (again) in danger of "death."

The cure for this disease is for the readers to be "brought back" to the "truth" (5:20) that God is "pure good." James proffers the cure on their behalf by his insistence that "God tests no one" (1:13b), that indeed God is "the Father of Lights, with whom there is neither varia- tion nor shadow cast by turning" (1:17). He also encourages those believers who have not "wandered" to fulfill their vocation of doing the "works" of providing care, prayer and forgiveness (5:13-16) that was "implanted" in them when they received the "word/wisdom" (1:21). Once these errant believers again come to know God as "pure good," they will be able to ask God for the wisdom which they lack, and since their request will be accompanied by "faith" rather than "doubt" they will receive it as a "generous gift" (1:5-6). Then they will both know how and be willing to perform their vocation of 'acting as God acts' in providing good for others and be "blessed in/for their doing" (1:25, cf. 2:20-26) by having their "souls saved from death" (1:21, 5:20).

Thus, James's errant implied readers have not "wandered" by a failure of orthodoxy *or* orthopraxis, but rather by a failure of orthodoxy *and* orthopraxis. It is the loss of belief in God as "pure good" that leads to their ethical failures. They will not be "restored" to orthopraxis unless they first are "restored" to orthodoxy by seeing God as "pure good" and not as "both good and bad;" but unless this orthodox "faith" leads to not only "hearing" but also "doing the word" regarding God's will (1:22-25), it will be of no "benefit" (2:14). "Faith [orthodoxy] separated from works [orthopraxis] is dead" (2:26). Thus, causing his readers to once again believe that God is "pure good" (by adopting his system of convictions) is the dominant function while causing them to "do the word" remains the ultimate objective of the religious paraenetic discourse "the Epistle of James."

An Overarching Figure: The "Epistle" of James

The function of causing the readers to once again believe as he does and so meet the objective of causing them to "do the word" are among the chief purposes which led the author to compose the Epistle. As with any skillful writer, we may assume that James carefully selected not only the individual figures but also the overall organizing structure or genre to effectively communicate this function and objective to the implied readers so that he might achieve these purposes for writing. These "inside" functions and objectives ("deep structures") should, therefore, be able to assist our understanding of such "outer limits" of the discourse ("surface structures") as its use of generic conventions. To phrase it differently, how does our understanding of James's religious purposes for writing provide insight into his choice and use of generic conventions such as the epistolary prescript which opens the discourse?

One of the findings of studies on Greco-Roman epistolography has been that letters were "primarily a function of a previous relationship."[10] Could it be that James utilizes epistolary conventions to figurativize the relationship between himself and his readers? If so, what can we learn about the author's perception of that relationship from these figures? To answer these questions, we need to determine what epistolary conventions have been used in the text and then inquire as to their rhetorical function.[11]

Epistolary Elements in the Epistle of James

There has been widespread agreement among historico-critical scholars that the prescript in Jas 1:1 is "the only epistolary element in the entire document" with the corollary conclusion being drawn that the apparent epistolary form which it provides is little more than a "literary veneer."[12] But, as we saw in reviewing the work of redaction critics on the Epistle, this scholarly consensus has now been challenged by Fred O. Francis. Thus, before we can determine whether this overture to

---

[10]William G. Doty, *Letters in Primitive Christianity* (GBS, NT series; Philadelphia: Fortress Press, 1973), 70; cf. John L. White, "New Testament Epistolary Literature in the Framework of Ancient Epistolography," *ANRW* II.25.2 (1984): 1731-1732.

[11]In what follows we will ultimately be moving outside the limits of the discourse itself to envision a possible *Sitz im Leben* for the Epistle. If it should seem somewhat more imaginative than proposals offered by historical critics, it will be in part because its musings are primarily related to a possible rhetorical setting and function of the Epistle rather than to historical ones. But it must be asserted that reconstructions of an historical *Sitz im Leben* are no less exercises of the imagination; cf. the comments on the "historical imagination" by Elisabeth Schüssler Fiorenza, *In Memory of Her: A Feminist Theological Reconstruction of Christian Origins* (New York: Crossroad Publishing Company, 1986), xx.

[12]Dibelius, *James*, 1-2. Virtually any commentator could be cited for a similar assessment; cf. also Doty, *Letters in Primitive Christianity*, 70.

epistolary forms and generic expectations serves a rhetorical purpose or is only a "literary veneer," we first need to determine whether other epistolary features are indeed employed in the text.

Drawing upon a study of primary and secondary letters (i.e. letters embedded within other literary genres), Francis argued that other traits typical of the opening and closing paragraphs of Hellenistic public and private letters can be discerned within the Epistle of James. We have already noted his argument regarding a parallel development between two sections in the opening division of letters and the presence of such a pattern in the Epistle at the conclusion of our discussion of the discursive semantic structure of Jas 1:2-21 (see the closing comments on "Discursive Semantic Structure" in chapter 3). It remains for us to consider his observations regarding the closings of such letters, and whether there is evidence of similar features in the final verses of the Epistle. Although Francis's specific interest in the "form and function of the opening and closing paragraphs" of epistles led him not to discuss the epistolary prescript itself, we will begin with an analysis of the figurativization of this most obvious epistolary feature of the Epistle.

The Epistolary Prescript (Jas 1:1)

There can be no doubt that the opening phrasing of the Epistle predisposes the reader to employ epistolary conventions in reading the text which follows. His salutation "James, a servant of God and of the Lord Jesus Christ, to the twelve tribes of the Diaspora: Greeting!" is in the classic epistolary form of address "A- to B- χαίρειν" of Hellenistic letters.[13] Indeed, this address is even more typical of the contemporaneous epistolary style than the more elaborate Pauline salutations familiar to modern readers of the New Testament.[14]

Having already discussed the figure of the "twelve tribes of the Diaspora" in the chapter two, it remains for us here to consider the remaining figure of the opening salutation, namely the author's self-appellation "James (Ἰάκωβος), a servant (δοῦλος) of God and of the Lord Jesus Christ." While it is possible that a simple name may be used as a figure,[15] more often names are only 'blanks' or 'gaps' which must

---

[13]See White, "New Testament Epistolary Literature," 1734 and 1755.

[14]Cf. Dibelius, *James*, 67-68; and White, "New Testament Epistolary Literature," 1740-1741.

[15]This was essentially the position taken by Meyer when he argued that Ἰάκωβος here designates the patriarch Jacob who addresses the "twelve tribes" by allegorical allusions to the sons of Jacob and other important characters in the patriarchal

be filled in either by other elements of the text or the previous knowledge of the readers.[16] By using only a name rather than a full biographical description (whether authentic or fictive), an author leaves large "gaps" about the identity of the person so named. Many models of reading emphasize the role of readers in "filling in" these gaps either from their knowledge[17] or their imaginations. This emphasis is true both of "reader-response criticism"[18] and historical criticism. As a consequence, commentators have attempted to identify who "James" is.

The means that have been employed to solve this "who-dun-it" are both interesting and instructive because they all emphasize the large "gap" left by the Epistle in providing information about "James." The size of the gap itself becomes evidence for some that "James" must be "James the Just," the first 'bishop' of Jerusalem and "brother of Jesus," because no one else named "James" could have had the authority and stature within the early church to issue such strong admonitions.[19] In that the practice of pseudonymity in early Jewish and Christian writings seems to have stemmed from the desire to relate a writing to an authoritative tradition,[20] even those who consider the ascription of the Epistle to "James" as pseudonymous often still link this name with James the

---

narratives of Genesis (e.g. Leah, Rachel, Isaac, and Rebekah); see Meyer, *Rätsel des Jacobusbriefes*, 240-279 and 298-300.

[16]For discussions of names from a semiotic perspective, see Louis Marin, *The Semiotics of the Passion Narrative: Topics and Figures* (PTMS 25; Pittsburgh: The Pickwick Press, 1980), 16-18; and Greimas and Courtés, *Semiotics and Language*, "name/naming," 202-203.

[17]Thus, publishers often provide brief biographical sketches about authors on back covers or dust jackets so that readers can know something about the author whose "name" appears on the book. Critical readers may even discern something about the author on the basis of knowledge about the general kinds of works the particular publisher usually prints.

[18]See Wolfgang Iser, *The Act of Reading: A Theory of Aesthetic Response* (Baltimore: Johns Hopkins University Press, 1978), 163-70.

[19]Cf. Davids, *James*, 63 (who allows the Epistle may have been redacted later either by this James or a disciple); Cantinat, *Jacques et Jude*, 57; Moo, *James*, 57; Homer A. Kent, *"Faith that Works:" Studies in the Epistle of James* (Grand Rapids: Baker Book House, 1986), 34; and David P. Scaer, *James, the Apostle of Faith: A Primary Christological Epistle for the Persecuted Church* (St. Louis: Concordia Publishing House, 1983), 26.

[20]See David G. Meade, *Pseudonymity and Canon: An Investigation into the Relationship of Authorship and Authority in Jewish and Earliest Christian Tradition*, WUNT 39 (Tübingen and Grand Rapids: J. C. B. Mohr [Paul Siebeck] and William B. Eerdmans Publishing Company, 1986), especially 103-105.

Just.[21] To others, the fact that no apostolic titles are given proves the work must be authentic since a pseudonymous writer would have sought to make the identification with James the Just unmistakable.[22] For still others, the absence of mention of apostolic rank only opens the question of whether James the Just was technically an apostle,[23] or the failure to capitalize on his familial relationship to Jesus only suggests the Epistle was written by some otherwise unknown "James."[24]

All of these concerns, then, relate to readers' possible investments in the name "James" which opens the Epistle. But more important than the "gaps" which readers must "fill in" are those elements of the person's identity that the author makes pertinent by explicitly mentioning them in the text.[25] In this instance, that "James" may be an apostle, the leader of the Jerusalem church, and/or even the brother of Jesus (or more to the point, the perceptions that readers may have about "James" in these regards), are not pertinent to the identity of the "narrator"[26]

---

[21]See Dibelius, *James*, 65-66; Ropes, *St. James*, 48; Martin, *James*, 19; and Reicke, *James, Peter, and Jude*, 12. Both Martin and Reicke, however, believe the pseudonymous redactor may have been a disciple of James the Just who may have included some authentic materials from him.

[22]See Kent, *"Faith that Works"*, 20-21. For Kugelman (*James and Jude*, 12) this 'argument from silence' proves the work is not pseudonymous (the author's name was actually "James"), but does not establish the Epistle as an authentic work of James the Just (see n. 24 below).

[23]See L. P. Trudinger, "ΕΤΕΡΟΝ ΔΕ ΤΩΝ ΑΠΟΣΤΟΛΩΝ ΟΥΚ ΕΙΔΟΝ, ΕΙ ΜΗ ΙΑΚΩΒΟΝ: A Note on Galatians i 19," *NovT* 17 (1975): 200-202; and George Howard, "Was James an Apostle? A Reflection on a New Proposal for Gal. i 19," *NovT* 19 (1977): 63-69. For Mußner (*Jakobusbrief*, 7-8), the fact that "der Herren-bruder Jakobus" was not an apostle and the lack of the apostolic title within the prescript, coupled with the anti-Paulinist dispute within the letter, indicates that indeed James the Just was its author.

[24]So Kugelman, *James*, 12. He argues this "unknown James" was a Hellenistic Jewish convert who had a familiarity with "the hortatory literature of Judaism and the ethical teaching of Jesus."

[25]This point is even clearer in the process of actorializing the enunciator named within a discourse. On the process of actorialization and the role of pertinent qualifications of will, ability, and knowledge as they are made explicit by a text, see Patte, *Religious Dimensions*, 176-202, especially paragraph 5.125 on 183-84, and idem, *Structural Exegesis for New Testament Critics*, 33-36.

[26]We must speak of the "narrator" at this point since the name "James" is here used to actorialize the enunciator at the level of the discursive syntax of the Epistle. That is to say, within the epistolary salutation, the "implied author" behind the text emerges explicitly into the text itself under the name "James."

constructed by the writer.[27] What is crucially important for the readers to know about the author of the Epistle if they are to understand this
text is that "James [is] a servant of God and the Lord Jesus Christ," not
that he may (also) be an apostle and brother of Jesus.[28] Thus, the real
emphasis should be placed on the designation "servant of God and the
Lord Jesus Christ" rather than on the name "James."

So what meanings can be invested in the figure "servant/slave"
(δοῦλος)? Dibelius suggested two possibilities for its application to
"James." If one concludes that the Epistle is an authentic work of James
the Just, then the figure "servant" is "a modest self-designation, with
which the author places himself on the same level with the other Christians."[29] If however the Epistle is pseudonymous, as Dibelius argued,

> the actual writer would have prefaced his document with the name of the
> brother of the Lord precisely because he esteemed him as one of the greats
> of the classical period. Attaching to him no other predicate than this term
> 'slave,' he obviously has in mind something special and is comparing James
> to Israel's men of God [e.g. Moses, David, and the prophets] rather than to
> the mass of Christians.[30]

---

[27]To return to our analogy of biographical information about authors supplied
by publishers, only those aspects of their lives that contribute to their authority to
speak on the topic addressed by the book are usually treated. Thus, scholarly works
usually make mention of such things as the author's academic degrees, teaching
posts, and other publications. But a study on marriage and family issues might also
include reference to how long the author has been married and the number of her or
his children.

[28]Having said this, let me emphasize that there is a reason why the writer,
whoever he or she may have been, chose the self-appellation "James" (as is
particularly obvious if the Epistle is pseudonymous). Had that name not been
capable of establishing the implied author as someone worth hearing for the implied
readers—had it not been capable of contributing to the fiduciary contract between the
writer and the recipients—then we might expect the author to have adopted a different
name, unless all that was necessary to establish such credibility was one's
designation as a "servant of God and of the Lord Jesus Christ" (so Laws, *James*, 46)
in which case presumably any name might have been used.

[29]Dibelius, *James*, 65. This position is adopted by Cantinat (*Jacques et Jude*,
58) and Reicke (*James, Peter and Jude*, 11), though for Reicke the Epistle is still
a pseudonymous work associated with James the Just.

[30]Dibelius, *James*, 65-66. So also Martin, *James*, 4; and Vouga, *Jacques*, 37.
It has been suggested, based on an emendation of a Hegesippus fragment preserved
by Eusebius, that James the Just had the nickname "Obadiah" (≈ עֹבֵד יהוה ≈ δοῦλος
θεοῦ). See Klaus Baltzer and Helmut Koester, "Die Bezeichung des Jakobus als
ΏΒΛΙΑΣ," *ZNW* 46 (1955): 141-42.

Other commentators have tried to maintain the aspects of humility and authority in tension by arguing that "the servant does not come in his own name, ... [and yet] the bearer of the title is in the service of a great king."[31] Ropes, on the other hand, argued it was neither a designation of humility nor honor; "[t]he writer simply declares himself to belong to Christ as his worshipper, and so commends himself to readers who are also Christians."[32]

Yet none of these proposals gives particular attention to the context of the Epistle. Given the prominence of Wisdom theology and the "piety of the poor" that we have discerned in the beliefs of the implied readers,[33] I would suggest that James anticipated this "servant" language would evoke the "servant of Yahweh" imagery among his readers.[34] In particular, it seems likely that James anticipated the readers would hear in this description an allusion to the "righteous sufferer" *par excellence*.[35] But it does not seem possible to reach much more precision regarding their investments in this figure because it is never resumed within the Epistle; no other occurrences of the δοῦλος word group appear in either nominal or verbal form. Nevertheless, it would seem this specific "servant" image was of great importance to the implied readers since it was chosen for use at the outset of the Epistle to establish the fiduciary contract between the author and readers.

But in what sense does James consider himself a "servant of God and of the Lord Jesus Christ"? On the basis of the inverted parallelisms with Jas 5:19-20 and the overall pattern of his system of convictions, it seems probable that James understands himself as a "servant" because

---

[31]Davids, *James*, 63. Cf. also Moo, *James*, 57; and Mußner, *Jakobusbrief*, 60-61.

[32]Ropes, *St. James*, 117-18. See also Laws, *James*, 46; and Sidebottom, *James, Jude, 2 Peter*, 26. Such positions would be in keeping with Dibelius's remarks regarding the use of δοῦλος among devotees of the Mystery Religions: "The designation of man as 'slave' (δοῦλος) is the correlate to the predication of God as 'Lord' (κύριος) .... [T]he term 'slave' expresses a definite relationship to the God to whose cult a person is committed" (*James*, 65).

[33]Cf. the discussion of the "Diaspora" figure in chapter two and the discussion of Jas 1:2-12 in chapter 3.

[34]Cf. also Cantinat, *Jacques et Jude*, 58. This despite the objections of Ropes (*St. James*, 117) and Sidebottom (*James, 2 Peter, Jude*, 26). The fact that the Septuagint renders עֶבֶד יהוה by the Greek words παῖς κυρίου rather than by δοῦλος θεοῦ/κυρίου is insufficient justification for ruling out any influence by this important theological motif on Jas 1:1.

[35]See Martin, *James*, xciii-xcviii.

he "restores those who wander away from the truth" by acting as God acts in doing good and providing for the needs of others. Thus, this "slave/master" (δοῦλος/κύριος) imagery would figurativize his conviction that believers must adopt God's will as their own so that their actions arise from that divine will rather than their own "desires." One might then consider "doing the word" to be "serving God," although no such connections are explicitly drawn in the Epistle. To be a "servant of God" is for James to be one who 'acts as God acts' in endeavoring to "restore" others to the "truth."

This connection between Jas 1:1 and 5:19-20 also points toward the separation between James and his implied readers. They have "wandered" from the "truth"—have become people of God who are now separated from the author ("to the twelve tribes of the Diaspora")—and so James addresses himself to them as a "servant of God" who will "restore them to the truth." Thus, it is clear that the figures which describe the author ("servant of God") and the recipients ("Diaspora") within the epistolary prescript figurativize the relationship between the implied author and implied readers. They have become separated from one another by the differences in their beliefs and their practices arising from those beliefs. In order to bridge this separation, James writes an "epistle" in the hopes of 'correcting' their beliefs (the religious function of his paraenesis) and so also their praxis (the religious objective).

Conventions for Closing Epistles
and Jas 5:7-20

Returning to Francis's arguments regarding epistolary features within the Epistle of James, he divided these features into two basic categories: 1) those which were characteristic of developments among early Christian letter writers in particular, and 2) those characteristic of Hellenistic letters more generally. The more formulaic of these characteristics are those typical of Hellenistic letters in general, and so let us begin with them.

Francis began by addressing the objection that the Epistle does not follow established epistolary conventions because it does not conclude with an epistolary closing formula (e.g. greetings to and from mutual acquaintances). He responded to this objection by noting that "many Hellenistic letters of all types have no closing formulas whatsoever; they just stop." Thus, by not employing such a device, the author "has simply identified what was a live option in Hellenistic epistolary form."[36] Francis then observed that the author does utilize, however, some of the formulaic language identified by Exler as typical of epistolary closings, namely the use of the phrase πρὸ πάντων with a health wish and oath formulas[37] (cf. Jas 5:12-16). Francis concluded, "It would seem that James 5:12-20 may be occasioned by epistolary forms providing for oath formulas and expression of concern for the recipients' health at the end of the letter."[38]

In terms of more particularly Christian forms for closing letters, Francis pointed to three features in the closing verses of the Epistle of James that are well attested in other early Christian epistolary writings. The first two of these features are generally closely related; an eschatological injunction is joined with a thematic reprise of the letter as a whole.[39] Francis argued that these elements are present in the call for patient endurance in the light of the approaching "advent of the Lord" in Jas 5:7-11. The third element typical of Christian epistolary closings is prayer, and indeed one finds a discussion of prayer in Jas 5:13-18.[40]

Yet, it must be noted that with regard to several of these closing conventions James does not directly employ them so much as to play on them. He does not wish the readers health or offer a prayer on their behalf, but rather instructs them to pray for one another when they are ill (Jas 5:13-16). He does not utilize an oath formula, but rather prohibits the use of oath formulas (5:12). It is perhaps for such reasons that Francis's article has received such diverse response, ranging from abrupt dismissal to enthusiastic support.[41] Nevertheless, it seems

---

[36]Francis, "Form and Function," 124-125. He provided examples of such abrupt conclusions from private and public, primary and secondary letters from the Hellenistic period.

[37]Citing F. X. J. Exler, *The Form of the Ancient Greek Letter: A Study in Greek Epistolography* (Washington: Catholic University of America, 1923), 114 and 127-132. See also the discussion of Exler's work in White, "New Testament Epistolary Literature," 1733-1736.

[38]Francis, "Form and Function," 125.

[39]For examples from other New Testament letters, cf. the citations given at ibid., 124 nn. 47 and 49. Francis's identification of the particular thematic reprise in the Epistle of James as being "intimated in the relation of the opening (1:16) warning against being deceived on the source of adversity and the closing concern with those in adversity (5:13-18) and those who are deceived (5:19-20)" (ibid., 125-126) is very close to our identification of the theme of the Epistle as "restoring" to the "truth" of God as "pure good" those who have "wandered" because they have come to believe God is the source of both good and bad.

[40]See ibid., 125.

[41]Kümmel (*Introduction*, 408 nn. 15 and 17) dismisses Francis's proposal

certain that first century readers would have perceived more epistolary features within this writing than just its prescript. They would have recognized the two part introduction and the variations on epistolary closing conventions and associated the book with the epistolary genre. The question then becomes, why did the author employ this particular genre? What, if anything, does this choice of genre contribute to achieving his purposes for writing?

Rhetorical Effect of the Epistolary Genre

Since most scholars have operated from the assumption that the only epistolary feature of the Epistle of James is its prescript, they generally have not been concerned with why the author chose to begin the book in this way.[42] Those who have speculated regarding this choice of opening generally assumed that it functions to associate the book with other apostolic letters, and thereby to give it an air of apostolic authority.[43] A more appropriate starting point, however, is to begin with the more general socio-rhetorical function of letters within Hellenistic society.

The primary social function of letters was as a means of maintaining contact between parties who had become separated. While they might be used simply to 'keep in touch,' they were also used as a means of exchanging specific information and of making requests of the recipients. In most cases letters were "primarily a function of a previous relationship" and were "understood as the representative of [their] writer."[44] They functioned rhetorically to create an 'epistolary

---

without discussion. Davids (*James*, 24-28 and 29), Vouga (*Jacques*, 18-23), Martin (*James*, xcviii-civ) and Reese ("Exegete as Sage," 82-85) are all favorable of his proposal and utilize slight modifications of it in their own work. Both White ("New Testament Epistolary Literature," 1756) and Popkes (*Adressaten, Situation und Form*, 15-16) summarize his argument without themselves taking clear positions either for or against his proposal.

[42]Ropes (*St. James*, 9) explained the prescript by arguing that it was "altogether natural and appropriate for a tract" in this period to have such epistolary trappings; cf. also Reicke, *James, Peter and Jude*, xxix-xxxii; and Sidebottom, *James, Jude, 2 Peter*, 1-3.

[43]Cf. Martin, *James*, lxxvii. On the importance of the Pauline letters in the development of epistolary literature as a form of authoritative discourse in early Christianity, see White, "New Testament Epistolary Literature," 1751-1755.

[44]Doty, *Letters in Primitive Christianity*, 16-17; see also White, "New Testament Epistolary Literature," 1731-1732.

presence' for the author who was physically absent, a presence which was essential to maintaining the bonds between the parties and, in the case of apostolic letters, to exercising apostolic authority and power.[45]

Returning to the particular case of the Epistle of James, most scholars asserted that James is not a genuine letter, i.e. it was not written and then mailed to its recipients at some other location(s).[46] It is possible that the author's playing with epistolary conventions in the closing sections is deliberate evidence of this fact. How might the socio-rhetorical functions of the epistolary genre have served the author's purposes in such a case? Since there would be no physical separation to be overcome by a rhetorically created 'epistolary presence' of the author, the epistolary prescript would function rhetorically to establish the 'epistolary absence' of the readers/hearers. We can imagine "James" rising within a setting of Christian worship to read this 'open letter' to the "Diaspora" within the congregation who had "wandered from the truth." And this very "wandering" and resultant separation of author and audience are figurativized by the epistolary genre.[47]

Discursive Structure and Purpose
in the Epistle of James

Our summary of the religious purposes of the Epistle highlighted James's interest in modifying his readers' beliefs (they believe God is good, but is also a source of bad; James believes God is "pure good") so that they may also modify their actions (their actions must arise from God's will revealed in "wisdom" rather than from their own "desires"). We have also seen how James utilized variations on epistolary convictions to figurativize the separation which has opened between the readers

---

[45]See Robert W. Funk, "The Apostolic *Parousia*: Form and Significance," in *Christian History and Interpretation: Studies Presented to John Knox*, ed. W. R. Farmer, C. F. D. Moule, and R. R. Niebuhr (Cambridge: Cambridge University Press, 1967), 263-266.

[46]The notable exceptions in this regard are Mayor (*St. James*, 31) and Mußner (*Jakobusbrief*, 11) who each suggested it may have been an actual encyclical letter circulated among churches.

[47]This interpretation of the rhetorical function of the epistolary features technically corresponds to the thematic investment in the epistolary figurativization. That is to say, it describes the author's investment in the epistolary figures in terms of the theme of the discourse as a whole established by the inverted parallelism between Jas 1:1 and 5:19-20. Thus, it does not foreclose the possibility that the readers would have made other investments in these figures, such as seeing them as indicative of authoritative apostolic discourse (see again Martin, *James*, lxxvii).

and James himself as a result of their 'improper' belief about the divine. It remains for us, then, to review how the overall structure of the Epistle seeks to persuade the readers of their "wanderings" and to "restore" them to the "truth."

James opens the "epistle" by developing his own system of convictions about achieving blessedness over against his readers' "piety of the poor" and "wisdom theology." Whereas they have come to believe that they will become "perfect and complete, lacking in nothing" by "patiently enduring" the "trials" which God sends to them (1:2-4), James counters that "God tempts/tests no one" (1:13b) and "generously" (1:5) provides only "good and perfect gifts" (1:17). Whereas they believe they must learn "wisdom" through their "endurance" (1:4) and divine "reprimands" (1:5b) James responds that those who "lack wisdom" need only "ask with faith" and God will give it to them (1:5-6). By the end of the two-fold introduction in Jas 1:2-21,[48] James has presented virtually the full system of convictions, the *micro*-semantic universe of this discourse.

He then proceeds to complete the system of convictions by emphasizing that believers must not "only hear"/"receive the implanted word" but must also be "doers of the word" if they are to "blessed" (1:21-25). In the short compass of Jas 1:22 - 2:13, James constructs no less than five oppositions of actions to emphasize this point. He follows this with an essentially thematic sub-unit in 2:14-26[49] drawing extensively on figures from their pattern of beliefs in an attempt to persuade them that they should accept his system of convictions which only modifies their own. Most striking is his use of the tradition regarding the "testing of Abraham" to support his contention that it was Abraham's "faith" in God as "pure good" that was "working with his works" in offering Isaac and resulting in his justification (2:20-24). The opening unit (1:2-21) focused on elaborating the general system of convictions that James considers orthodoxy, the second unit (1:22 - 2:26) on what constitutes orthopraxis within the context of that pattern of beliefs.

Having thus completed his 'argument,' James proceeds to persuade the implied readers of their need to "repent" (cf. 4:7-10). He exposes their attitudes as "earthly, unspiritual, demonic" (3:15) by once again drawing his figures from their own pattern of beliefs. The readers are in need of the "wisdom that is from above" (3:17), but it can only be

---

[48]See the end of the section on "Discursive Semantic Structure and Thematization" in chapter 3 above.

[49]It contains but a single opposition of actions, OPP 2:16.

received by "humbling themselves in the presence of the Lord" (4:10). If they will "submit to God" (4:7), then God will give "grace" to them (4:6) and will "exalt" them (4:10). Convinced that the implied readers will heed his call to repentance, James exhorts them in the final unit (4:11 - 5:20) to follow his example by "restoring" others within the community who may be "wandering" from the truth (5:19-20). The readers should fulfill this vocation by directing the wanderer's attention to God's goodness and provision through communal prayer, praise and confession (5:13-16), just as James has restored them in the course of his Epistle.

Conclusion: One Reading Among Many

We began our study of the Epistle of James with two basic questions: how could someone have written such an apparently disorganized and disjointed text, and what could he or she have hoped to accomplish by writing it in this way? The structural semiotic analysis which we have pursued has enabled us to find far more organization and structure within the text than the day-to-day reading conventions of our modern, Western culture would normally allow. It has also provided us both with a clear sense of two of the religious purposes of paraenetic discourse and with the methodological means to isolate and study those purposes within the particular discourse of the Epistle of James. By reading the Epistle "from the inside out," we have found promising answers to the questions with which we began.

Yet we must also acknowledge that while these semiotic lenses have brought certain meaning producing dimensions more clearly into focus, they have done so at the expense of occulting other possible answers to our questions. The combination of "textpragmatic" linguistic analysis and ancient rhetorical theory applied to the Epistle by Wuellner and Frankemölle[50] holds great promise for assisting our understanding of its argumentative structure and purpose. The Mujerista reading of the Epistle from the three angles of "oppression-suffering," "hope," and "praxis" that has been offered by Elsa Tamez[51] is both engaging and

---

[50]See Wuellner, "Jakobusbrief im Licht der Rhetorik und Textpragmatic," and Frankemölle, "Semantische Netz des Jakobusbriefes."

[51]Elsa Tamez, *The Scandalous Message of James: Faith Without Works is Dead*, trans. John Eagleson (New York: The Crossroad Publishing Company, 1990. For her discussion of these three reading angles, see 9-14. She likewise begins with the problem of twentieth century Christians attempting to make sense of an "intercepted letter," but focuses her attention on a "Latin American reading of the letter."

challenging. Not even the historico-critical analyses, which we have seen are less satisfying in their answers given the emerging paradigms of meaning in our culture, are disproved by these other approaches.[52] Each in their own way sheds light on the multi-dimensional meaning producing effects of the Epistle.

Moreover, there are other questions which not only may but must be asked about the Epistle of James. How are we to respond to the clear androcentric bias of the language in the Epistle? How can we appropriate its sense of eschatological imminence after almost two thousand years have passed? How are we to relate James's conviction of God as "pure good" and his unwillingness to specify the source of "miseries" (5:1) while maintaining that "trials" are a product of an individual's own sinful human "desires" (1:14) with our post-Holocaust experience of the world and its social structures? Other readings and methods of reading will be needed to find answers to these and similarly pressing questions.

And so, I have offered only a reading of the Epistle of James among many possible and necessary readings. What is important is not that we as readers find closure in our encounter with this text, but that we continue to explore new ways of making its messages meaningful to us that we may be challenged to see that our faith is working with our works and that our faith is completed by works (cf. Jas 2:22). We must be "restored" from our own "wanderings," that we may then fulfill our vocation as believers of restoring others.

---

[52]And indeed, without the insights into the 'cultural dictionary' of possible semantic investments in the figures of the Epistle provided by historical critics, our own semiotic analysis could not have been conducted.

An Interpretative Translation
of the Epistle of James

[1:1]James, a servant of God and of the Lord Jesus Christ, to the twelve tribes of the Diaspora: Greeting!

[2]You considered it complete joy, my brothers and sisters, when you encountered diverse trials [3]because you knew that the testing of your faith produces patient endurance. [4]But you must let endurance have its complete work in order that you might be complete and whole, lacking in nothing.

[5]If anyone among you lacks wisdom, let that one ask of the God who gives to everyone generously, without reprimanding, and God will give it to him or her.[a] [6]But let that one ask with faith, without doubting—for the one who doubts is like the waves of the sea that are wind-blown and tossed. [7]Do not let such persons suppose they will receive anything from the Lord, [8]being double-minded persons, unstable in all their ways.

[9]Let the lowly brother and sister boast in their exaltation, [10]and the rich boast in their abasement, for they will pass away like a wildflower. [11]As the sun rises with scorching heat and dries the grass causing its

---

[a]The Greek text here is masculine singular (αὐτῷ). The translation in this appendix is not as "literal" in its rendering of gender specific language as that found within the citations in the body of the text. In this "interpretative translation" I have followed current conventions of inclusive language by including both masculine and feminine vocatives, substituting plurals for masculine singular references where gender assignment is not restrictive, etc.

flower to fall and the beauty of its appearance to be ruined, so even the rich will die in the midst of their way of life. [12]Blessed is the person who endures trial, because that one will receive the crown of life which has been promised to the ones who love God.[b]

[13]Let no one who is being put to a test say, "I am being put to the test by God;" for God is unable to be put to the test by evil, and God puts no one to the test. [14]Rather, each one is put to the test when dragged away and enticed by one's own evil desire. [15]Once it has conceived, desire gives birth to sin; and when it has matured, sin gives birth to death. [16]Do not continue to be deceived, my beloved brothers and sisters.

[17]Every good gift and every perfect present is from above, coming down from the Father of Lights, with whom there is neither variation nor shadow cast by turning. [18]According to the divine will,[c] God gave birth to us by the word of truth, in order that we might be a kind of first fruit of God's creations. [19]You know this, my beloved brothers and sisters.

Let every person be quick to hear, slow to speak, slow to anger; [20]for human anger does not accomplish godly righteousness. [21]Therefore, having put aside all filth and abundance of wickedness, by meekness, receive the implanted word which is able to save your souls.

[22]Be doers of the word and not only hearers who deceive themselves. [23]If anyone is a hearer of the word and not a doer, this one is like a person who observes one's own face in a mirror; [24]for observing oneself and going away, one immediately forgets[d] what one was like. [25]But the ones who look into the perfect law of freedom and remain, who are not forgetful hearers but doers of the work, these ones will be blessed for their doing.

[26]If any consider themselves to be religious who are not bridling their tongue but rather deceiving their heart, their religion is useless. [27]Pure and undefiled religion before God the Father is this: to care for orphans and widows in their distress, and to keep oneself untainted by the world. [2:1]My brothers and sisters, do not hold the faith of our glorious Lord Jesus Christ with partiality. [2]For if a man in splendid clothing and wearing a gold ring should enter your assembly and a poor person in filthy clothing should also enter, [3]and you should look at the

---

[b]Greek, αὐτόν.

[c]Greek, βουληθείς. Cf. BAGD, "βούλομαι" 2b, 146.

[d]Taking the aorist participles as having gnomic force and therefore translating as English present tense (cf. Dibelius, *James*, 115).

one wearing the splendid clothing and say, "Sit here, please," but to the poor person you should say, "Stand there," or "Sit on the floor," ⁴have you not discriminated among yourselves and become judges with evil reasonings? ⁵Listen, my beloved brothers and sisters. Did not God choose the poor with respect to the world to be rich with respect to faith and heirs of the kingdom which God promised to the ones who love God?ᵉ ⁶Yet you have dishonored the poor. Is it not the rich who are oppressing you, and themselves dragging you into court? ⁷Are not they themselves blaspheming the good name which was invoked upon you? ⁸If you perform the royal law according to the scripture, "Love your neighbor as yourself," you do well; ⁹but if you show partiality, you commit sin, being convicted by the law as transgressors.

¹⁰For whoever should keep the whole law, but should trip in one thing, that one has become guilty of the whole thing. ¹¹For the one who has said, "Do not commit adultery," also said, "Do not commit murder." If you do not commit adultery but do commit murder, you have become a transgressor of the law. ¹²So speak and so act as ones who are about to be judged by the law of freedom. ¹³For judgment is without mercy for the one who does not perform mercy, yet mercy triumphs over judgment.

¹⁴What is the benefit, my brothers and sisters, if someone claims to have faith but does not have works? Is the claimed faith able to save that one? ¹⁵If a brother or sister is naked and lacking sustenance,ᶠ ¹⁶and someone among you should say to them, "Go in peace, be warm and well fed," but you do not give them the things needed by the body, what is the benefit? ¹⁷So also faith by itself, if it does not have works, is dead. ¹⁸But someone will say, "Do you have faith?" And I would respond, "I have works. Show me your faith separated from works, and I will show you faith by my works. ¹⁹You believe that God is one, and so you should.ᵍ Yet even the demons believe that, and they tremble!"

²⁰Do you desire proof,ʰ O Vain Person, that faith separated from works is useless? ²¹Was not our ancestor Abraham justified by works when he offered his son Isaac upon the altar? ²²You see that faith was working with his works and faith was completed by the works, ²³and the scripture was fulfilled which says, "Abraham believed God, and it was

---

ᵉGreek, αὐτόν.

ᶠLiterally, "lacking the daily food" (λειπόμενοι τῆς ἐφημέρου τροφῆς).

ᵍLiterally, "you do well" (καλῶς ποιεῖς). See the discussion of 2:19 in the "Exegesis and Commentary" of chapter 4.

ʰLiterally, "do you wish to know" (θέλεις δὲ γνῶναι).

accounted to him as righteousness," and he was called God's friend.
²⁴You see that a person is justified by works and not by faith alone.
²⁵Likewise, was not Rahab the harlot also justified, having shown
hospitality to the spies and sending them out by another way? ²⁶For just
as the body separated from spirit is dead, even so also faith separated
from works is dead.

³:¹Not many of you, my brothers and sisters, should desire to
become teachers, knowing that we will receive a stricter judgment.
²Indeed, we all sin in many things. If anyone does not sin in speech,
this one is a mature person who is able to bridle even the whole body.
³If we put bridles into the mouths of horses in order to make them obey
us, we also guide their whole body. ⁴Consider also that the ships—big
though they are[i] and being driven by strong winds—are guided by a very
small rudder wherever the will of the pilot desires. ⁵Likewise the tongue
is also a small part, yet it boasts great things.

How small a flame ignites so large a brushwood! ⁶And the tongue
is a fire. The tongue has been established among our members as the
unrighteous world, staining the whole body and setting ablaze the course
of life, having itself been set ablaze by Hell.[j] ⁷Indeed every species of
both beasts and birds, of both reptiles and sea life, is controlled and has
been controlled by the human species, ⁸but no one among humanity[k] is
able to control the tongue. It is an unstable evil, full of lethal poison.
⁹With it we bless the Lord and Father, and with it we curse the human
beings who have been made according to the likeness of God; ¹⁰from out
of the same mouth comes blessing and curse. My brothers and sisters,
these things ought not to be so! ¹¹Can a spring pour sweet and bitter
water from the same opening? ¹²Can a fig tree, my brothers and sisters,
bear olives or a grapevine figs? No more so than salty water can be
made sweet!

¹³Who is wise and intelligent among you? Let them by good
conduct show that their works are performed by humility characteristic
of wisdom. ¹⁴But if you have bitter rivalry and ambition in your heart,
do not degrade and lie against the truth. ¹⁵This is not the wisdom which
comes down from above, but is rather earthly, unspiritual, demonic.
¹⁶For where there is rivalry and ambition, there is rebellion and every

---

    [i]Concessive use of ὄντα; cf. Moulton, Howard and Turner, *Grammar*, 1:23 and
Robertson, *Grammar*, 1129.

    [j]Greek, γεέννης, "Gehenna."

    [k]Taking ἀνθρόπων with οὐδείς (see Martin, *James*, 117; and Ropes, *St. James*,
240) rather than with γλῶσσα (which would result in "human tongue").

bad deed. [17]But the wisdom from above is first of all pure, then peaceful, gentle, obedient, full of mercy and good fruits, impartial. [18]And the fruit of righteousness is sown in peace by those who make peace.

[4:1]From where do quarrels and disputes among you arise? Do they not originate here, from your passions which are at war within your members? [2]You desire but do not have, so you murder. You are envious but are unable to obtain, so you battle and wage war. You do not have because you do not ask; [3]and you ask but do not receive because you ask with evil motives in order that you might squander it on your passions. [4]Adulterers![l] Do you not know that friendship with the world is enmity with God? Therefore, whoever desires to be a friend of the world is made an enemy of God.

[5]Or do you think that the scripture speaks for no reason? God longs jealously for the spirit which God caused to dwell in us [6]and gives even more grace; for this reason it says, "God opposes the arrogant, but gives grace to the humble." [7]Therefore submit to God. Resist the devil, and he will flee from you; [8]come near to God, and God will come near to you. Cleanse your hands, sinners, and purify your hearts, double-minded ones. [9]Lament, and mourn, and weep; let your laughter turn to sadness and your joy to dejection. [10]Humble yourselves in the presence of the Lord, and the Lord will exalt you.

[11]Do not speak against one another, brothers and sisters. The one who speaks against a brother or sister or who judges one's brother or sister speaks against the law and judges the law. And if you are judging the law, you are not a doer of the law but a judge. [12]There is one Lawgiver and Judge who is able to save and to destroy—so who are you who judges the neighbor? [13]Go now, you who say,[m] "Today or tomorrow we will go to such and such a city, and we will work there for a year and will conduct business and will make a profit," [14]whereas actually[n] you do not know about tomorrow. What is your life? For you are a vapor appearing for a short time, and then disappearing.

---

[l]This English form is used in its now generic sense of "one who commits adultery" without respect to that one's gender. It should be noted, however, that the Greek text uncharacteristically uses a feminine vocative form (μοιχαλίδες, "Adulteresses!"); see the discussion of 4:4 in the "Exegesis and Commentary" of chapter 5.

[m]Literally, "the ones who say" (οἱ λέγοντες), but joined with the interjection and the second-person verb of 4:14 (ἐπίστασθε) it is clearly second-person vocative.

[n]On this adversative use of the relative pronoun οἵτινες, see Moulton, Howard and Turner, *Grammar*, 1:124.

[15]Instead you should say, "If the Lord wills, we will both live and will do this or that." [16]But now you boast in your pretensions; all such boasting is evil. [17]Therefore, for the one who knows to do good but is not doing it, it is sin for that one.

[5:1]Go now you who are rich, wail greatly° on account of your miseries that are coming upon you. [2]Your wealth has rotted and your garments have become moth-eaten. [3]Your gold and silver are tarnished, and their corrosion will be a witness against you and will eat your flesh as fire. You have stored up treasure even in the Last Days. [4]Listen!ᴾ The wage that was robbed from the laborers who reap your fields cries out against you, and the cries of the harvesters have entered the ears of Lord Sabaoth. [5]You have revelled upon the earth and lived indulgently; you fattened your hearts for the day of slaughter. [6]You condemned, you murdered the righteous. Does not God oppose you? [7]Therefore have patience, brothers and sisters, until the advent of the Lord. Consider how the farmer waits for the precious fruit of the ground, having patience concerning it until it receives the early and late rains. [8]So be patient, strengthen your hearts, because the advent of the Lord has come near. [9]Do not grumble against one another, brothers and sisters, so that you may not be condemned. Behold, the Judge stands before the door.

[10]Brothers and sisters, take as an example of perseverance in suffering the prophets who spoke by the authority of the Lord. [11]Indeed, we consider as blessed the ones who endured. You have heard about the perseverance of Job, and you know the end that the Lord accomplished, how that the Lord is compassionate and merciful.

[12]But above all things, my brothers and sisters, do not swear either by Heaven or Earth or any other oath. But let your "Yes" be yes, and your "No" be no so that you will not fall under condemnation. [13]Are any among you suffering misfortune? Let them pray. Are any happy? Let them sing praise. [14]Are any among you sick? Let them call the elders of the church, and let the elders pray on their behalf after anointing them in the name of the Lord. [15]The prayer offered with faith will save the sick, and the Lord will raise them. And if the sick person has committed sins, they will be forgiven. [16]Therefore, confess your sins to one another and pray on behalf of one another so that you may be healed. The effective prayer of a righteous person is capable of much. [17]Elijah was a person with the same nature as us, and he prayed

---

°Literally, "cry crying aloud/wailing" (κλαύσατε ὀλολύζοντες).
ᴾLiterally, "Behold!" (ἰδού).

fervently[q] and it did not rain upon the ground for three years and six months. [18]Then he prayed again, and the sky gave rain and the ground produced its fruit.

[19]My brothers and sisters, if any among you should wander from the truth and someone should restore them, [20]let that one know that the one who restores sinners[r] from the error of their way will save their[s] souls from death and will cover a multitude of sins.

---

[q]Literally, "prayed a prayer" (προσευχῇ προσηύξατο).   On the cognate accusative, see BDF §198.6 (106-107).

[r]The Greek text here and in the related terms which follow is masculine singular.

[s]The pronoun αὐτοῦ is ambiguous (and in fact, textually problematic; cf. *TCGNT*, 686). It may take as its antecedent either the noun ἁμαρτωλόν (as in the translation given here) or the participle ἐπιστρέψας (and thus it is the one who restores another whose "soul is saved from death"). See the exegetical treatment of these verses in chapter 6.

OPPOSITIONS OF ACTIONS IN THE
EPISTLE OF JAMES

This appendix provides a listing of all of the oppositions of actions in the Epistle of James. Each opposition is designated by the chapter and verse numbers in which it appears. By convention, the positive action of each opposition of actions is presented in the left column, the negative in the right.[1]

OPP 1:5

διδόντος θεοῦ πᾶσιν ἁπλῶς	μὴ ὀνειδίζοντος
Divine ([gift] ≻ believer)	Divine (rebuke ≻ believer)

OPP 1:6

αἰτείτω δὲ ἐν πίστει	μηδὲν διακρινόμενος
Believer (request with faith ≻ God)	Believer (request with doubt ≻ God)

---

[1]For a discussion of the principles for identifying oppositions of actions, see Patte, *Structural Exegesis for New Testament Critics*, pp. 23-45.

OPP 1:13-14

πειράζει δὲ αὐτὸς οὐδένα. ἕκαστος δὲ πειράζεται ὑπὸ τῆς ἰδίας ἐπιθυμίας ἐξελκόμενος καὶ δελεαζόμενος·

μηδεὶς πειραζόμενος λεγέτω ὅτι 'Απὸ θεοῦ πειράζομαι·

Elliptic Polemical Dialogue:

Tempted Person, "God (temptation ⊁ person), but desires (temptation ≻ person.)"

Tempted Person, "God (temptation ≻ person)."

OPP 1:22

ποιηταὶ λόγου

Believer (doing ≻ word)

μόνον ἀκροαταὶ

Believer (only hearing ≻ word)

OPP 1:25

ποιητὴς ἔργου

Believer (doing ≻ works of word/Law)

ἀκροατὴς ἐπιλησμονῆς

Believer (forgetting ≻ word/ Law)

OPP 2:1, 4

μὴ ἐν προσωπολημψίαις ἔχετε τὴν πίστιν τοῦ κυρίου ἡμῶν Ἰησοῦ Χριστοῦ τῆς δόξης.

Believers (partiality ⊁ believers)

οὐ διεκρίθητε ἐν ἑαυτοῖς καὶ ἐγένεσθε κριταὶ διαλογισμῶν πονηρῶν;

Believers (distinctions ≻ fellow believers)

OPP 2:5, 6

οὐχ ὁ θεὸς ἐξελέξατο τοὺς πτω- χοὺς τῷ κόσμῳ πλουσίους ἐν πίστει καὶ κληρονόμους τῆς βασιλείας ἧς ἐπηγγείλατο τοῖς ἀγαπῶσιν αὐτόν;

ὑμεῖς δὲ ἠτιμάσατε τὸν πτωχόν.

Divine (honor ≻ poor)   Believers (dishonor ≻ poor)

OPP 2:8, 9

εἰ μέντοι νόμον τελεῖτε βασιλικὸν κατὰ τὴν γραφήν, Ἀγαπή-
σεις τὸν πλησίον σου ὡς σεαυ-
τόν, καλῶς ποιεῖτε·

Believers (love ≻ believers)

εἰ δὲ προσωπολημπτεῖτε, ἁμαρτίαν ἐργάζεσθε

Believers (partiality ≻ believers)

OPP 2:16

δῶτε δὲ αὐτοῖς τὰ ἐπιτήδεια
τοῦ σώματος

Believer (necessities ≻ believer)

εἴπῃ δέ τις αὐτοῖς ἐξ ὑμῶν,
Ὑπάγετε ἐν εἰρήνῃ, θερμαίνεσθε καὶ χορτάζεσθε

Believer (only word of blessing
≻ believer)

OPP 4:11A

Μὴ καταλαλεῖτε ἀλλήλων,
ἀδελφοί·

Believer (speaking against ≁
believer)

ὁ καταλαλῶν ἀδελφοῦ ἢ κρίνων τὸν ἀδελφὸν αὐτοῦ

Believer (speaking against =
judging ≻ believer)

OPP 4:11B

εἶ ποιητὴς νόμου

Believer (doing ≻ law)

καταλαλεῖ νόμου καὶ κρίνει
νόμον·

Believer (judging ≻ law)

OPP 4:13, 15-16

ἀντὶ τοῦ λέγειν ὑμᾶς, Ἐὰν ὁ
κύριος θελήσῃ, καὶ ζήσομεν
καὶ ποιήσομεν τοῦτο ἢ ἐκεῖνο.

οἱ λέγοντες, σήμερον ἢ αὔριον
πορευσόμεθα εἰς τήνδε τὴν
πόλιν καὶ ποιήσομεν ἐκεῖ ἐνι-
αυτὸν καὶ ἐμπορευσόμεθα καὶ

κερδήσομεν· ... καυχᾶσθε ἐν
ταῖς ἀλαζονείαις ὑμῶν·

Polemical Dialogue:

Believers say, "If the Lord
wills, we will both live and
will do this or that."

Believers say or boast, "Today
or tomorrow we will go to
such and such a city, and we
will work there for a year
and will conduct business
and will make a profit."

OPP 5:1, 5

ἐπὶ ταῖς ταλαιπωρίαις ὑμῶν
(=οἱ πλούσιοι) ταῖς ἐπερχομέναις.

Unspecified (miseries > rich)

ἐτρυφήσατε ἐπὶ τῆς γῆς καὶ
ἐσπαταλήσατε, ἐθρέψατε τὰς
καρδίας ὑμῶν

Rich (luxury > themselves)

OPP 5:19

ἐπιστρέψῃ τις αὐτόν

Believer (restores truth > fellow
believer)

τις ἐν ὑμῖν πλανηθῇ ἀπὸ τῆς
ἀληθείας

Believer (departure from truth
> self)

BIBLIOGRAPHY

Adamson, James B. *The Epistle of James*. New International Commentary on the New Testament. Grand Rapids, Michigan: William B. Eerdmans Publishing Company, 1976.

Aland, Kurt; Matthew Black, Carlo M. Martini, Bruce M. Metzger, and Allen Wikgren, eds. *Novum Testamentum Graece*. 26th ed. Stuttgart: Deutsche Bibelgesellschaft, 1979.

_____. *The Greek New Testament*. 3rd ed., corrected. New York: United Bible Societies, 1983.

Amphoux, C. B. "A propos de Jacques 1,17." *Revue d'histoire et de philosophie religieuses* 50 (1970): 127-136.

Applebaum, Shimon. "Judaea as a Roman Province; the Countryside as a Political and Economic Factor." In *Aufstieg und Niedergang der römischen Welt: Geschichte und Kultur Roms im Spiegel der neuern Forschung*, ed. H. Temporini and W. Haase, II.8:355-396. Berlin and New York: Walter de Gruyter, 1978.

Baasland, Ernst. "Der Jakobusbrief als Neutestamentliche Weisheitsschrift." *Studia theologica* 36 (1982): 119-139.

Bal, Mieke. *Murder and Difference: Gender, Genre, and Scholarship on Sisera's Death*. Trans. Matthew Gumbert. Indiana Studies in Biblical Literature. Bloomington: University of Indiana Press, 1988.

Baltzer, Klaus, and Helmut Koester. "Die Bezeichung des Jakobus als ΏΒΛΙΑΣ." *Zeitschrift für die neutestamentliche Wissenschaft und die Kunde der älteren Kirche* 46 (1955): 141-142.

Barton, John. *Reading the Old Testament: Method in Biblical Study*. Philadelphia: Westminster Press, 1984.

233

Bauer, Walter. *A Greek-English Lexicon of the New Testament and Other Early Christian Literature*. Trans. William F. Arndt and F. Wilbur Gingrich from 4th ed., rev. F. Wilbur Gingrich and Frederick W. Danker from Bauer's 5th ed. Chicago: University of Chicago Press, 1979.

Berger, Peter L., and Thomas Luckmann. *The Social Construction of Reality: A Treatise in the Sociology of Knowledge*. New York: Anchor Doubleday, 1967.

Black, Matthew. "Critical and Exegetical Notes on Three New Testament Texts: Hebrews 6:11, Jude 5, James 1:27." *Zeitschrift für die neutestamentliche Wissenschaft und die Kunde der älteren Kirche* 30 (1964): 39-45.

Blass, F. and A. Debrunner. *A Greek Grammar of the New Testament and Other Early Christian Literature*. Trans. and rev. Robert W. Funk from the 9th and 10th German eds. Chicago: University of Chicago Press, 1961.

Bultmann, Rudolf. *Theology of the New Testament*. 2 volumes. Scribner Studies in Contemporary Theology. New York: Charles Scribner's Sons, 1951-55.

Burchard, Christoph. "Zu Jakobus 2,14-26." *Zeitschrift für die neutestamentliche Wissenschaft und die Kunde der älteren Kirche* 71 (1980): 27-45.

Burge, G. M. "'And Threw Them Thus on Paper': Rediscovering the Poetic Form of James 2:14-26." *Studia Biblica et Theologica* 7 (1977): 31-45.

Cantinat, Jean. *Les Epîtres de Saint Jacques et de Saint Jude*. Sources biblique. Paris: Libraire Lecoffre, 1973.

Cargal, Timothy B. "The Generative Trajectory in Certain non-Western Cultures." In *The Religious Dimensions of Biblical Texts: Greimas's Structural Semiotics and Biblical Exegesis*, by Daniel Patte, 265-75. Society of Biblical Literature, Semeia Studies. Atlanta: Scholars Press, 1990.

Childs, Brevard S. *The New Testament as Canon: An Introduction*. Philadelphia: Fortress Press, 1984.

Culley, Robert C. "Action Sequences in Genesis 2-3." *Semeia* 18 (1980): 25-33.

Dana, H. E. and Julius R. Mantey. *A Manual Grammar of the Greek New Testament*. New York: Macmillan, 1957.

Dautzenberg, Gerhard. "Ist das Schwurverbot Mt 5,33-37; Jak 5,12 ein Beispiel für die Torakritik Jesu?" *Biblische Zeitschrift*, Neue Folge 25 (1981): 47-66.

Davids, Peter H. *The Epistle of James*. New International Greek Testament Commentary. Grand Rapids, Michigan: William B. Eerdmans Publishing Company, 1982.

_____. "The Epistle of James in Modern Discussion." In *Aufstieg und Niedergang der römischen Welt: Geschichte und Kultur Roms im Spiegel der neueren Forschung*, ed. H. Temporini and W. Haase, II.25.5:3621-3645. Berlin and New York: Walter de Gruyter, 1988.

_____. "James and Jesus." In *The Jesus Tradition Outside the Gospels*, ed. David Wenham, 63-84. Sheffield: JSOT Press, 1984.

_____. "The Meaning of ἀπείραστος in James i. 13." *New Testament Studies* 24 (1978): 386-392.

_____. "Themes in the Epistle of James that are Judaistic in Character." Ph.D. dissertation, University of Manchester, 1974.

_____. "Tradition and Citation in the Epistle of James." In *Scripture, Tradition and Interpretation*, Festschrift for E. F. Harrison, ed. W. W. Gasque and W. S. LaSor, 113-26. Grand Rapids: William B. Eerdmans Publishing Company, 1978.

Delling, Gerhard. "ἀλαζών, ἀλαζονεία." In *Theological Dictionary of the New Testament*, ed. Gerhard Kittel and Gerhard Friedrich, trans. Geoffrey W. Bromiley, 1:226-227. Grand Rapids: William B. Eerdmans Publishing Company, 1964-76.

Dibelius, Martin. *From Tradition to Gospel*. Trans. Bertram Lee Woolf. New York: Charles Scribner's Sons, 1935.

_____. *James*. Rev. Helmut Greeven, trans. Michael A. Williams, and ed. Helmut Koester. Hermeneia—A Critical and Historical Commentary on the Bible. Philadelphia: Fortress Press, 1975.

Donker, Christiaan E. "Der Verfasser des Jak und sein Gegner: Zum Problem des Einwandes in Jak 2,18-19." *Zeitschrift für die neutestamentliche Wissenschaft und die Kunde der älteren Kirche* 72 (1981): 227-240.

Doty, William G. *Letters in Primitive Christianity*. Guides to Biblical Scholarship, New Testament Series, ed. Dan O. Via. Philadelphia: Fortress Press, 1973.

Easton, B. S. "The Epistle of James: Introduction and Exegesis." In *The Interpreter's Bible*, 12 volumes, ed. George A. Buttrick, 12:3-74. New York and Nashville: Abingdon Press, 1957.

Eco, Umberto. *Semiotics and the Philosophy of Language*. Advances in Semiotics. Bloomington: University of Indiana Press, 1984.

_____. *A Theory of Semiotics*. Advances in Semiotics. Bloomington: University of Indiana Press, 1976.

Edsman, Carl-Martin. "Schöpferwille und Geburt. Jac 1, 18: Eine Studie zur altchristlichen Kosmologie." *Zeitschrift für die neutestamentliche Wissenschaft und die Kunde der älteren Kirche* 38 (1939): 11-44.

_____. "Schöpfung und Wiedergeburt: Nochmals Jac. 1:18." In *Spiritus et Veritas*, Festschrift for Karl Kundzin, 43-55. Eutin: Ozolin, 1953.

Eisenman, Robert. "Eschatological 'Rain' Imagery in the War Scroll from Qumran and in the Letter of James." *Journal of Near Eastern Studies* 49 (1990): 173-184.

Elliott-Binns, L. E. "James I.18: Creation or Redemption?" *New Testament Studies* 3 (1956/57): 148-161.

_____. "The Meaning of ὕλη in Jas. iii. 5." *New Testament Studies* 2 (1955/56): 48-50.

Ekstrom, J. O. "The Discourse Structure of the Book of James." Typed Manuscript [photocopy]. International Linguistics Center, Dallas, 1975.

Exler, F. X. J. *The Form of the Ancient Greek Letter: A Study in Greek Epistolography.* Washington: Catholic University of America, 1923.

Fabris, Rinaldo. *Legge della libertà in Giacomo.* Supplementi alla Rivista Biblica, 8. Brescia: Paideia Editrice, 1977.

Felder, Cain. "Partiality and God's Law: An Exegesis of James 2:1-13." *The Journal of Religious Thought* 39 (1982/83): 51-69.

Fiorenza, Elisabeth Schüssler. *In Memory of Her: A Feminist Theological Reconstruction of Christian Origins.* New York: Crossroad Publishing Company, 1986.

Forbes, Peter B. R. "The Structure of the Epistle of James." *Evangelical Quarterly* 44 (1972): 147-153.

Francis, Fred O. "The Form and Function of the Opening and Closing Paragraphs of James and 1 John." *Zeitschrift für die neutestamentliche Wissenschaft und die Kunde der älteren Kirche* 61 (1970): 110-126.

Frankemölle, Hurbert. "Gespalten oder ganz: Zur Pragmatik der theologischen Anthropologie des Jakobusbriefes." In *Kommunikation und Solidarität: Beiträge zur Diskussion des handlungstheoretischen Ansatzes von Helmut Peukert in Theologie und Sozialwissenschaften*, ed. Hans-Ulrich v. Brachel and Norbert Mette, 160-178. Freiburg and Münster: Edition Exodus, 1985.

_____. "Das semantische Netz des Jakobusbriefes: Zur Einheit eines umstrittenen Briefes," *Biblische Zeitschrift*, Neue Folge 34 (1990): 161-197.

Funk, Robert W. "The Apostolic *Parousia*: Form and Significance." In *Christian History and Interpretation: Studies Presented to John Knox*, ed. W. R. Farmer, C. F. D. Moule, and R. R. Niebuhr, 249-268. Cambridge: Cambridge University Press, 1967.

Gertner, M. "Midrashim in the New Testament." *Journal of Semitic Studies* 7 (1962): 267-292.

Genuyt, F. "Le chapitre 1 de l'Epître de Jacques. Compte-rendu d'une séance du séminaire 'Littérature Biblique' du C.A.D.I.R. (1979-1980)." *Sémiotique et Bible* 17 (1980): 38-45.

_____. "Epître de Saint Jacques—Chapitre 2." *Sémiotique et Bible* 19 (1980): 25-31.

_____. "Epître de Jacques—Chapitre 3." *Sémiotique et Bible* 22 (1981): 55-59.

_____. "Epître de Jacques 4,1 - 5,6." *Sémiotique et Bible* 23 (1981): 44-56.

_____. "Epître de Saint-Jacques, ch. 5,6-20." *Sémiotique et Bible* 24 (1981): 28-36.

Goppelt, Leonhard. *Theology of the New Testament.* 2 vols. Translated by John E. Alsup. Grand Rapids, Michigan: William B. Eerdmans Publishing Company, 1982.

Gordon, Robert P. "ΚΑΙ ΤΟ ΤΕΛΟΣ ΚΥΡΙΟΥ ΕΙΔΕΤΕ (Jas v.11)." *Journal of Theological Studies* 26 (1975): 91-95.

Greimas, Algirdas J. and Joseph Courtés. *Sémiotique: dictionaire raisonné de la théorie du langage.* Paris: Hachette, 1979. English Translation: *Semiotics and Language: An Analytical Dictionary,* trans. Larry Crist and Daniel Patte, and James Lee, Edward McMahon II, Gary Phillips, and Michael Rengstorf. Bloomington: Indiana University Press, 1982.

Harder, Günther. "στηρίζω, ἐπιστηρίζω, στηριγμός, ἀστήρικτος." In *Theological Dictionary of the New Testament,* ed. Gerhard Kittel and Gerhard Friedrich, trans. Geoffrey W. Bromiley, 7:653-657. Grand Rapids: William B. Eerdmans Publishing Company, 1964-76.

Hartin, Patrick J. *James and the Q Sayings of Jesus.* Journal for the Study of the New Testament Supplement Series, 47. Sheffield: JSOT Press, 1991.

_____. "James: A New Testament Wisdom Writing and Its Relationship to Q." D.Th. thesis, University of South Africa, 1988.

Hartmann, Gerhard. "Der Aufbau des Jakobusbriefes." *Zeitschrift für katholische Theologie* 66 (1942): 63-70.

Harvey, Van A. *The Historian and the Believer: The Morality of Historical Knowledge and Christian Belief.* New York: Macmillan, 1966.

Hill, Ralph. "An Analysis of James 3-5 to the Paragraph Constituent Level." Typed Manuscript [photocopy]. International Linguistics Center, Dallas, 1978.

_____. "An Overview of the Discourse Structure of the Epistle of James: Comments." Typed Manuscript [photocopy]. International Linguistics Center, Dallas, 1978.

Hoppe, Rudolf. *Der theologische Hintergrund des Jakobusbriefes.* Forschung zur Bibel, 28. Würtzburg: Echter Verlag, 1977.

Hort, F. J. A. *The Epistle of St. James.* London: Macmillan, 1909.

Howard, George. "Was James an Apostle? A Reflection on a New Proposal for Gal. i 19." *Novum Testamentum* 19 (1977): 63-69.

Iser, Wolfgang. *The Act of Reading: A Theory of Aesthetic Response.* Baltimore: Johns Hopkins University Press, 1978.

Johanson, B. C. "The Definition of 'Pure Religion' in James 1:27 Reconsidered." *Expository Times* 84 (1973): 118-119.

Johnson, Luke Timothy. "Friendship with the World/Friendship with God: A Study of Discipleship in James." In *Discipleship in the New Testament*, ed. Fernando F. Segovia, 166-183. Philadelphia: Fortress Press, 1985.

_____. "James 3:13-4:10 and the *Topos* περὶ φθόνου." *Novum Testamentum* 25 (1983): 327-347.

_____. "The Mirror of Remembrance (James 1:22-25)." *Catholic Biblical Quarterly* 50 (1988): 632-645.

Kadushin, Max. *Organic Thinking: A Study in Rabbinic Thought*. New York: Bloch, 1938.

_____. *The Rabbinic Mind*. 3rd ed. New York: Bloch, 1972.

Kee, Howard Clark and Franklin W. Young. *Understanding the New Testament*. Englewood Cliffs, New Jersey: Prentice-Hall Inc., 1957.

Kennedy, George. *New Testament Interpretation through Rhetorical Criticism*. Studies in Religion, ed. Charles Long. Chapel Hill and London: University of North Carolina Press, 1984.

Kent, Homer A. *"Faith that Works:"* *Studies in the Epistle of James*. Grand Rapids: Baker Book House, 1986.

Kilpatrick, G. D. "Übertreter des Gesetzes, Jak. 2,11." *Theologische Zeitschrift* 23 (1967): 433.

Kirk, J. A. "The Meaning of Wisdom in James: Examination of a Hypothesis." *New Testament Studies* 16 (1969/70): 24-38.

Kittel, Gerhard. "Die geschichtliche Ort des Jakobusbriefes." *Zeitschrift für die neutestamentliche Wissenschaft und die Kunde der älteren Kirche* 41 (1942): 71-105.

Kreissig, Heinz. "Die landwirtschaftliche Situation im Palästina vor dem judäischen Krieg." *Acta Antiqua Academiae Scientiarum Hungaricae* 17 (1969): 223-254.

Kugelman, Richard. *James and Jude*. New Testament Message, 19. Wilmington, Delaware: Michael Glazier, 1980.

Kuhn, Thomas S. *The Structure of Scientific Revolutions*. 2nd ed. Chicago: University of Chicago Press, 1970.

Kümmel, Werner Georg. *Introduction to the New Testament*. Revised English edition, trans. Howard Clark Kee. Nashville: Abingdon Press, 1975.

Ladd, George E. *A Theology of the New Testament*. Grand Rapids: William B. Eerdmans Publishing Company, 1974.

Lake, Kirsopp. *The Apostolic Fathers*. 2 volumes. Loeb Classical Library. London and New York: William Heinemann and G. Putnam's Sons, 1912-13.

Laws, Sophie. *A Commentary on the Epistle of James*. Harper's New Testament Commentaries. San Francisco: Harper and Row, 1980.

_____. "Does Scripture Speak in Vain? A Reconsideration of James iv. 5." *New Testament Studies* 20 (1973/74): 210-215.

Lee, E. Kenneth. "Words Denoting 'Pattern' in the New Testament." *New Testament Studies* 8 (1961/62): 166-173.

Légasse, Simon. "Les pauvres en esprit et les 'volontaires' de Qumran." *New Testament Studies* 8 (1961/62): 336-345.

Liddell, Henry G., and Robert Scott. *A Greek-English Lexicon*. Rev. Henry Stuart Jones, 9th ed., 2 vols. with supplement. London: Oxford University Press, 1948.

Lodge, John G. "James and Paul at Cross-Purposes? James 2,22." *Biblica* 62 (1981): 195-213.

Lohse, Eduard. *The Formation of the New Testament*. Trans. M. Eugene Boring from the 3rd German ed. Nashville: Abingdon Press, 1981.

_____. "Glaube und Werke—Zur Theologie des Jakobusbriefes." In *Die Einheit des Neuen Testaments*, 285-306. Göttingen: Vandenhoeck und Ruprecht, 1973.

Lorenzen, Thorwald. "Faith without Works Does Not Count before God! James 2:14-26." *The Expository Times* 89 (1978): 231-235.

Louw, Johannes P. "Discourse Analysis and the Greek New Testament." *The Bible Translator* 24 (1973): 101-118.

_____. *Semantics of New Testament Greek*. Society of Biblical Literature Semeia Studies. Atlanta: Scholars Press, 1982.

Louw, Johannes P., and Eugene A. Nida, eds. *Greek-English Lexicon of the New Testament based on Semantic Domains*. 2 volumes. New York: United Bible Societies, 1988.

Luck, Ulrich. "'Weisheit' und Leiden: zum Problem Paulus und Jakobus." *Theologische Literaturzeitung* 92 (1967): 253-258.

Malbon, Elizabeth Struthers. "The Theory and Practice of Structural Exegesis. A Review Article." *Perspectives in Religious Studies* 11 (1984): 273-282.

Manns, Frédéric. "Une tradition liturgique juive sous-jacente à Jacques 1:21b." *Revue des sciences religieuses* 62 (1988): 85-89.

Marconi, Gilberto. "La struttura di Giacomo 2." *Biblica* 68 (1987): 250-257.

Marcus, Joel. "The Evil Inclination in the Epistle of James." *Catholic Biblical Quarterly* 44 (1982): 606-621.

Marin, Louis. *The Semiotics of the Passion Narrative: Topics and Figures*. Trans. Alfred M. Johnson, Jr. Pittsburgh Theological Monograph Series, 25. Pittsburgh: The Pickwick Press, 1980.

Martin, Ralph P. *The Epistle of James*. Word Biblical Commentary, 48. Dallas: Word Books, 1988.

_____. "The Life-Setting of the Epistle of James in the Light of Jewish History." In *Biblical and Near Eastern Studies*, Festschrift for William Sanford LaSor, ed. G. A. Tuttle, 97-103. Grand Rapids: William B. Eerdmans Publishing Company, 1978.

Marxsen, Willi. *Introduction to the New Testament: An Approach to its Problems.* Trans. G. Buswell. Philadelphia: Fortress Press, 1968.

Maynard-Reid, Pedrito U. *Poverty and Wealth in James.* Maryknoll, New York: Orbis Books, 1987.

Mayor, Joseph B. *The Epistle of St. James. The Greek Text with Introduction, Notes and Comments.* 3rd ed. London: MacMillan and Co., 1910.

McKnight, Scot. "James 2:18a: The Unidentifiable Interlocutor." *Westminster Theological Journal* 52 (1990): 355-364.

Meade, David G. *Pseudonymity and Canon: An Investigation into the Relationship of Authorship and Authority in Jewish and Earliest Christian Tradition.* Wissenschaftliche Untersuchungen zum Neuen Testament, 39. Tübingen and Grand Rapids: J. C. B. Mohr (Paul Siebeck) and William B. Eerdmans Publishing Company, 1986.

Metzger, Bruce M. *A Textual Commentary on the Greek New Testament.* Corrected edition. New York: United Bible Societies, 1975.

Meyer, Arnold. *Das Rätsel des Jakobusbriefes.* Beihefte zur *Zeitschrift für die neutestamentliche Wissenschaft und die Kunde der älteren Kirche*, 10. Giessen: Töpelmann, 1930.

Minear, Paul S. "Yes or No. The Demand for Honesty in the Early Church." *Novum Testamentum* 13 (1971): 1-13.

Moo, Douglas J. *James.* Tyndale New Testament Commentaries. Grand Rapids: William B. Eerdmans Publishing Company, 1985.

Moulton, James Hope, and George Milligan. *The Vocabulary of the Greek New Testament Illustrated from the Papyri and Other Non-Literary Sources.* London: Hoddin and Stoughton Limited, 1930.

Moulton, James H., Wilbert F. Howard, and Nigel Turner. *A Grammar of New Testament Greek.* 4 volumes. Edinburgh: T and T Clark, 1908-63.

Mußner, Franz. *Der Jakobusbrief.* Herders theologischer Kommentar zum Neuen Testament, XIII/1. Freiburg und Basel: Herder, 1964.

Nauck, Wolfgang. "Lex insculpta (חוק חרות) in der Sektenschrift." *Zeitschrift für die neutestamentliche Wissenschaft und die Kunde der älteren Kirche* 46 (1955): 138-140.

Neitzel, Heinz. "Eine alte crux interpretum im Jakobusbrief 2:18." *Zeitschrift für die neutestamentliche Wissenschaft und die Kunde der älteren Kirche* 73 (1982): 286-293.

Nötscher, F. "'Gesetz der Freiheit' im NT und in der Mönchsgemeinde am Toten Meer." *Biblica* 34 (1953): 193-194.

Oepke, Albrecht. "κενός, κενόω, κενόδοξος, κενοδοξία." In *Theological Dictionary of the New Testament*, ed. Gerhard Kittel and Gerhard Friedrich, trans. Geoffrey W. Bromiley, 3:659-662. Grand Rapids: William B. Eerdmans Publishing Company, 1964-76.

Ogletree, Thomas W. *The Use of the Bible in Christian Ethics*. Philadelphia: Fortress Press, 1983.

Patte, Daniel. *The Gospel According to Matthew: A Structural Commentary on Matthew's Faith*. Philadelphia: Fortress Press, 1987.

_____. "Method for a Structural Exegesis of Didactic Discourses: Analysis of 1 Thessalonians." *Semeia* 26 (1983): 85-129.

_____. *Paul's Faith and the Power of the Gospel: A Structural Introduction to the Pauline Letters*. Philadelphia: Fortress Press, 1983.

_____. *The Religious Dimensions of Biblical Texts: Greimas's Structural Semiotics and Biblical Exegesis*. Society of Biblical Literature, Semeia Studies. Atlanta: Scholars Press, 1990.

_____. *Structural Exegesis for New Testament Critics*. Guides to Biblical Scholarship, New Testament Series, ed. Dan O. Via. Minneapolis: Augsburg Fortress, 1990.

_____. "A Structural Exegesis of 2 Corinthians 2:14-3:6 and 6:11-7:4." In *Society of Biblical Literature Seminar Papers*, 26, ed. Kent Harold Richards, 23-49. Atlanta: Scholars Press, 1987.

_____. *What is Structural Exegesis?* Guides to Biblical Scholarship, New Testament Series, ed. Dan O. Via. Philadelphia: Fortress Press, 1976.

Patte, Daniel and Aline Patte. *Structural Exegesis: From Theory to Practice*. Philadelphia: Fortress Press, 1978.

Pearson, Birger A. "James, 1-2 Peter, Jude," in *The New Testament and Its Modern Interpreters*, ed. Eldon Jay Epp and George W. MacRae, 371-406. Society of Biblical Literature, The Bible and Its Modern Interpreters. Atlanta: Scholars Press, 1989.

Peck, George. "James 5:1-6." *Interpretation: A Journal of Bible and Theology* 42 (1988): 291-296.

Perdue, Leo G. "Paraenesis and the Epistle of James." *Zeitschrift für die neutestamentliche Wissenschaft und die Kunde der älteren Kirche* 72 (1981): 241-256.

_____. "The Social Character of Paraenesis and Paraenetic Literature." *Semeia* 50 (1990): 5-39.

Perrin, Norman. *The New Testament, An Introduction: Proclamation and Paraenesis, Myth and History.* San Francisco: Harcourt, Brace, Jovanovich, 1974.

Popkes, Wiard. *Adressaten, Situation und Form des Jakobusbriefes.* Stuttgarter Bibelstudien, 125/126. Stuttgart: Verlag Katholisches Bibelwerk GmbH, 1986.

Powell, Cyril H. "'Faith' in James and its Bearings on the Problem of the Date of the Epistle." *Expository Times* 62 (1951): 311-314.

Prockter, Lewis J. "James 4.4-6: Midrash on Noah." *New Testament Studies* 35 (1989): 625-627.

Reese, James M., O.S.F.S. "The Exegete as Sage: Hearing the Message of James." *Biblical Theology Bulletin* 12 (1982): 82-85.

Reicke, Bo. *The Epistles of James, Peter and Jude.* Anchor Bible, 37. Garden City, New York: Doubleday, 1964.

Riesenfeld, Harald. "ΑΠΛΩΣ: Zu Jak. 1,5." *Coniectanea neotestamentica* 9 (1944): 33-41.

Roberts, D. J. "The Definition of 'Pure Religion' in James 1:27." *Expository Times* 83 (1971/72): 215-216.

Robertson, A. T. *A Grammar of the Greek New Testament in the Light of Historical Research.* Nashville: Broadman Press, 1934.

_____. *Word Pictures in the New Testament.* Volume 6, *The General Epistles and the Apocalypse.* New York and London: Richard R. Smith, Inc., 1933.

Ropes, James Hardy. *A Critical and Exegetical Commentary on the Epistle of St. James.* International Critical Commentary. New York: Charles Scribner's Sons, 1916.

Ross, Alexander. *The Epistles of James and John.* New International Commentary on the New Testament. Grand Rapids: William B. Eerdmans Publishing Company, 1954.

Rountree, Catherine. "Further Thoughts on the Discourse Structure of James." Typed Manuscript [photocopy]. International Linguistics Center, Dallas, 1976.

Sanders, E. P. *Paul and Palestinian Judaism: A Comparison of Patterns of Religion.* Philadelphia: Fortress Press, 1977.

Sanders, J. T. *Ethics in the New Testament: Change and Development.* Philadelphia: Fortress Press, 1975.

Scaer, David P. *James, the Apostle of Faith: A Primary Christological Epistle for the Persecuted Church.* St. Louis: Concordia Publishing House, 1983.

Schlier, Heinrich. "ἐλεύθερος, ἐλευθερόω, ἐλευθερία, ἀπελεύθερος." In *Theological Dictionary of the New Testament*, ed. Gerhard Kittel and Gerhard Friedrich, trans. Geoffrey W. Bromiley, 2:487-502. Grand Rapids: William B. Eerdmans Publishing Company, 1964-76.

Schmidt, Karl Ludwig. "διασπορά." In *Theological Dictionary of the New Testament*, ed. Gerhard Kittel and Gerhard Friedrich, trans. Geoffrey W. Bromiley, 2:99-104. Grand Rapids: William B. Eerdmans Publishing Company, 1964-76.

Schmitt, John J. "The Gender of Ancient Israel." *Journal for the Study of the Old Testament* 26 (1983): 115-125.

_____. "You Adulteresses! The Image in James 4:4." *Novum Testamentum* 28 (1986): 327-337.

Schneider, Johannes. "ὄνειδος, ὀνειδίζω, ὀνειδισμός." In *Theological Dictionary of the New Testament*, ed. Gerhard Kittel and Gerhard Friedrich, trans. Geoffrey W. Bromiley, 5:238-242. Grand Rapids: William B. Eerdmans Publishing Company, 1964-76.

Schökel, Luis Alonso. "James 5,2 [sic, '5,6'] and 4,6." *Biblica* 54 (1973): 73-76.

Segal, Alan F. "'He who did not spare his own son ...': Jesus, Paul, and the Akedah." In *From Jesus to Paul: Studies in Honor of Francis Wright Beare*, ed. Peter Richardson and John C. Hurd, 169-184. Waterloo, Ontario: Wilfrid Laurier University Press, 1984.

Seitz, Oscar J. F. "Afterthoughts on the Term 'Dipsychos.'" *New Testament Studies* 4 (1957/58): 327-334.

_____. "Antecedents and Signification of the Term ΔΙΨΥΧΟΣ." *Journal of Biblical Literature* 66 (1947): 211-219.

_____. "Relationship of The Shepherd of Hermas to the Epistle of James." *Journal of Biblical Literature* 63 (1944): 131-140.

Shogren, Gary S. "Will God Heal Us? A Re-examination of James 5:14-16a." *Evangelical Quarterly* 61 (1989): 99-108.

Sidebottom, E. M. *James, Jude, 2 Peter*. New Century Bible. Grand Rapids, Michigan: William B. Eerdmans Publishing Company, 1967.

Stählin, G. "Zum Gebrauch von Beteuerungsformeln im Neuen Testament." *Novum Testamentum* 5 (1962): 115-143.

Stanton, Graham. Review of *The Gospel According to Matthew: A Structural Commentary on Matthew's Faith*, by Daniel Patte. *Interpretation: A Journal of Bible and Theology* 43 (1989): 184-86.

Stauffer, Ethelbert. "Das 'Gesetz der Freiheit' in der Ordensregel von Jericho." *Theologische Literaturzeitung* 77 (1952): 527-532.

Stowers, Stanley K. "The Diatribe." In *Greco-Roman Literature and the New Testament*, ed. David E. Aune, 71-84. Society of Biblical Literature Sources for Biblical Studies, 21. Atlanta: Scholars Press, 1988.

Strobel, A. *Untersuchungen zum eschatologischen Verzögerungsproblem: Auf Grund der spätjüdischen-urchristlichen Geschichte von Habakuk 2,2 ff.* Novum Testamentum Supplements, 2. Leiden and Köln: E. J. Brill, 1961.

Tamez, Elsa. *The Scandalous Message of James: Faith without Works is Dead.* Trans. John Eagleson. New York: The Crossroad Publishing Company, 1990.

Thayer, James. "On James." Typed Manuscript [photocopy]. International Linguistics Center, Dallas, 1974.

Thompson, W. Ralph. "The Epistle of James: A Document on Heavenly Wisdom." *Wesleyan Theological Journal* 13 (1978): 7-12.

Thyen, Hartwig. *Der Stil de Jüdisch-Hellinistischen Homilie.* Forschungen zur Religion und Literatur des Alten und Neuen Testaments, Neue Folge 47. Göttingen: Vandenhoeck und Ruprecht, 1955.

Tolbert, Mary Ann. *Sowing the Gospel: Mark's World in Literary-Historical Perspective.* Minneapolis: Augsburg Fortress, 1989.

Torakawa, Kiyoko. "Literary-Semantic Analysis of James 1-2." Typed Manuscript [photocopy]. International Linguistics Center, Dallas, 1978.

Townsend, Michael J. "James 4:1-4: A Warning against Zealotry?" *Expository Times* 87 (1976): 211-213.

Trocmé, Etienne. "Les Eglises pauliniennes vues du dehors: Jacques 2,1 à 3,13." *Studia Evangelica* 2 (1964): 660-669.

Turner, Victor. *The Forest of Symbols.* Ithaca, New York: Cornell University Press, 1967).

_____. *The Ritual Process.* Ithaca, New York: Cornell University Press, 1967).

Trudinger, L. P. "ΕΤΕΡΟΝ ΔΕ ΤΩΝ ΑΠΟΣΤΟΛΟΩΝ ΟΥΚ ΕΙΔΟΝ, ΕΙ ΜΗ ΙΑΚΩΒΟΝ: A Note on Galatians i 19." *Novum Testamentum* 17 (1975): 200-202.

Verheul, Ambrosius. "The Paschal Character of the Sacrament of the Sick: Exegesis of James 5:14-15 and the New Rite for the Sacrament of the Sick." In *Temple of the Holy Spirit: Sickness and Death of the Christian in Liturgy*, trans. Matthew J. O'Connell, 247-257. New York: Pueblo Publishing Company, 1983.

Via, Dan O. Foreword to *What is Redaction Criticism?*, by Norman Perrin. Guides to Biblical Scholarship, New Testament Series. Philadelphia: Fortress Press, 1969.

_____. "The Right Strawy Epistle Reconsidered: A Study in Biblical Ethics and Hermeneutics." *Journal of Religion* 49 (1969): 253-267.

von Rad, Gerhard. *Wisdom in Israel.* Nashville and New York: Abingdon Press, 1972.

Vouga, François. *L'Epître de Saint Jacques.* Commentaire du Nouveau Testament, 2d ser., XIIIa. Genève: Labor et Fides, 1984.

Wall, Robert W. "James as Apocalyptic Paraenesis." *Restoration Quarterly* 32 (1990): 11-22.

Wanke, Joachim. "Die urchristlichen Lehrer nach dem Zeugnis des Jakobusbriefes." In *Die Kirche des Anfangs*, Festschrift für Heinz Schürmann zum 65. Geburtstag, ed. by Rudolf Schnackenburg, Josef Ernst, and Joachim Wanke, 491-499. Erfurter theologische Studien, 38. Leipzig: St. Benno-Verlag, 1977.

Ward, Roy Bowen. "Partiality in the Assembly: James 2:2-4." *Harvard Theological Review* 62 (1969): 87-97.

_____. "The Works of Abraham: James 2:14-26." *Harvard Theological Review* 61 (1968): 283-290.

White, John L. "New Testament Epistolary Literature in the Framework of Ancient Epistolography." In *Aufstieg und Niedergang der römischen Welt: Geschichte und Kultur Roms im Spiegel der neuern Forschung*, ed. H. Temporini and W. Haase, II.25.2:1730-1756. Berlin and New York: Walter de Gruyter, 1984.

Wilckens, Ulrich. "σοφία, σοφός, σοφίζω." In *Theological Dictionary of the New Testament*, ed. Gerhard Kittel and Gerhard Friedrich, trans. Geoffrey W. Bromiley, 7:465-476 and 496-528. Grand Rapids: William B. Eerdmans Publishing Company, 1964-76.

Williams, Robert Lee. "Piety and Poverty in James." *Wesleyan Theological Journal* 22 (Fall 1987): 37-55.

Windisch, Hans. *Die katholischen Briefe*. 3rd ed., rev. Herbert Preisker. Handbuch zum Neuen Testament, 15. Tübingen: J. C. B. Mohr (Paul Siebeck), 1951.

Wolverton, Wallace I. "The Double-minded Man in the Light of Essene Psychology." *Anglican Theological Review* 38 (1956): 166-175.

Wuellner, Wilhelm H. "Hermeneutics and Rhetorics: From 'Truth and Method' to 'Truth and Power'." *Scriptura: Journal of Bible and Theology in South Africa* S 3 (1989): 1-54.

_____. "Der Jakobusbrief im Licht der Rhetorik und Textpragmatic." *Linguistica Biblica* 43 (1978): 5-66.